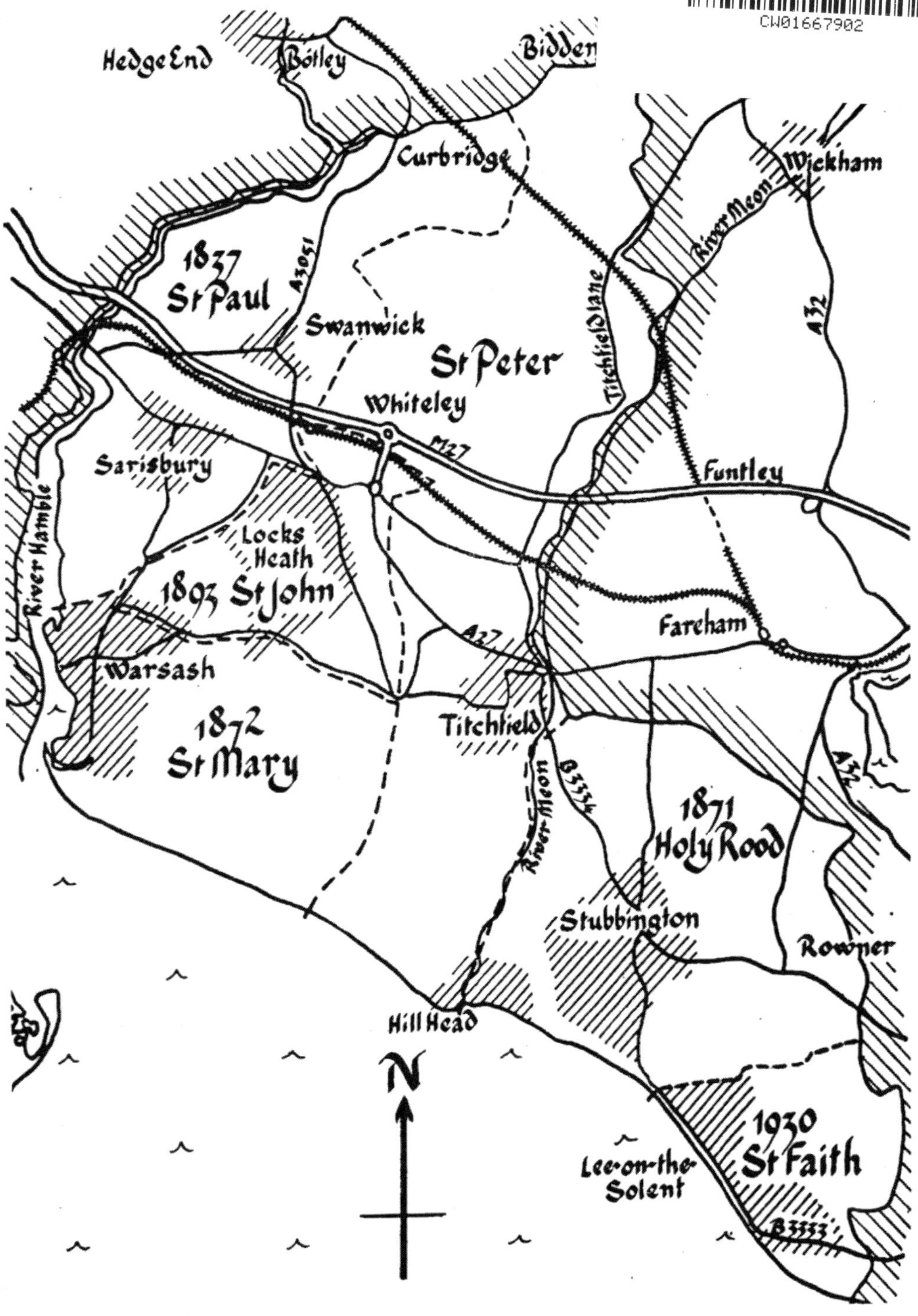

The parishes, which made up the Ancient Parish of Titchfield. Reproduced with kind permission of the Earl of Southampton Trust

Village Voices 1914 - 1964 - Peoples' stories in their own words

Published by Titchfield Spirit

Website www.titchfieldspirit.uk

Email titchfieldspirit@hotmail.co.uk

October 2015

British Library Cataloguing-in-publication Data:
A catalogue record of this book is available from the British Library

ISBN: 978-0-9508131-8-9

Printed by:

Spinnaker Print Limited,
Unit 4 Claylands Park,
Claylands Road,
Bishops Waltham,
Southampton,
SO32 1QD

Contents

		Page
Acknowledgements		vi
About the book		viii
Part One	**Introduction to Titchfield**	1
Part Two	**1914 - 1938**	
	Childhood and families	9
	School	20
	Celebrations and leisure	22
	Food and farming	24
	Work	25
	Church, chapel and religion	26
	What's that in old money?	36
	Titchfield Telephone Directory 1932	37
	Part Two Bonus Pictures	39
	Significant dates	41
Part Three	**1939 - 1945**	
	Childhood and families	43
	Bellfield Road revisited	52
	School	53
	Celebrations and leisure	57
	Food and farming	58
	Work	64
	Church, chapel and religion	65
	War and fighting	66
	Military bases	84
	Plan of the D-Day invasion	96
	War's End	108
	World War Two terms explained	110
	Part Three Bonus Pictures	112
	Significant dates	114
Part Four	**1946 - 1964**	
	Childhood and families	115
	School	128
	Celebrations and leisure	129
	Food and farming	136
	Work	143

Church, chapel and religion 154
Groups, clubs and societies, 156
Shopping in Titchfield 168
Bus stop names 178
ABC of Hampshire dialect 179
Part Four Bonus Pictures 180
Significant dates 182

Bibliography and further reading. 183

Foreward

"How can we raise some money to repair the church organ?"

This was our question that would launch a play, a book, a web site and a school resource pack, but unfortunately no money for the church organ!

2014 marked the centenary of the outbreak of the First World War, (WW1), and the 75th anniversary of the start of the Second World War (WW2). This was the background to the development of Titchfield Spirit. It was decided, from the outset, that Titchfield Spirit would be a community project involving as many local people as possible.

With the support of a Heritage Lottery grant a stage play, which dramatised the Titchfield Tapestries, was written and produced. The Tapestries are six sewn panels which tell the history of the village from Saxon times up to the Millennium. The play was originally intended to be for one night with a few friends playing all the parts but it rapidly grew into an 'all-singing, all-dancing event'! The Great Barn on Mill Lane was offered by Titchfield Festival Theatre, (TFT), as the venue. In addition to TFT, Titchfield Youth Theatre, Titchfield Art and Community Theatre, Titchfield Primary school children, some additional friends made up a cast of 70 players. Together they brought to life 200 characters, including eight monarchs. William Shakespeare and Jane Austin also put in an appearance. The drama played to full houses with three performances in June 2014 and was very well received.

The Lottery funding also allowed for a second part of the project, which was to carry out oral-history research work in the area. Together with a team of volunteers we have spent a further year collecting local people's stories, memories and pictures. We chose as our boundaries for this research, the ancient parish of Titchfield for a wider perspective of the area. This has proved a fascinating and exciting project; the material gathered has been published in this book.

As part of the community approach, Titchfield Spirit arranged a visit to the Titchfield Primary School by six of the people who had been involved with the book. This was the culmination of the school's Local Studies Week, which proved interesting for the children and visitors alike. The visitors told the children about their childhood, and their school days (most of which were spent at that very school). They commented on how much schooling had changed since their day, as one person said:

"Oh! It was so dark and cold when I was here and I was frightened".

The children made their guests very welcome and listened attentively to their presentations. When the time came, they showed that they could ask many very sensible questions. They did however show an alarming interest in corporal punishment! Some children's comments were:

"We thank you for coming to our school to share your interesting information about your childhood. It was exciting having a person who came to our school in the 1930s and '40s."

"We liked it when you told us you got caned."

"They even had a fire in their classroom." (a coke-burning open stove)

"It was really interesting to see how different things are now and how it has changed. It was good to get our visitors perspective as it was hard for us to understand that they had been here before us. We complain about school but it is good to know what they found hard and what we find hard."

"I liked it when you told us that you loved playing football, the same as I do. Also when you told us about your favourite lesson, literature."

Some of the learning opportunities that the visit provided for the children were: letter writing; taking notes; debating corporal punishment; poster presentations; art and drama as well as research skills.

A resource pack for schools entitled 'Local Study Pack: Titchfield Area 2015.' has been produced to help children in the future to understand what it was like to live through this 50 year period of momentous change.

Titchfield Spirit has also developed a website www.titchfieldspirit.uk so that the material will be available for anyone to access now and in the future.

The Heritage Lottery funding covered the cost of the production of the book so that copies could be distributed free of charge to the participants, schools, local libraries and societies. There is also a DVD of the stage play.

The project finale was an open celebration event where the local community met the people who contributed their stories and heard them retold.

Ross and Jill Underwood

Acknowledgements

Village Voices has been compiled and produced by Ross Underwood ably assisted by his wife, Jill. Ann Wheal has brought her wealth of experience to editing the book and together we would like to thank everyone who has helped in any way with this production. We have made every attempt to mention all the people who have contributed, but please accept our utmost apologies if we have missed anyone out.

We would especially like to thank the following people who willingly gave us stories and pictures about their lives and the lives of their families between 1914 and 1964. We would also like to thank all the other people who contributed additional material to help us fill in the gaps from our research.

Alan Brind, Ken Bayley, Mary Burner (Chase), Paul Catcheside, Ken Charman, Robert Chase, Victor Chase, Paul Cousins, Annette DeVoil, Lesley Downs, Tony Dugan, Catherine Palmiter (Earles), John Ekins, Douglas Elkins, Lesley Ellis, Linda Felton (Tunbridge), Mike Ferris, Kevin Ford, Jean Faulds (Godbehere), Dorothy Francis (Sainter), John Freemantle, Pamela Fullick (Price), Margaret Groves (Gardner), Irene Harris (Gearing), Sheila Hignell (Harris), Jenny Hill, Amanda Laws (Werge-Hartley), Rachel McGuire (Harris), John Maginnis, Eddie Matthews (Windsor), Andrew Mills, David Mugford, Margaret Mugford (Rousell), Anthony Norris, Margaret Noyce (Whitmore), Pete Noyce, Mary Parrett (Harris), Brian Patten, June Pellatt (Bowers), Kitty Potter (Evans), Wally Pratt, Michael Prior, Rita Prior (Etherington), Gerald Read, John Rousell, Aimee St. John (Dwyer), Kate Scott (Sentanse), Tessa Short (Collins), Chris Smith, Louis Stamp, Judy Stokes (Maddocks), Sister Valeria, Bessie Traves (Harris), Tony Traves, Suzanne Traves (Buxey), Donald Upshall, Joseph Waldron, Ben Waterfall, George Watts, Paula Weaver (Rogers), Debbie West (Stiles), Sylvie Whittaker (Taylor), Colin Wilton-Smith, John Williams and Kim Young.

We would also like to thank the researchers: Joan Anglides, Jan Davies, Edwina and Roger Day, Peter and Julia Mills, Steve Nash, Ros Seward, Suzanne Traves and Marilyn Wilton-Smith for their diligence and patience. Thanks also go to Barbara Le Sueur and Caryl Larkin, who spent many hours typing up relevant documents.

Thank you also to Karen Postle and Peter Wheal for their clear heads and support when we become somewhat overwhelmed with all the material. Many thanks also go to Sheila Hignell, Peter Mills, Margaret Pace, Anna Sketchley, and Paula Weaver our critical readers. Their efforts are much appreciated.

We are also very grateful to Titchfield Remembers

titchfieldremembers@gmail.com

and Titchfield Nostalgia

https://www.facebook.com/groups/275757209258079/

for allowing us to use some of their material.

Also our thanks go to the cast of 'Titchfield Spirit, the play' (2014). Their names are listed on the DVD of the play.

Titchfield Spirit has been made possible by the financial support of The Heritage Lottery, especially awarding the project more than was originally bid. This has made it possible to distribute the first run of Village Voices free of charge so that everyone can enjoy it.

An acknowledgements page would not be complete without a special thanks to the Titchfield History Society for their help, support and advice.

About the book

The aim of the book has been to record the lives of the people of Titchfield during the 50 momentous years, 1914 to 1964. It is written in the words of the people themselves and recorded in an easy to read style. The book also contains photographs and diagrams.

The book is organised as follows:

Part 1 Introduction to Titchfield
Part 2 1914 - 1938
Part 3 1939 - 1945
Part 4 1946 - 1964
Bibliography and further reading

The stories within sections 2 - 4 have been divided under the following headings:

Childhood and Families
School
Celebrations and Leisure
Food and Farming
Work
Church, Chapel and Religion
War and Fighting (Part 3)
Shopping (Part 4)

Many people were interviewed, others wrote their own stories. We hope you find these stories as fascinating as we did and enjoy reading about, and looking at, to find out about the lives of the local residents in the recent past.

The material in the book is in the words of the people themselves. We are deeply grateful to the contributors who gave us so much material. Unfortunately we were not able to use all of it but all their stories are on our website, www.titchfieldspirit.uk

Different people may remember things slightly differently but the book is about memories so no one memory can be more accurate than another, just slightly different.

"These histories disappear with us if they're not written down."
Contributor.

Note: we have tried to use only material that does not infringe on other people's copyright. However, if you find something that you feel is not original, please contact titchfieldspirit@hotmail.co.uk and appropriate amendments /acknowledgements will be made in the future.

Many of our contributors have mentioned Spitfires: building them, repairing them, or watching them overhead. This picture was taken on 15th September 2015. It shows the first two flights of Spitfires and Hurricanes that took off from Goodwood (RAF Westhampnett) to commemorate the 75th anniversary of the Battle of Britain. In 1940, this was the crucial day in a four-month defence against the German air force (Luftwaffe), where our airmen repelled all that was thrown at them.

As a result Hitler cancelled his invasion of England.

Part One - Introduction to Titchfield

Titchfield lies between Fareham and the Solent in Hampshire. Records show that there was a village of some sort before 900 AD. The church of St Peter's in the heart of the village also dates back to approximately this time. The ancient Parish of Titchfield ran from what is now Lee-on-the-Solent to Warsash and to the edge of Shedfield in the north.

The Meonwara, a war-like group, were one of the last tribes to be converted to Christianity by St Wilfred's missionaries in approximately 680 AD. The church they founded was built as a minster church to serve the whole of the Meon Valley. If you look at St Peter's Church porch you can still see the Roman bricks that were robbed from Portchester Castle.

An early postcard of Titchfield

History runs deep in this area. It has seen visits from eight kings and queens to Titchfield Abbey. This became the seat of an influential family, the Earls of Southampton. After the Abbey became a ruin, the area settled down again to be quiet country villages, farms and small holdings.

The village has a canal, which is one of the earliest man-made waterways in the country. It runs from the tannery, now a small industrial estate, to the open sea. There are many stories about the canal and it is believed that it was originally constructed by the third Earl of Southampton in 1611. The village once had a market hall in the centre of the Square but it was allowed to fall into disrepair. It was eventually given to the Weald and Downland Open Air Museum in

Sussex where it has been restored to its former glory and is available for all to see.

By the first half of the 20th century many people worked for the tannery, the gas works, or Fielder's brewery. Some worked in the shops, but most people worked on the land. Titchfield has rich soil which is ideal for market garden produce such as strawberries, lettuce and tomatoes.

Titchfield and World War 1 (WW1)

Sleepy Titchfield was rocked by the devastation of WW1. Its ordinary men-folk, some of whom had never strayed further than Fareham, went off to fight for king and country. Of these men, 51 lost their lives. Their families had to learn to cope without them, but cherished the memory of their men folk when naming their new-born sons.

'Titchfield Remembers', a separate local research project was set up in 2014 to find out more details of the men whose names are recorded on the village War Memorial (see page 10). From their research we mention here just four of the men who didn't come back.

Frank Biddle, Private in 10th B Hampshire Regiment

Frank, the third child and the eldest son of Henry and Jane Biddle, who had ten children. The census shows that he was a 'carter on farm' in Titchfield. Frank joined the 10th Hampshire Regiment and his military record shows he entered the Balkan theatre of war on 5th August 1915. Shortly after joining the Gallipoli Campaign in northern Turkey, he died on 10th August, aged 22.

Albert George Biddle, Private in Kings Royal Rifle Corps

Albert was one of Frank's younger brothers. By November 1911 he had enlisted as a regular soldier, as had his elder brother Frank. Albert was in the King's Royal Rifle Corps and they were in Blackdown when war broke out. They proceeded to France, landing at Le Havre on the 13th August 1914. They fought on the Western Front throughout the War, taking part in most of the major actions including the first Battle of Ypres in October.

Albert died on 10th January 1915 in Le Touquet, south of Calais. It is not clear exactly how he died, but extracts from a dispatch from the Commander in Chief of the British Armies in France and Flanders at that time said: 'Weather conditions were abnormally bad, the snow and floods precluding any active operations during the first three weeks of January.' From this it can be concluded that Albert George Biddle may have been injured in December, possibly by a stray bullet. He was 21.

Donald B.E. Upshall, Private in 1st Northumberland Fusiliers

Donald was one of five siblings, whose father was a schoolmaster, first at the Endowed Boys School in Broughton and then at the National School at the top of West Street in Titchfield. Donald joined the army in 1913 and so, unlike many of the Titchfield lads, he was a regular soldier and one of the first to leave for France in 1914. He joined the Northumberland Fusiliers who were part of the British Expeditionary Force. He was engaged in the major actions on the Western Front. On Easter Monday, 9 April 1917, at 5.30 a.m., with poor visibility and snow, the Canadian and British First Army set out to take control of Vimy Ridge in southern Belgium. This was a high point, the capture of which, would allow the Third Army to advance to take an important road and rail junction and liberate the coal-mining region. During this first day's offensive Donald Upshall was killed. He was 22.

Benjamin Waterfall, Chief Petty Officer, HMS Research

Benjamin was the second of five children to Benjamin, an engine driver from Deptford, and his wife Christiana. Benjamin junior joined the Royal Navy in 1889. He married Matilda Frampton in 1899. They had four children and lived in West Street, Titchfield. Whilst serving on HMS Research at Portland, a depot ship for locally employed armed trawlers, he died from an unstated disease. He was 43. He is buried in the graveyard of St Peter's, Titchfield.

'Remembrance of things past, The Vicar of Titchfield visits the Front in France in 1915', *written by Brian Patten for the Titchfield Parish Magazine in November 2008.*

This month marks the 90th anniversary of the end of the First World War when on the 11th November 1918 the guns fell silent on the Western Front. The fact that this terrible conflict still looms large in our consciousness is not really surprising given the vast amount of contemporary accounts, photographs and artistic works that have been handed down to us. Added to which are the many books written by historians, novelists and veterans since the event, and the films, radio and TV programmes that continue to bring home the suffering and ordeals of the men and women who fought in that War.

Of course, every town and village in the country has that most visible of signs of remembrance, the War Memorial, each of which lists the names of the fallen and where in many cases, including here in Titchfield, they are read out on Remembrance Sunday. It is extremely difficult to put ourselves back in time to understand the different emotions that affected people at different stages of the War but as early as 1915 it was beginning to dawn on many people that this was not going to be a quick walk-over as the troops from both sides dug in for three more years of trench warfare.

One man, whom I am sure realised this, was the Rev. Charles Matthews, Vicar of Titchfield. It was he in April 1915 arrived in France to serve as chaplain and minister to the wounded in a base hospital 40 kilometres from Calais. In June he wrote of his experiences in the St Peter's Parish Magazine saying that since arriving he had witnessed some very wonderful sights which had brought home to him the tragic horrors of the War, in a manner which could not be realised, in England.

"Every man I speak to acknowledges the mercy of God in sparing his life, and many have made their communions with deep thankfulness," he writes. "I could tell you many a story of the sufferings, the patience, and even cheerfulness of many a poor lad who is lying here - one especially interests me - who has lost both his arms. He always smiles when I visit him, and he is making slow but sure strides towards recovery. He was very devout and thankful when I gave him communion after his second operation."

He uses the euphemism 'crossing the bar' for those who had died of their wounds. He says that he had written letters to the bereaved parents and wives and he had accompanied several relatives to the cemetery for the last rites. They had gone over to France to see their loved ones but had arrived too late. The funerals of the troops took place daily at 8.00 a.m. and the officers' funerals at 2.30 p.m.

Construction of WW1 cemetery

He writes of the several Sunday services he conducted at the hospital and at other base camps and says that the heartiness of the singing is most inspiring. He discovers that one feature stands out prominently, the intense feeling of the value of prayer and intercession.

"Every man I have spoken to believes in the power of prayer," he wrote. "One dear lad told me that he and his chums had said the 23rd Psalm daily in the trench while the Germans were shelling our front"; and he added, "I believe, Sir, God heard and answered our prayer, as four out of five of us were spared."

Charles Matthews then goes on to issue a mild rebuke to his parishioners. "I mention this, because I know that there are some at home who do not come to Church to pray for our brave lads out here. I can only say to such as these; if you could come out here and visit this hospital for half an hour with me you would be absolutely convinced of the need and the value of intercession for as long as this ghastly war lasts."

It was to last for another three and half years during which time many thousands were killed and millions more wounded and damaged by their experiences. It still goes on in the conflicts which followed and those which are continuing today. As we remember our war dead at the War Memorial on Remembrance Sunday and think of those servicemen and women currently engaged in conflicts on our behalf we should recall the words of Charles Matthews and convince ourselves of the value of intercession.

Peace celebrations 1919

Titchfield after WW1

Although the War left its mark, the people of Titchfield soon made every effort to return to normal life as the baby show in 1921 and the opening of the bowls club in 1923 show. The Queen's Head public house is also mentioned during this time.

Baby Show 1921

Visitors also started to come to the village again. The Rev. E. C. Bedford, Rector and Rural Dean of Holborn in London wrote in his Parish leaflet in June 1924 under the heading 'Parish History':

The Queen's Head pub

'The writer was fortunate enough to have a week's holiday at Easter and spent it in a place probably little known to his readers, namely Titchfield - in Hampshire. The small town, or large village, two miles from Fareham, lies in a beautiful green valley through which the River Meon winds swiftly towards the sea. The wide street, as in many another country town, is bordered by shops, a few private houses and two old fashioned hotels with bow windows. At one time the quiet of the street was only disturbed twice a day by the arrival of the coach and the stream of life ran very placidly for the inhabitants. But now all through the day, charabancs pass and repass, motors and cycles go noisily by and the village dog can never compose himself for slumber for any length of time.

But those who visit Titchfield will not complain; for these same charabancs enable them to visit many more important places, as Portsmouth and Southampton and many beauty spots beyond the reach of the ordinary pedestrian. Above the town are woods and fields, particularly of strawberry plants, and houses and bungalows are springing up rapidly around.

St Peter's Church and the River Meon

There are two special objects of interest to the antiquarian here. The old Parish Church is one, dedicated to St Peter, with chancel, aisle and western tower showing different style of architecture, a fine Norman west door and early English decorated and perpendicular windows. In beautiful order and well restored, it repays a visit. But what is especially attractive is the magnificent tomb of the Earls of Southampton. This is fashioned of different coloured marbles with pillars and carving, and recumbent figures of the first Earl and his Countess and their son the second Earl. A welcome touch of colour is given to the sombre mass of marble by heraldic shields covered with armorial bearings in red and blue and gold, and gilded lettering giving the names and family history of those who lie beneath. The tomb is in perfect preservation, having been carefully restored under the direction of an artist.

The other object of interest to which the visitors direct their steps lies a little way to the north of the town, in the fields. This is the ruin of the great house called Place House (short for Palace House) once the stately residence of the Wriothesley family, Earls of Southampton.

An imposing gateway still stands with flanking battlemented towers and, stretching out on either side, two wings of the house with handsome chimney stacks and corner turrets. Roofless now, it is yet possible to trace various rooms, kitchen, hall and solar and imagine, at a later date, King Charles I

Titchfield Abbey

taking shelter here after his escape from Hampton Court and finding a brief rest before the storm broke and his fate sealed.

HM Board of Works has lately stripped away the ivy which mantled the whole building, and have made safe the existing portions of the house. All the rest of the structure has disappeared but excavations are being made which show part of the Abbey, upon the site of which, the great house was built. One can trace the walls of the cloister and can, with a little imagination, picture the monks of old strolling about, pursuing their various tasks, crossing the meadow and catching fish in the little river for the Friday fast.

A fascinating place, and known to history, as here King Henry VI married Margaret of Anjou. But it may be asked, what connection has it with St Andrew's, that it is written about under 'Parish History?' The answer is that Wriothesley, Earl of Southampton, Chancellor to King Henry VIII, was patron of St Andrew's. He lived in Holborn and was buried in our church. His son removed the bodies of his father and mother from their resting place here and conveyed them to Titchfield, where they lie under the marble tomb above described in the chancel aisle of the Parish Church.'

Thomas Wriothesley

Part Two 1914 - 1938

Childhood and Families

Alan Brind

My granddad was Herbert Allen (Jack) Laxton 1884 - 1936. He married Eva Whitear from Titchfield in 1913 and they lived at 81 West St. Titchfield.

Jack Laxton

Jack served for 24 years in the 108th Heavy Battery Royal Garrison Artillery which, as Sergeant, he left in 1926. He was a horseman par excellence and served the whole of WW1 in France and Belgium coming through numerous engagements uninjured. He was awarded a Mons Star with Clasp and Roses, British Army War Medal and Victory Medals.

He left the army in 1926 and became a bricklayer and worked on the building of Titchfield Primary School and also the Embassy and Savoy cinemas in Fareham. It was ironic that despite having worked with horses throughout his army career, he died, aged 52, following an infection due to a bite from a horse fly.

Donald Upshall

As I was the first grandchild in the Upshall family I was named after my uncle who was killed in WW1. If you look in the church you will see his name on the remembrance plaque. My father started the garage on East Street when I was born. Now, in 2015, we've been in business 89 years.

Today you don't realise how narrow the roads were then. There were no kerbs. You just walked along the edge of the road. But there wasn't much traffic then. It is so different now of course. I remember the main A27 road. I used to push my brother in his pushchair all the way in to Fareham where they had all these Hornby toys. I used to look at them in the window as I was a big Hornby train enthusiast at the time.

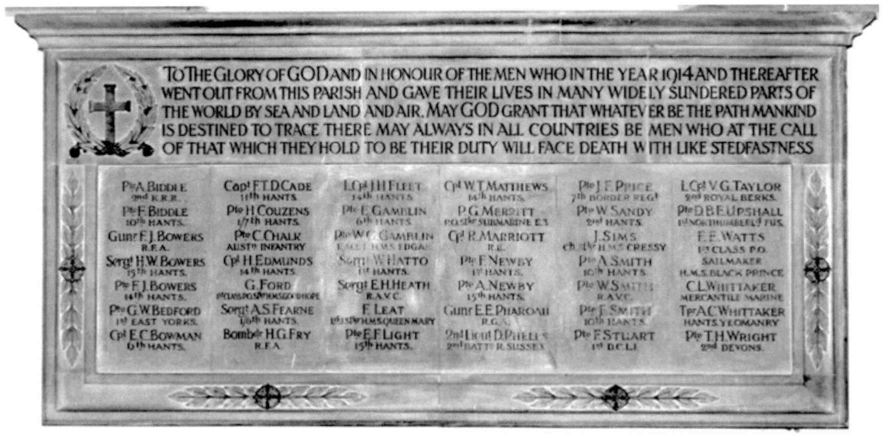

St Peter's War Memorial

My grandfather was the headmaster of the old Titchfield Primary School, when it was in West Street, back in the '20s and '30s; it was called the National School. In those days headteachers were respected and strict, and when we went to tea with him you had to be careful. When the new school was opened in 1934, he was on the board as a governor so he helped select the new headmaster. I was at West Street for about a year but I didn't used to see him. He had a motto, 'Manners Maketh Man' He had it right across the entrance to the assembly hall. Then we moved to the new school and he retired.

When we used to go to his house for tea in the '30s we used to sit there and he might have another friend, a headmaster, round and you certainly thought he was special! He used to tell me that people used to raise their hat to him in the street. They were respected then. He used to wear gentleman's boots, nice polished brown lace-up ones. When he caught a bus he always went upstairs to keep fit. I know he was connected to the church. I don't know if he played the organ but he used to go to the church because of the children, his students.

If you had to go to the doctor's you did not need an appointment so you sat and waited for your turn. Dr Windermer and the vicar were very well respected. Mr Mason was the chemist but there were no pills. He mixed up the prescription in medicine form.

I was the eldest of ten children whom my mother had to bring up. We used to live in the house opposite the garage, next to the Wheatsheaf pub in East Street. There were no supermarkets, double glazing or central heating and we had an outside toilet. I left home before I was 16 and my sister left for a secretarial job. Otherwise we were a bit crammed but the War was on and we had to put up with it. You look back and think how did we exist? I gave six sisters away in marriage as my father died near the end of WW2.

Ben Waterfall

"Brother married sister, and sister married brother"

Four generations with Audrey, Em (with baby Bev) and Tilly Waterfall

I am the grandson of the Ben Waterfall listed on the Titchfield War Memorial but I never knew my grandfather. Nobody ever told me about him and it wasn't until I started looking up the family tree that I found out about him. My gran wouldn't talk about him. I also didn't know, until after gran had died, that my great aunt Flo (Florence) was granddad's sister - no one ever told me. I just knew her because she was married to Grandma Tilly's (Matilda's) brother.

Ben Waterfall senior

Granny had a telegram from the Navy to say that granddad was on his last legs down at Portland and she should get down and see him so she went down there and was with him when he died. Gran lost her husband and son, Berty, in the same year. My dad was the only boy who survived, along with his sisters - aunts Rose, Minnie, Annie (Beryl's Mum), and Em (Emily).

Ben Waterfall's ship HMS Research

Douglas Elkins

Once in my boyhood I had to be seen by a doctor, Dr Weir from Lee-on-the-Solent. He lifted my shirt tail and said I had chicken pox! "That will be half a crown," (12.5p) said the doc to my mother. Children in those days suffered mumps, measles, jaundice, chicken pox, conjunctivitis, thread worms and every other malady known to school children and many never saw a doctor because of the cost.

I remember I used to cycle into Fareham town and, on one occasion, stood my bike against the kerb to go shopping, for my mother. On my return the cycle had vanished so I had a three mile walk back home. Several weeks later I was astonished to see a boy of about my age riding through Fareham on my bike. I promptly grabbed him and my bike and marched him up to the police station. The police station then was in the large house which is now the Registry Office in Osborn Road South, behind the Magistrates Court.

The sergeant sat me in a room on my own and took the other boy into another room to 'talk' to him. After some time the sergeant returned and said that he had left the boy in another room for a short while but on his return he found the boy had run away! I was re-united with my bike and went off upon my way. Thinking about this many years later, I think the sergeant gave the boy advice and time to get away before sending me away rejoicing.

Paula Weaver

My dad, George Rogers, known as Tom, was a Londoner. He joined the Royal Artillery as a boy soldier in 1925 as he wanted to work with horses. His assessment documents state that he was 'a first class gunner and a promising groom, fond of horses.' He was based at Fort Wallington. He left the army in 1931 and worked in the building trade.

George Rogers

I think he must have met my mum, Flo Ford, here in Titchfield. He told us that all his mates in the army, including him, had to say goodnight to the girls at the bridge in East Street because they were not allowed any further. The villagers did relent eventually because several of the soldiers, including my dad, married local girls and stayed in the village.

George Watts

George was born in 1931 at number 26 West Street. It was his grandparents' house and when his parents got married they had the upper rooms. Later the council built new houses at the top of West Street and he moved with his family to the new house, number 72.

June Pellatt

My great grandfather, William Burgess was the last Town Crier/Knocker-Up in Titchfield. He had three children, William, Ada and my gran Pat. Pat married Harry Bowers and they had four children, my dad was one of them, George Bowers.

William Burgess

George worked at Arthur Hales cycle shop from the age of 12 and was later apprenticed at the Upshall's garage. Arthur Hales used to be partners in the combined cycle shop and accumulator battery business with Edward 'Eddy' Upshall, but they separated and he left to open the cycle shop in the Square. Eddy carried on repairing cars at the same site. His grandson Phillip still runs the garage.

My granddad on mum's side was Sidney Russell, and his sister was Poppy. Their dad was an educated man who had become a farmer in the area. Sidney didn't want to go into farming so he joined the Royal Marines. Poppy married Archibald Freemantle whose father ran a pub. Although it was hoped that Archi would join his dad in the pub trade, he became a carpenter and later an undertaker. His grandson John Freemantle still works as an undertaker in the village.

I think my gran, with a couple of friends, did munitions work, filling shells in WW1. They went by transport and it was all a bit 'hush hush'. They had to stop though because the chemicals they were using started to turn them yellow. (*The munitions workers, or munitionettes, were called 'canary girls' because their skins turned yellow.*)

Kate Scott

'Granddad cycled down to Fareham from Nottingham in a day.'

Maud was my great granny on my mother's side. Granddad, Arthur Stanley Sentanse (Stan), came from Grantham in Lincs. He met granny on the 11th of the 11th 1929, funny wasn't it? He was in the army, the Royal Artillery and stationed at Fort Fareham. There were dances in Titchfield and the village girls enjoyed going to them. They often married the in-comers. I think it made the gene pool better!

Great granny Maud with brother Thomas, dad John Carse and Mrs Carse senior

As a married person great granny was entitled to an extra one shilling (5p) a week from the Government so she married on the 15th February 1930. Great granddad sailed to India on the 20th February 1930. Granny carried on working at Gudge Heath Lane, Fareham. When granddad came out of the army he couldn't get a job so he went to Nottingham.

Great grandfather got him a job. As granddad was an ex-serviceman he had experience with horses so he cut the grass with a team of horses at RAF Siskin and RAF Fort Grange. When granddad heard there was a job near here he got on his bike and cycled down to Fareham from Nottingham. It was one of the old bikes without gears. They were then together and my dad was born later.

Leslie Ellis

Leslie Ellis was born in Harrogate. He was the youngest of six children, four boys and two girls. The boys attended a Methodist boarding school in Colwyn Bay, North Wales. The choice of school came about because of his father's fear of Germans in WW1. His father thought that he and his brothers would be safer in North Wales. Leslie's eldest sister taught him to drive when he was just 14 years old.

Mike Ferris

"The gas holders were very large and ugly and they smelt very unpleasant"

I was born in 1937 at number 2 Frog Lane, which at that time formed the main entrance to the gas works. The gas holders were very large and ugly. They smelt very unpleasant although I was too young to realise this at the time. The weighbridge for the vehicles leaving the gas works still exists in Bridge Street on the driveway of the last of the terraced cottages.

We then moved to the Bellfield estate which was built in three phases with lower Bellfield being Phase one and Coach Hill and what we knew as middle Bellfield forming phase two. Numbers 81 and 82 on Posbrook Road, opposite the cemetery, were the last to be built before construction ceased during the War. We eventually moved to one of the cottages on Posbrook Road but then purchased land in Brownwich Lane where a nursery was established .

Rita Prior

Rita as a baby

Rita, a twin, was born on Monday 7th July 1930 at North Hill, Fareham. Her parents were Lillian Maggie and Leonard Etherington.

My twin is Roy. He was born first. My aunt, Amy, was present at the birth, being asked to assist the nurse. My mother was not too well following the births so nanny, Mary Ellen Bown, and aunt Amy said they would look after me 'until I could walk' but in the end I was brought up with them at Catisfield, 2 Fairthorne Cottages where I lived until I was married.

Rita celebrating the Coronation 1937

My early memories are of always visiting my mum and dad at North Hill regularly, spending birthdays together, I also remember, at Christmas, looking out of the window to see my own mum and dad and brothers and sister coming to spend Christmas Day with us all - nanny, aunt Amy, uncle Alec, aunt Elsie, and uncle Fred. Granddad, George Bown, died in 1933. I have been told he used to take me to watch the men building the Titchfield by-pass, the A27. I remember being taken on the bus to visit his grave at Titchfield Cemetery.

In early June 1935 a little baby wrapped in a shawl was placed in bed with me. Sylvia Annie Ruth Etherington was born on May 31st 1935. Her mother Annie died shortly after her birth. Once again aunt Amy came to the rescue and Sylvia became one of our family, believed by many to be my sister. Her father was Harold my father's nephew, her grandmother was my grandmother's sister, so closely related, we grew up as sisters really. Stanley George Weychan was aunt Amy and uncle Alec's only child and was like a brother to me. At five I caught whooping cough and was sent home from school, to stay home for six weeks. Sylvia was only a little baby and I remember her being quite ill with it. We also shared chicken pox, mumps and measles. Aunt Amy was a marvellous nurse and looked after us when we were sick.

Leslie Downs

I was born in Titchfield, in the Square. The village green at the bottom of West Street is where the house was but it was pulled down. I had three sisters and one brother, five of us all together. I am the only one left. My father worked in the building trade.

Kitty Potter

"The horses were not always willing to be caught"

I was born on 12th June 1913, in Mill Street, Titchfield, in the first of three cottages on the left hand side (as you face the A27). I had three brothers and two sisters in my family and now I am the only surviving sibling. My father Albert was the youngest of ten children born to William and Harriet Evans, both from Titchfield families. They were married in Titchfield church in 1855. William, my grandfather, was an agricultural labourer born about 1836. He died in 1925. I remember him as being a stern man. My grandmother, Harriet, died in 1915. My father's sister Mary, with her husband Jack and children lived in the cottage opposite and next door to the 'big house' - the home of the Parr family. Aunt Mary worked at the big house and before school each day I had to go across the road and help my aunt clean out the fireplaces.

Kitty Potter, Sunday School Concert

The Titchfield fire engine was horse-drawn and I think it came from what was the site of the Drill Hall and later the Community Centre. The horses were not always willing to be caught and harnessed up.

Kitty died 7th August 2015 aged 102.

Linda Felton

I have traced my family back to Henry and Hannah Mondey living in Titchfield in 1788. My great grandparents were George and Beatrice Frampton who owned two cottages in Church Street, Titchfield. My grandmother Gertrude Mary Frampton married John Austin, from Kent in 1925. They had three children, Betty Joan, John and my mother, Joy Evelyn, who was born in 1930. Her father had tuberculosis, TB, at the time and they were told that she would not be a normal baby. When she was born she was perfect and her father held her up and named her Joy so that she would always bring happiness to the family. Sadly, he died nine weeks later.

My grandmother was left with four children to look after as she also had her step-daughter Cathy. As the family were struggling financially, my grandparents' family took custody of Cathy. Gertrude married again and the family moved to 30 Bellfield. I was born there in 1951 and now live 18 doors away on Coach Hill.

Victor Chase

"My mother didn't christen me, didn't even give me my name or anything"

I was born in 1926 above the grocery store run by my father and mother. It was next to the chapel in Titchfield and what is now a Chinese take-away restaurant. When I was born my mother, Ada, was very ill and my father had to run the shop. I had three brothers and a sister. My sister went to stay with one of my aunties because my mother was so ill. My mother didn't even christen me, didn't give me my name or anything - it was touch and go as to whether she lived or not. She was a music teacher and had five sisters and

High Street, Titchfield

two brothers. One, Fred, was killed in WW1. My sister, Brenda, went to stay with my aunty and never came back.

Ada

We had to get out of the shop in 1926 - the recession. My dad said that there was hardly anyone in Titchfield that didn't owe him money. They used to say "Oh we'll pay you next week Ted" or whatever.

My grandfather worked at Hollam House and we used to get invited there as kids. New Year's eve they used to have the bell ringers in to ring in the New Year, and they had a party there which we went to. My grandfather worked there and my grandmother was cook so we got invited to all that lot.

I suppose we were fortunate in a way because my father, when he came out of the shop, worked for a Mr Bradley, headmaster of Prices School in Fareham. It was up Fishers Hill and we were more or less their kids, we were always up there, tennis court and all they had. Mrs Bradley used to take us out for car rides. In them days, there was hardly any cars about. We used to go to Cosham very often because she was interested in the Portsmouth Voluntary Association for the Welfare of the Blind which was there. She was one of the benefactors and she would take us there for a ride. In those days we were not used to a car and she would go over Portsdown Hill turning round to talk to us. We were shaking in the back! So we were privileged in a way.

Wally Pratt

"One of the last people alive who spoke with Lawrence of Arabia"

My brother was eight years older than me. He joined the RAF in 1929. Whilst stationed at RAF Calshot in the early thirties he went on a night out with some other airmen to Southampton and caught the ferry from Hythe. Whilst on the ferry he was approached by another airman who questioned him about supplies from Calshot for the RAF rescue launches he was building at Hythe. After they parted someone asked my brother if he knew who he had spoken to. It was Aircraftsman Lawrence - Lawrence of Arabia. My brother died 3 years ago this week. Up until then he must have been one of the last people alive who spoke with Lawrence of Arabia.

Bessie Traves

"We couldn't afford to pay for the bells to be rung"

I was born on the 21st December 1915 at Milvil Farm near to the entrance of what was later to become HMS Daedalus at Lee-on-the-Solent. I was the eighth child of ten, six girls and four boys born to Albert and Blanche Harris. Some of my older brothers and sisters were already out at work. Milvil Farm was the home of my maternal grandmother and grandfather.

I went back to our family home with my mother to join some of my siblings at Enterprise House in Peak Lane. It still stands alone on the east side of the road. It was a smallholding with what we called the 'large field' and the 'small field' a greenhouse and an orchard. We kept pigs and chickens as most smallholders did .The house had four bedrooms and the then luxury of an indoor toilet. The family had to help with the work on the smallholding. Sadly, in 1925, as the result of a serious accident to my father we had to give up the smallholding. After this, the family lived at various addresses in Stubbington and Hill Head. In 1931 my mother was offered the tenancy of No. 3 Posbrook Cottages so the family moved to Titchfield.

Wedding of Bessie and Cyril

In August 1935, I married Alfred Cyril Traves. He was a Leading Seaman in the Royal Navy and was serving in HMS Hood. I still have his cap ribbon from then. We were married by Canon Morley at St Peter's Church, Titchfield, and were the first couple to be married at three o'clock following a then recent change in the law. We couldn't afford to pay for the bells to be rung.

My first job was at a bungalow in Crofton Avenue 1929-1930. I then went to work in service for Colonel and Mrs House and their family at Crofton Manor. I was there until 1935. When I married, Mrs House' dress maker made my wedding dress, which I still have.

Cyril was away with the Navy a good deal of the time and then in 1937 his ship was sent to join the Mediterranean fleet. He did not return until early in

Graf Spee at Spithead, Coronation 1937 with HMS Resolution and HMS Hood (rear)

1941. During this period I was in service in Stubbington. Upon Cyril's return to the United Kingdom he was involved with North Sea convoy escort duties. His ship was based at Grimsby and, in order to have some time together, I joined him there, where we lived with a family who, after the War, became firm friends.

School

Donald Upshall

Titchfield School about 1934

The new school on the A27 was opened in 1934, I think, and I went to that school. I enjoyed school, but in those days you were always a bit nervous as teachers weren't so familiar. You respected teachers with 'Sir' and 'Mr So and So'. Miss Sarr the headmistress lived on Coach Hill, the second turning on the corner of Bellfield. Some children had to walk from Hook to school. When you got older you were allowed to use ink but it came as a powder and had to be mixed up and poured into an ink well. The blackboard was on an easel and the teacher used chalk.

Douglas Elkins

I began school at the age of five years at Crofton Council Junior School in Gosport Road, Stubbington, in the Autumn of 1934.

A toilet block sat in the middle of the playground. There was just a peat urinal and bucket lavatories for boys. Girls had bucket lavatories too. Two hand basins were provided in the playground. There was just cold water, no soap, no towels. Drinking water was provided by a standpipe in the playground. In winter there was often no water because the tap was frozen.

Queen Mary luggage tag

Around 1935/7 the new steam passenger ship, HMS Queen Mary, was launched and its maiden voyage was from Southampton. This vessel displaced over 80,000 tons and the occasion drew such attention that all of the pupils were marched to the Coast Guard Cottages by Saltern Park (Hill Head) to see the ship sail past and out to sea.

Mrs Upson terrified me as she did other children. I was seven years old. Afternoon play time ended at 3.10 p.m. and there was then a 50 minute lesson until 4.00 p.m. I suddenly developed severe stomach discomfort and raised my hand to ask to go to the toilet. The formidable teacher promptly made it clear that I could not leave the class until 4.00 p.m. Well, soon after that, I had diarrhoea but I sat in silence contemplating the mess that I was in. Eventually children around me raised their hands and reported that there was a nasty smell. Mrs Upson then came to investigate and decided that I could go to the toilet after all. Bucket loos, no paper, no soap, no hot water. AD 1936!

The next class was taught by Mrs Dyer. When I was aged eight, one day a girl in the class reported that I had sworn in class - untrue. Mrs Dwyer told me to sit at the front of the class, behind her desk, until lunchtime when I would be taken to the head master. I used to walk home at noon for lunch, a distance of about a mile but on this day I had first to be taken to Mr Farthing. He listened to Mrs Dyer's account and decided I should be caned! However, there were children sitting in classrooms eating their packed lunch so they found somewhere else to cane me so I wouldn't upset their lunch. It was a large classroom out of sight of all. Afterwards I ran home in order not to be late back for the afternoon lesson at 1.30 p.m.

George Watts

I attended Titchfield Junior School and my favourite teacher was Miss Carden who wore a bottle green jumper. Although I was only six I fell in love with her. There were only four classes then and I went to the new school which is still on its present site. The other teachers were Mrs Croucher and young Miss Morgan, and the headmistress was Miss Sarr, who took the top class.

Titchfield Junior School

Kitty Potter

"We left school then aged 14"

I started school on the 8th July 1918 at the old school in West Street.
The teachers that I remember were:
Miss Cardin - 'Babies'
Miss Richards - 'Infants'
Miss Godley - 'Standards I and II'
Mrs Croucher - 'Standards III and IV'
Miss Ings was the headmistress and taught the older girls of 13 and 14 years. We left school then aged 14. A corrugated metal fence separated the girls' and boys' schools. I went home for dinner.

Bessie Traves

I attended the old Stubbington School on the Gosport Road, leaving at 14 to go into service. My school friends were all Stubbington girls. I remember going by horse and cart on a Sunday School outing to Newlands farm for a picnic.

Celebrations and Leisure

Douglas Elkins

Around 1936/7 there was a 'Flying Circus' which came to Lee-on-the-Solent and put on an Air Day. A man stood between the wings of a biplane which then took off and circled around allowing us to see him jump off and descend by parachute. Quite exciting for a small boy! At this display a very small airplane named the 'Flying Flea' was presented and this was claimed to be the smallest flying aircraft. Many years later I stumbled across one of these in a museum. I think it was said to have been French-built and unstable because of its design.

The Flying Flea

Irene Harris

Mrs Harris, known as Rene, recalled how she went with her husband Steve to an air show in Lee-on-the-Solent in about 1932 when they were courting.

Amy Johnson and Amelia Earhart, her American counterpart, were both there and Rene and Steve went on an exhilarating flight over the Solent. That must have been an incredible experience for those days! The flight cost five shillings (25p), which was a lot of money then!

Rene died on 8th April 2015 on her 101st birthday.

Victor Chase

The Tower complex at Lee-on-the-Solent

My father built one of them seaside huts at Hillhead for Mr Bradley. It was the first one built down there and it's nearest the harbour. At Brinnage, (Brownwich) the long lane had all the families going down there on a weekend or sunny day, all walking. On the right hand side there was a field with a stream going through. We used to spend weekends there, loads of tents down there on the beach and the fields behind. We had fresh water from the stream. That was our holiday really. For a proper holiday we went to Lee-on-the-Solent cause they had the Tower there and all that. And a real holiday, like going abroad, was one day in the year, the Sunday School would go to Southsea on coaches. Yes, that was a real holiday that was. In those days you had to go to Sunday School, to get out of the way of parents, cos it was mostly big families in them days. So talk about holidays that was our holidays. My father used to organise coach trips like the one in the photo.

Coach trip

As kids it was football and actually my father who owned strawberry fields separated a bit off and made a football pitch out of it up Hunts Pond Road. We used to have proper football matches there and our place was popular for football - that was the main entertainment then. My father was chairman of Titchfield Football Club and they won a cup in the end, in fact I think they won several cups but the last cup they played in Botley and we won. It was the only time I know that they had a dance in the Square. They put a platform down and had some piano accordion players and plenty of beer. I think that was just before the War.

Food and Farming

Victor Chase

Then in the summer us kids, we used to go strawberry picking for about three weeks. And the money we used to get, part of it, went towards our clothes you know to help out, and the other part we used to get cycles.

Victor and his bike

In the Square at the end there was a cycle shop so we used to take our bike down and get another one. That was your travel, your bikes.

Kitty Potter

My father, a market gardener, rented the ground in what is now Protea Gardens, Titchfield, and we kept a pony. At that time it was possible to walk down to the river to water the horses. This was before the A27 was built and is approximately where the bridge that carries the A27 across the river now stands. Some cottages in Mill Street were demolished to make way for the road. We had a well in the back garden to supply the cottages but if it dried up we had to wait for the water-carrier to come round.

Douglas Elkins

Peel Farm and House were accessed from Peel Common. Henry Smith was the farmer and his son Quentin also farmed around the area. Henry Smith ran the dairy and supplied all locals with milk, served from urns with measures poured into milk tins placed on householders' doorsteps. When old enough, I sometimes did jobs at Peel Farm. The pay for gathering acorns was two shillings (10p) per bushel. (One bushel = 8 gallons = 36.4 litres.)

Quentin Smith would sometimes ask my father if I would go and lead the horse when horse-hoeing brassicas, this I did and the pay was three pennies (1.2p) per hour. Quentin would also take me to the annual Wickham Fair in his van.

A hare at speed

Henry Smith would sometimes arrange a shoot for hares, on land where HMS Collingwood playing fields are now, back to his farm house. We boys would be paid 3d per hour to 'beat', driving the game through the fields, brassicas and foliage onto the guns. This was 1930-40. Jugged hare or a hare-cup would be unheard of nowadays.

Work

Kitty Potter

When I left school in 1927 I went to work for Captain and Mrs May at a house called Langalla in Catisfield. Most girls then went into service. In 1933 while I was working for Captain May, Paul Robeson, who was appearing locally, stayed there with them. He gave me a signed photo of himself which I still have. Mrs May died in 1939 and Captain May in 1943.

Paul Robeson

Victor Chase

Paul Robeson, he come to Titchfield once. He was such a big bloke, I think he stayed at Hollam House. The maid had a shock once, they didn't have a bed big enough for him and she saw him with his feet stuck out the end of the bed.

Leslie Ellis

Leslie attended Cambridge and Leeds universities to study medicine. When he qualified, he assisted a G.P. in Ackworth, Yorkshire.

Church, Chapel and Religion

Donald Upshall

Mr Upshall senior, 2nd from the right

I remember the names of the vicars, in the '30s. The Reverend Moorley, he was well known and very sociable with his parishioners. He'd go round for a glass of port. The next one was Reverend Spurway. He was quite a good chap and he got us choirboys formed in to a football team and we played West Hill School. And the third one after that was Reverend Miller. He married my wife and me. In those days you respected them more, the vicar, choirmaster and organist. When I was in the choir we had lady members, men, girls and boys. The men would look over the boys and tap you on the shoulder and tell you to keep quiet. We had a hand pump to drive the organ.

I remember my grandfather insisted I became a junior choirboy. Being the first grandson I had to join the choir. I used to have a pretty good voice and I became head choirboy. I showed my son, Philip, exactly where I used to sit. We used to sit in the middle and the younger ones were last and went into the choir stalls. I used to lead as I was head boy, I was 13 or 14. I used to sing solos and my grandfather said something about going to Winchester, but nothing came of it because of the War. I was confirmed in St Peter's and then I acted as a server at communion. We had different coloured cassocks. We used to have choir practice on Tuesday. The choirmaster was called Smith and he used to come all the way from Southampton to take the choir.

The children's choir

Once a month, we would have a procession. The servers would start and we'd all form up and walk slowly around the perimeter of the church, singing a hymn and then go back to our seats. Being a Naval area there were lots of admirals and rear admirals around and academic types and they would ask the vicar if we choirboys would go out and sing Christmas hymns, by appointment, in their houses. So the vicar and organist would take us in their cars to sing carols in these houses and we would have lemonade and cake. That was in the '30s. Some of these houses have been knocked down but St Margaret's is still there. We used to be thrilled with that! It was quite an event. We used to get a little money to keep the interest up. Where the chapter rooms are now, we had a vestry with changing rooms, one for the men. The girls were separate, outside the vestry so they would pull a curtain across.

In those days a lot of the older congregation had their name-plates in the places they always sat. On the left hand side right at the top were the three spinster sisters, the Miss Hewetts, who were well known. They owned a lot of land. They lived next to the garage, not the one I lived in but the one on the other side. They had their own little plate with their name on it, on the pew, where they sat all the time. Mr Mason, the chemist read the lesson every Sunday morning.

Douglas Ekins

The 'Tin Tabernacle'

I moved to Peel Common, (Newgate Lane) in 1933; the southernmost house known as Willow Cot.

I believe Albert Holgate built the Peel Common Mission Hall. Hitherto the mission was carried on in a corrugated iron building (tin tabernacle) situated by Peel House, just down into Woodcote Lane. I, together with many other children on the Common, was sent to a Sunday School there long before starting day school. That continued until I was past 14 years of age.

John Williams

"I earned my first 6d for pumping the organ at the morning and evening services in chapel"

I earned my first wage of 6d (2.5p) for pumping the organ at the morning and evening services at the chapel. My family were quite religious. My father was secretary of the chapel and among his duties he was responsible for arranging for the lay preachers each Sunday. These lay preachers came mainly from Southampton so usually came to our house for Sunday lunch. So my mother provided a good Sunday lunch from what little rations we had.

There was a canteen set up in the Sunday School hall of the chapel for the service personnel to relax in. My mother was one of the ladies who served tea and sandwiches for them.

Paula Weaver & Pamela Fullick

We remember, aged about four, going to watch magic lanterns at Sunday School with Mr Cousins. We used to get in the back room, Pam played and I pumped the organ. We played all sorts of music before everyone came. We pulled the curtains and played.

Mary Burner and her brother Robert Chase, The Chase Family

The name Chase goes back a long way in Titchfield and we have managed to trace our family history to the 18th century. Our family has mainly lived in East Street. The building trade was always part of the Chase family. Our claim to fame is that we are fortunate enough to still have a few manhole covers in some streets or gardens in the village, with 'D. Chase & Son' on them! Apart from properties within the village, we have papers which show that David Chase, our great-grandfather, bought 'Bellfield House', and other buildings on Coach Hill, in an auction.

David Chase was born in Frog Lane. His parents were George and Catherine Chase and they had 11 children - George, Jane, Caroline, David, Mary-Ann, Alfred, Ellen, Robert, Harriet, Elizabeth, and William. When David married and had children he rented 31 East Street from Miss Rose Green, the owner, who had a large estate in Catisfield and Titchfield. The house was eventually bought from Miss Green.

David Chase and his wife Elizabeth had four girls Elizabeth, Mary, Emma and Sarah, and one boy William (our grandfather). Three girls married, and presumably left the village, leaving my grandfather, William, and great aunt Sarah in the house. The 1911 census shows William registered as a builder and great aunt Sarah as a spinster. Great aunt Sarah later moved out to a cottage in Warsash Road when our grandparents got married. David and Elizabeth Chase are buried in a tomb in the churchyard.

William Chase, our grandfather, was in his 40s when he got married to Bertha May. Miss May came from Bradford-upon-Avon and worked as a milliner at Hudson's, formerly Collihole's and now One Stop in

David Chase

the Square. We have a letter from when grandfather was 'courting' her, where he wrote to her, posted the letter, even though she only lived round the corner in the Square, to ask her to come to tea in East Street and got a reply from her later in the day! Our grandfather did not serve in WW1; I assume partly because he was too old and partly because he was in the building business.

William and Bertha only had one child, our father, William David Robert Chase, known as David, who was born in October 1916. Sadly, grandmother Bertha died when David was 18. She pricked her finger on a rose whilst gardening and died of septicaemia. Grandfather died in 1938 and they are both buried in Posbrook Lane cemetery.

Our father, David Chase, went to the local primary school in Titchfield in about 1920 and then went to Price's Grammar School in Fareham. David then worked for his father in the building business and studied architecture at Portsmouth College of Art. He qualified in 1936. All his studies were painted in watercolour and were delicate - a real work of art. On his right hand, his little finger was permanently bent under and he couldn't straighten it. He said it was because it was where his hand was always pressing down on the drawing board. He drew and produced beautiful plans for various people in the village and surrounding area. Some plans we found we gave back to the people when father died; for example, to Linda Gardner, her father Roy Gardner was a carpenter for my father, and dad designed her bungalow.

When David was in his twenties he decided to buy a car. He went to Southampton and came back with a foreign car – no driving test then! My grandfather immediately told him to take it back and get a British car. That was in 1936. He did as he was told. When he eventually took his driving test in 1937, the hill start was taken by the Old Portsmouth walls on a gravel bank. A matchbox was put behind the back wheel and he had to do a hill start without disturbing gravel or running back over the matchbox. We have his first driving licence!

After he completed his training as an architect, and after grandfather died, David took over the building business and management of the properties owned by the Chase family. At that time the family had properties in East Street, Church Path, South Street, West Street and Southampton Hill, one of which was the old police house.

Most of the houses in the village would have had some sort of work done to them by Chase. For example, Old Lodge in the High Street - grandfather was running the business when two cottages were demolished to make way for a new entrance to Old Lodge.

Josephine Doherty

At some point the building yard moved from 31 East Street to Southampton Hill. It was situated between Sisman & Goatcher garage and the fire station, backing onto Barry's meadow. Our father married Josephine Bridget Doherty (Joey) in November 1938. Joey was born at Cheekpoint, Waterford, Southern Ireland. She left home at 18 to go to London to St Thomas's hospital where she did her training. On qualifying she moved to Southampton, to the Royal South Hampshire Hospital, to be near some of her family.

My parents met at the Royal South Hampshire Hospital where my father was visiting a sick friend. When they married, she gave up nursing and moved to No. 31 East Street. Women did not usually work after marriage then. She used to say that No. 31 was a dark and scary house - it had stuffed birds and animals in glass boxes in the alcoves, which she soon got rid of. It was our grandfather's dying wish that our parents should marry. With her nursing background, my mother had cared for him and it sounds like he took a shine to her.

George Edward Ferris, 1885-1964

The Ferris family were engaged in the local Titchfield farming and agricultural community from the early part of the 19th century, principally on the farms at Brownwich, Little Posbrook and Great Posbrook.

George Ferris married the daughter of the head shepherd at Brownwich farm and was initially a carter before becoming a skilled

George Edward and son George H. Ferris

ploughman. He was, however, a man of initiative and after the end of WW1 he purchased from his employer some land at Brownwich Lane. Here he established one of the regions early market gardens and a nursery. At the same time he acquired an ex-WW1 army hut, which was converted into a bungalow where his family of three girls and four boys grew up. They were also engaged, at various times, in the activities of the market garden.

The principal crops he grew were strawberries and, under glass, tomatoes. However he was also an early pioneer grower of off-season winter lettuce and chrysanthemums in the greenhouses. He also grew crops such as anemones off-season in the strawberry fields together with all the normal produce from a market garden. He enjoyed a particularly high reputation for the quality of the strawberries, he produced. Much of the crop of this fruit from the region, was shipped daily by horse and cart to Swanwick station and then to markets in London and Scotland.

In 1929 George won the coveted accolade for producing the best 20 baskets of Hampshire strawberries in Covent Garden for that year, for which he was presented with an engraved silver cup.

George was a founding shareholder in the Swanwick Basket Factory, which produced all the containers for the fruit industry in the region. He was similarly involved with the establishment of Titchfield Mill, which specialised in providing fertilisers, seeds and general farming supplies.

George's affinity with horses remained with him throughout his working life and one was employed on his land for all the heavy work until the early 60s. After his eventual retirement, two of his sons took over the running of the business.

Ken Bayley, a walk around pre-war Titchfield

I was 12 when I moved to The Close in Bellfield with my parents and my brother and sister. These memories are of Titchfield in the years leading up to WW2. At Posbrook, the cemetery and the allotments were just as today, but there were fields everywhere else. White City, as it was known, which is an extension to Bellfield, was not built. There was Boyd's Nursery, then Jim and Steve Harris' land with strawberries and other horticulture. Then there was Mortimer's land; they farmed right down to the sea. Every sort of vegetable was grown as well as corn. But there was no rhubarb, sweetcorn or pumpkins. Behind the farm cottages was the copse, but all over the village anyone who had a bit of land grew strawberries.

Fielder's Brewery

Coach Hill was not built up as it is today. Just into Lower Bellfield was The Black Shop, a general store run by the Downes family. Further down was the doctor's house, where Dr Ellis now lives. Dr Windermer worked on his own there in the '30s. You had to go in and queue up. Some families paid into a medical insurance, like the Foresters. The next house belonged to Mr Fielder who owned the brewery in Bridge Street. He employed four or five workers. I remember the bowling green on the right. Further on was the dairy farm run by Miss Hewett of Mill Street. When Titchfield Road bypass was constructed it cut through her farm. I think she sold out before this.

South Street

In South Street, Freemantle's builders and funeral directors occupied its present site. The Coach and Horses pub on the corner of Coach Hill was the pub my parents went to occasionally. The main entrance to the gasometer was on the right in Frog Lane. The surrounding land was meadows. We would go there for the fair and the circus. You could walk round to the churchyard which had metal railings then. These were later handed over for the War effort. There was a walkway through to the tannery. Back to South Street: The Red House was a pub. Next door was a sweet shop and general store, and adjacent to the Tudor cottages, a fish and chip shop. A piece of fish and some chips wrapped in newspaper cost four pennies (1.6p).

Beyond the old cottages was a black shed. This was the snooker club. I never went in there. Then there was Beards, a barber shop, which also sold cigarettes and newspapers which he also delivered. Where the hairdresser is now was the blacksmith's. Oily William's shop was next. He sold everything from tin baths to chocolate. He owned two vans which he would drive around the district delivering paraffin. The last shop in South Street was Arthur Hale's bicycles. Arthur would also re-charge the batteries for our accumulators before we had electricity. You could buy a Raleigh bike for about £6. I had a bike.

The Bradley family would cycle down to Meon to collect winkles. They would bring them home, sort them and then cycle to Fareham to sell them.

Church Street: there was a National Provincial Bank on the right. Close to the church on the left was the harness shop. Saddles and tack were made on the premises and were displayed on large pegs on the wall on the left. These are still visible and now serving as flower pot holders.

Church Street

Back into the Square, sited where the Co-op is now, on the corner of Church Street, was the gasometer shop, where I remember people went to buy coke. Past the Bugle pub was Anne's sweet shop. There was a large shop, Colihole, employing six or seven staff, selling clothes, curtains and material. There was a chemist where it is today, called Masons back then. The Earl of Southampton's Rooms were not there. The next building was the chapel. After this were a series of cottages. I remember a cobbler called Charlie who lived in one cottage. Then came the barber's shop, Worleys. He charged 6d (2.5p) for an adult shave and haircut. For children, it was 3d (1.2p), but he gave you back ½d (0.2p) for sweets on the way home. But if you turned up with 2½d, he wouldn't cut your hair!

Returning to the west side of South Street, past the Coach & Horses pub, there was a grocer, Walters, then a butcher, Horlock's, then Jimmy Smith, another cobbler who also sold shoes, then another grocery and vegetable shop. On what is now the Green, I remember a Tudor house which was pulled down. Turning into West St, there was a sweet shop in the front room of the cottage where the Freemantles

The West End Inn

lived (the timber-framed white house). This was a common practice. The West End pub came next, then White's baker and general store. Opposite was another baker.

Back in the Square, on the west side, were three shops run by Lankester & Crooks. The first was a grocer, the second an ironmonger and the third another butchers. Next came Walt Lane, the tinsmith. Near the Bugle pub was the post office, and then another butchers. Next door was St John the baker. His bread was good and he delivered it too. He baked delicious cakes. The Queen's Head pub and the Parish Rooms have not changed from how they were then. Southampton Hill had no development on the right hand side. On the left was a builder's yard and a garage.

The milk delivery

In East Street there was a shop called Farrell's. I think it had been a clothes shop but it was closed and derelict. Then came Wally Way, the newsagent and tobacconist, working out from one room. Wally and his mate would cycle off very early to Fareham station every day to collect the papers from the train, bring them back and deliver them around the village. I remember yet another general store before you reached the Wheatsheaf pub.

The Territorial Army used the building where the Community Centre is now. We could walk or cycle along Mill Street all the way to Titchfield Mill (with no A27 to cross). We played football in the recreation ground. There was a nursery opposite the Fisherman's Rest pub. There were two farms to the west, Wolf's and Abraham's. Both farms delivered milk to the houses in the village. You took out your jugs and cans to be filled. However, I do remember seeing my first milk bottle about then.

Back in East St, Upshall's Garage was where it is now but there was a cut through to the tannery. On the corner of East St and Mill St is Bridge House, where the three Miss Hewetts lived. One was the farmer in Bridge Street, another grew flowers and arranged these in the church whilst the third was the choir mistress.

The village was a busy place. People would come to here to shop from Catisfield, Park Gate and Stubbington. The carnival was a great event every year, with a procession so long that sometimes it met up with its tail! Those were good days. Everyone said "Good Morning" and helped each other out, with a cup of sugar or whatever. My father worked in the tannery. My brother was in the army. He came home safely. I met my wife Peggy on the bus one day! She is a relative of Steve Harris. When we married we came to live in Common Lane where we brought up our three daughters and where I still live today.

Farmer's wisdom

One boy's a boy
Two boy's half a boy
Three boy's no boy at all

Farmers knew from experience that the more boys there were working together, the less work that was actually achieved.

What's that in Old Money?

Old Money	Type	Name	Current Value
1/4d	'copper'	Farthing	Nothing!
1/2d	'copper'	Halfpenny, 'Ha'penny'	0.2p
1d	'copper'	Penny	0.4p
3d	'copper'	'Thrupenny bit' 'Thrupence'	1.2p
6d	'silver'	Sixpence or 'Tanner'	2.5p
1s	'silver'	Shilling (12 pennies)	5p
2s	'silver'	Florin, '2 Bob bit'	10p
2/6s	'silver'	Half Crown	12.5p
5s	'silver'	Crown (only commemorative coins)	25p
10s	'note'	'10 Bob', 'half a Nicker'	50p
£1	gold coin until 1932	Sovereign	£1
	'note'	Pound,' Quid', 'Nicker'	£1
21s	gold coin until 1814	Guinea (for buying posh horses)	£1.05

Names that still apply today

£5	'note'	'Fiver'	£5
£6		'Sick squid'	sorry!
£10	'note'	'Tenner'	£10
£20		'Score'	£20
£50		'Bullseye'	£50
£100		'Ton'	£100
£500		'Monkey'	£500
£1000		'Grand'	£1000

Coins used to contain real silver and gold. A gold sovereign was a coin valued at one pound which was in circulation up to 1932. To stop people clipping bits off, they were given a textured (milled) edge. As gold is so heavy, even a lead copy would feel light. Later coins had no precious metals in them, but were made of harder metal for a long life.

Cash is ready money and sometimes referred to as 'readies' or 'dosh'. Coins in the pocket or purse are known as 'shrapnel' or 'loose change'. A 'wad' or 'wedge' is a bundle of paper 'notes'. Paper money is also known as 'folding money'.

Titchfield Telephone Directory 1932

Tel No	Name	Business	Address
2	Windermer,	Doctor	Coach Hill
3	McKenzie		Mayburys
5	Ransome		The Shack
6	Waters		EastStreet
8	Napier		Catisfield Cottage
9	Williams		Sarisbury House
10	Mason	Chemist	The Chemist
11	Wisbey		Orchardleigh, Catisfield
12	Bunney		Brodick Lodge, Catisfield
13	Standen		Laylands, Catisfield
14	Lambert		Larches, Catisfield
15	Freemantle	Builder/Undertaker	Gainsborough
17	Baxter		Stanraer, Catisfield
18	Villiers		Hollam House
19	Boyd		Bungalow, Meon Road
20	Lane		Elmshurst, Catisfield
21	Sanders	Market Gardener	Hollam
22	Wield		South Street
24	Morley		The Vicarage
25	Walker	Stationer & PO	
26	Mortimer		The Limes, Catisfield
27	Freemantle	Butcher	High Street
28	Williams		Segensworth House
29	Watkins	Tanner	
30	Titchfield Abbey Co-op		
31	Tibbitts		Abbey Cottage
34	Lumsden		Invery Lodge
35	Jackson		Great Posbrooke
36	Ransome		West Hill Park
37	Upshall	Garage	Garage, East Street
38	Lang		Corner House
39	Skey		Little Crofton, Catisfield
40	May		Langaller, Catisfield
41	Bone		Brownwich
42	Ottley		Clanconnel, Catisfield
43	General store		Lankester & Crook
44	Chalmers		Guessens
46	Dredge	Public House	Coach & Horses
47	West		High Street
48	Stevenson		Singlestock, Catisfield
49	Mathais		Catisfield House
50	Gorton		Little Crofton
51	Harvey		Heathfield
52	Waters	Grocer	
54	Parry		St Margaret's
55	Wadham		Drumbrae, Catisfield

Tel No	Name	Business	Address
56	Nobes	Shoe Shop	
57	Maltby		Catisfield House
58	Canham		Ingleby, Coach Hill
59	Halahan		Sunny Corner, Meon
60	Sisman & Goatcher	Garage	Southampton Hill
61	Blake		Heathfield, Catisfield
63	Seymour		Meadowland, Catisfield
64	Temple		Carnahalla, Catisfield
65	Harvey		Whitecraigs, Catisfield
66	Righton		Norsome, Sandringham Rd
67	Foote		Catisfield Croft
68	Boakes		Park Farm
70	Riches		Warbreccan, Catisfield
71	Webb-Bowen		Fairthorne, Catisfield
74	Snook	Garage	Southampton Road
75	Goatcher		Ashlyn
77	Harris	Meon Farm	Posbrook Lane
79	Titchfield Gas Co		
80	Nicholson		Ranvilles, Catisfield
81	Police		
82	Banks		Highcroft, Sandringham Rd
83	Edwards		Old Lodge
84	Harris		Rohallion
86	Hulley		24 Highlands Road
88	Williams	Ironmonger	South Street
93	McMinn		Singledge, Meon
94	Shaw		The Mount, Catisfield
95	Ulyat		Crofton Cottage
96	Fielder	Brewer	The Brewery House
98	Allen	Post Office	Catisfield PO
99	Bethell		Meon House
101	Darking		New Clements, Catisfield
102	Case		Mendip, Sandringham Road,
103	Bradshaw		Little Brownwich
104	Mugliston		Stoneleigh
105	Green		The Croft
107	Crosley		Highlands Road
109	Draper		Hawkley, Fareham
110	White		Crofton House
111	Mack		Lithgow Ct, Catisfield
112	Merriman		Rosecroft, Crofton
114	Robertson		Briar Wood
115	Spurgin		Elmside, Meon
116	Penny		Cliff Cottage
117	Hughes		Meon Marsh

This is a transcription of a one-sheet document with all the 1932 telephone numbers for Fareham and Titchfield, kindly supplied by John Freemantle. The original can be viewed at www.titchfieldspirit.uk

Part Two Bonus Pictures

Toffs in 1909 Carnival

Airplane lands at Locks Heath 1913

The new bypass

Brownwich Farm

The Water Carrier

West Street

East Street

Seaplane at Lee on the Solent

Coronation celebrations 1937

Michael Ferris

Mr Pannell and son Alf

Work involving axe, shovel, & two brooms

Bessie Traves (Harris) first day at school with brother Steve and sister Emily

Significant dates (Titchfield items in Bold)

1914 - Outbreak of the First World War, WW1
1914 - Mayburys (High Street), converted to a soldiers hospital
1915 - Gallipoli, Allies failed attempt to secure waterway at Istanbul
1916 - Irish Easter Uprising, leads to Partition and Civil War
1916 - Battle of Jutland in the North Sea, naval battle with battleships
1916 - Somme Offensive, north France, 1 million dead, we gain 6 miles
1917 - Russian revolution starts leading to Communist takeover
1917 - America enters the War on British side
1917 - Battle of Vimi Ridge in northern France. Allied gain
1918 - Spanish Flu pandemic kills 50-100 million people worldwide
1918 - WW1 ends with 10 million combatants and 7 million civilians dead
1918 - Parliament gives partial voting rights to women
1919 - Lady Astor becomes the first female Member of Parliament
1919 - **Titchfield Parish Council's 1st lady member, Agnes Hewett**
1922 - United Soviet Socialist Republic, USSR, formed
1923 - Irish Free State wins the Irish Civil War
1923 - **Titchfield streetlights are converted from gas to electric**
1926 - General Strike as Trade Union Congress supports the miners
1928 - Women get the same voting rights as men (all over 21)
1929 - Great Depression drops world GDP by 15% in a decade
1930 - English Amy Johnson flies solo England to Australia
1932 - American Amelia Earhart, first solo flight across the Atlantic
1932 -Amy Johnson and Amelia Earhart at Lee-on-the-Solent show
1933 - Adolf Hitler appointed Chancellor of Germany
1936 - Year of the three Kings. The abdication crisis
1938 - *Snow White & the Seven Dwarfs*, first full-length animation film

The year of the three Kings

Part Three 1939 - 1945

Childhood and Families

Andrew Mills

"We used to get Christmas cards from them with bayonets on!"

I had two aunts, Trixie and Molly Laxton. I think Alan Brind's sister, was named after Trixie. Both aunts married Irish commandos, Sam Brodison and Mac Maginnis, respectively, and they lived in Bellfield. We used to get Christmas cards from them with bayonets on! They all got on well with my grandfather, who was a Calver.

My great grandfather was originally an American from Michigan who came over here and married my great grandmother and they lived in Woolston, Southampton. He was a very clever philosopher who worked for Vickers designing aircraft engines. He designed a silent aircraft engine and someone said to him that that would be great for the War, which was looming. Being an absolute pacifist, he destroyed the plans. The rest of the family thought he was very religious. In fact he was an atheist but, because of the way he talked, no one trusted him except my mother who was fascinated by him. He passed his challenging way of thinking onto her and she passed it on to me a bit. I was forever grateful to him for talking to my mother because she was a pretty bright sort of person. He left home and went back to America, but I later discovered that he died in Newton Abbot, Devon.

Bessie Traves

My son, Tony, was born at the Naval Maternity Home that had been evacuated from Southsea to Wickham. I came back to Posbrook with him just before Christmas. Coal was very short during the War, so I used to push Tony in his pram and pick up sticks from the hedges in Posbrook Lane and in Road Copse (off Posbrook Lane) in order to light the fire to warm the room and heat the water for his bath.

Tony Traves Carnival Cowboy

In February 1944 we moved to Common Lane. We shared the house with another family. It was August 1944 before my husband, Cyril, came home and met Tony for the first time. My daughter Margaret was born at home in Common Lane in mid-1945. Cyril completed his service in the Navy in 1947 and worked as a postman in and around the Fareham area until his retirement.

Donald Upshall

I remember my mother sending me round to Titchfield, to Collihole's, a big draper shop in the Square where One Stop is now. Titchfield people used to buy their clothes there. I remember on the Friday, 1st September, my mother sent me round to buy black-out material to stick up across the windows for when you put the light on, in case the Nazi planes came along.

The other thing I remember was rationing; you went into shops and the shelves were bare, just a few things. But now you go into supermarkets and the choice! But the pubs, later on in the War even they ran out of beer. Sometimes they had to shut for two or three days as rationing was so severe.

Collihole putting up the sunshade

Freemantle was a butcher, Russell ran the mill and Mason was the chemist, and they all went out together in a car for a drink. (Not many people had a car then.)

In 1944, my father died suddenly, which was a shock. I was only 18 then. I had a week's leave. He died in May and D-Day was 6th June. It was difficult to get leave. I had been on a driving course and the officer said: "You had better have a 24 hour pass."

Donald Upshall

I got to Fareham by train on the 22nd May 1944. I walked along the road to Titchfield. There were no cars on the road until about seven o'clock when a car slowed down to give me a lift. It was my mother, and one of the chaps from the garage driving, coming back from the hospital. I had no idea dad had been so ill and that he had died. They had sent a telegram to my squadron, which would have enabled me to have a few more days' leave, for the funeral, but where everything was so confusing I never got it. I was nearly home and somebody was giving me a lift and it was my mother, telling me that they had just got back from the hospital that afternoon. It was quite a shock. I'll always remember that and it took some getting over.

George Watts

The War bought great excitement to the boys of Titchfield. It was on the route for bombers as they came over to blitz Southampton, so the four Bofors guns that George remembers would blaze away at the German planes. He would crouch under a small porch at his grandparents' house in West Street, which was an inadequate shelter, and wait for the shrapnel and empty bullet cases to land in the street. With chaos all around he would rush into the road to snatch up the hot metal before another boy beat him to it!

If they heard the gunfire and another boy gave the shout "It's up at Segensworth!" the Titchfield boys would jump on their bikes and peddle as fast as they could to claim their prize, such was the urge to collect and gain status with exciting pieces of war trophies.

George had to be confined, with scarlet fever, to Fareham Isolation Hospital at the top of Gudge Heath Lane during the War. It cared for about 30 children, with girls' and boys' wards. It had an air raid shelter in the garden but if there was no time to take cover the children were told to hide under their beds.

One day the air raid warning sounded and the children took cover in the ward. However George was too interested in what was happening so he went to the window. From his vantage point he saw a two-engined bomber aiming for the strategically important railway line between Portsmouth and Southampton. It was flying at a very low height and he saw it shooting at the railway track and heard it shooting at Fareham station. He heard later that it had dropped a bomb nearby. Luckily he recovered from his illness, and went back to collecting 'trophies' with the other boys.

Gerald Read

We used to go down on the beach. You know where it was all barbed wired off. Well me and my friend were down there and the sirens went off. So we jumped on our bikes and peddled as fast as we could. But as we were going past Thatcher's Copse the gun battery there started up.

You know Thatcher's Copse, in the opposite field they made a decoy gun emplacement out of scaffold poles to fool the Germans. The guns made me deaf for days, but I couldn't tell mum, she'd belt me!

June Pellatt

Titchfield Fire Station 1939

My great aunt Lizzie Smith cleaned for the commander of HMS Daedalus at Lee-on-the-Solent. She caught a parachutist. She was the sort who would stand no nonsense and she used the pointy end of her umbrella and made him go to the police station. My great aunt Annie lived in the bakery on the corner of East Street and aunt Alice married Bob Chant and they lived next to the fire station at the bottom of Southampton Hill.

We never locked our doors or shut our windows if we went out and nobody got burgled. We used to hang a key on a piece of string behind the front door so when we wanted to get in we just pulled it out through the letterbox. There were a few rogues in the village but everyone knew who they were.

Kate Scott

Sleeping in a Morrison Shelter

My dad and my aunty Marlene were evacuated to Edinburgh but they were unhappy there and so they were sent to relations in Doncaster. Marlene was born in 1930 and now lives at the top of Coach Hill. We had Morrison air raid shelters that looked like tables. They had steel legs and mesh in case the house fell down. But on Locks Heath Road they had Anderson shelters in the gardens.

Margaret Groves

At the outset of the War I was living with my parents at The Old School House, 1 Place House Cottages, Mill Lane. My mother was Nurse Gardner, the local district nurse/midwife, and my father was too old to participate in the War effort apart from a little bit of ARP work. Living in the cottages next door were two families, Willard and Joyce. Charlie Joyce had his own market garden in the Swanwick area. I do not remember any of them joining up.

Nurse Gardner

Mum had a car because she was called out at night so often, sometimes having to go from one birth to another because the air raids would bring on contractions. She would often drive into the ditch as her car had hooded headlamps and she couldn't see where she was going. She was sometimes brought home by soldiers after an accident. I remember one night she had dragged herself home from Segensworth with a broken leg and was out of action for a while.

Paul Cousins

Paul Cousins has lived in Titchfield ever since he was six months old. He was five when the Second World War broke out. Then, he lived with his mother, father and three brothers in the northeast corner of Titchfield Square, alongside the Congregational chapel. He now lives just next door.

Paula Weaver

Everyone seemed to have a nickname. In my family my aunts and uncles were:
Uncle Tickle
Uncle Bill
Uncle Arch
Bliss and Auntie Violet
Uncle Op

Land Army at work on the farm

On Whit Monday we used to run across the field to the Meon Road to catch Jim Harris with his horse and cart, and get a lift gymkhana at Cams Alders at Fareham.

During the War years my mum had two Land Army girls billeted with us.

If you had room in your house you had to have people billeted with you. I loved trying on their uniforms. After they left we had a WRAF from the Balloon Barrage, which was on the A27 where the old Plessey factory is now. We also had mum's brothers and their wives living with us when they got married. You just had to make room. There were no houses for them to move into.

Pamela Fullick

I was five years old when the War started. I was born, grew up and lived in Bellfield Road until I got married. We spent most nights in our air raid shelter in the garden, where dad would tell us stories about Titchfield and previous occupants and our relatives. We always found plenty to occupy us as children and even earned a few coppers sometimes. We did errands for elderly neighbours like going to the Brewery Tap pub, which was in Bridge Street, with a jug to get their milk stout. I don't know how we didn't upset it getting it from Bridge Street to Bellfield.

Rita Prior

My nanny suffered a stroke in 1940 when I was ten and passed away in July 1942. As I shared a bed with her I had to go to Aunt Elise's to sleep, and used to come home for all my meals and things; a strange situation. During this time we had the Battle of Britain and air raids. We spent many nights in the Anderson shelter. Strangely enough I can't remember being frightened.

Two Anderson shelters put to the test

I remember being very ill with jaundice at this time. It was an illness going round the troops. I had three weeks in bed and lost a lot of weight. Aunt Amy said she had nursed me through all sorts but never wanted to go through that again. Medicine had to be paid for then. We used to pay into the Foresters Club for this and I well recall her telling our GP, Dr Windermer, that she could afford to pay for another bottle of medicine if necessary. In these days of National Health Service care it is something I often think of.

I can remember sitting outside the air raid shelter during the summer holidays in 1942, when the War was at its worst, and being told, "Don't move far from the shelters."

I called my auntie 'mum'. During wartime my next-door neighbour's children came up from Portsmouth. I was a bit jealous of them with my mum so started calling my auntie 'mum' and carried on calling her 'mum' until the day she died. I still called my own mum, 'mum' too and visited her every week until I got married.

Titchfield Home Guard

My real father died when I was ten. He was injured during WW1. He had half a thumb and two fingers missing. We never took any notice. We just grew up with it. Dad was also very deaf because of the artillery. I never heard him speak about WW1, ever. He was in the Home Guard during WW2 and used to meet down at the Drill Hall (now the Community Centre). When the Home Guard disbanded they had a party there for the children. It was wonderful for us as we had things we hadn't had during the War.

We didn't have many toys. In 1942, when I was 12, we were in Gosport and we went into Woolworths. They had a consignment of dolls and I begged and begged, could I please have the dolly, and mum bought me one. It was the best thing she could have bought and I made clothes for the doll so that's how I got interested in sewing and knitting. I remember having a life-sized china doll. It was dressed in baby clothes and I had a cot for it. My sister, Sylvia, dropped and broke it.

During the War I used to play with the children next door and we used to play schools and make little books and do sums and things. We used to watch the troops going along the road, everywhere. There were tar barrels at the side of the road. We used to climb up and sit on them. I had a horrid blue wart on my finger and I accidentally cut it off on one of these barrels. Watching troops was our entertainment. The troops used to talk to us as they went by, mainly from the lorries and 'ducks' (DUKW's amphibious trucks).

***D** (designed in 1940), **U** (utility), **K** (all-wheel drive), and **W** (dual rear axles)*

Sheila Hignell

My twin sister Mary and I were born in May 1941. It was a terrible night, bombs falling everywhere. When they rang the midwife, Nurse Gardner, she said she wouldn't come out. My dad had to leave my mum to fetch the midwife and then I was born first and then my sister. Mum had no idea she was having twins.

Nurse Gardner was the village midwife for 32 years. She delivered almost every baby in the village. Jonathan, my nephew, was one of the last babies she delivered. That was in 1963. She delivered all seven of us - my eldest sister is 77 years old. Gardner Road, which is off Coach Hill, was named after her when she retired. Her daughter, Margaret Groves, still lives in Place House cottages, opposite the Abbey.

We had to go to Hill Head near Titchfield with the horse and cart. Dad rented the land during the War and for few years afterwards. We used to take tea and jam sandwiches for everyone who was working overtime. My mother was always there. We had an air raid shelter at the end of the garden. My sister, who was born in 1944, and a cousin, used to be carried to the air raid shelter in a linen box. When we grew up we knew everyone and everyone knew us.

Victor Chase

When the War come, obviously the money wasn't so good, so dad went to AST in Hamble where I used to work. Then he got transferred up to Swindon. I was working at Boniface and Cousins garage and I had a message come through that said your father has had an accident. Mother's going up to the hospital at Swindon. But he died before she got there.

This pilot had his own plane and he asked my dad to start it by swinging the propeller. It cut his head. My father was invalided out of the Army after the WW1 because of a dodgy leg, and we wondered whether it had given out on him or something. Anyway the propellor cut his head and by the time they got him to hospital he was dead, that was 1941.

Swinging the propeller in 1950s

Before that, my father was an ARP warden and we had a telephone put in the house because of that. We kept after the War but it wasn't any use because nobody had them then. At the end of the War mother paid to carry it on.

Wally Pratt

"First Xmas I have had off for almost 15 years and no one can get home."

Wally was in the RAF stationed at RAF Ringway (now Manchester airport) and this is a transcript of letter sent by his mother in December 1940.

Sunday

Dear Wally,

Glad to hear you are coming down for the New Year, have heard from Sonny he cannot get down. Don't look forward to a peaceful leave as they are over here every night doing something or the other.

I never get the chance to undress of a night, in fact every night pretty well from 6 until 12 or 1 o'clock I spend in the air raid shelter. Sometimes the firing goes on nearly all night.

I hear they have been pretty busy up that part again, it must be getting in a heck of a mess up there. Trusting every thing is OK, looking forward to seeing you at the end of the week.

Love Mother,

PS - Len Barton gets married on 8th Jan.
Sent you on a small parcel just for Xmas, let me know if you get it safe. Also the radiogram has gone wrong, cannot get anything out of it, am trying to get it fixed up before you come home, but everything is so difficult these days.

First Xmas I have had off for almost 15 years and no one can get home.

What a world!

Bellfield Road Revisited
(now Lower Bellfield)

Bellfield Road

View over George and Mary Ellen Bowns' grave shows Bellfield in 1942

Bellfield '50s Carnival Day

Thanks to June Pellatt and Paula Weaver for remembering the families who lived along Bellfield Road at the beginning of WW2

No.	Name	No.	Name
18	Mr & Mrs S Price	19	Mr & Mrs Smith
17	Mr & Mrs Martin	20	Mr & Mrs Cox
16	Mr & Mrs Bennett	21	Mr & Mrs Matthews
15	Mr & Mrs F Gregory	22	Mr & Mrs Burgess
14	Mr & Mrs Gourlay	23	Mr & Mrs Watkins
13	Mr & Mrs S Porch	24	Mr & Mrs Rogers
12	Mrs & Miss Roberts	25	Mr & Mrs Gregory
11	Mr & Mrs Bowers	26	Mr & Mrs Roxburgh
10	Mr & Mrs Fay	27	Mr & Mrs Guy
9	Mr & Mrs Whitear	28	Mr & Mrs Stanton
8	Mr & Mrs Biddle	29	Mr & Mrs Page
7	Mr & Mrs Snelgrove (Snelgar)	30	Mr & Mrs Oakes
6	Mr & Mrs Gregory	31	Mr & Mrs Johnson
5	Mr & Mrs Roberts, Garage S'thampton Hill	32	Mr & Mrs Light
4	Mr & Mrs Shawyer & family	33	Mr & Mrs Fielder
3	Mr & Mrs Amy Downes Shop in shed	34	Mr & Mrs Watkins
2	Mr & Mrs Stovold	35	Mr & Mrs Cobb
1	Miss Sarr Headmistress	36	Mr & Mrs Tomkins

››› Coach Hill ›››

School

Douglas Elkins

When War began in September 1939 I was 10 years old and I had just moved into Mr Farthing's class. Two boys from Mr Farthing's class were assigned to each shelter. When an air raid warning siren sounded, these boys had to run to the shelter, nip up the ladder and pull the metal cover over to keep out any flying debris. If an air raid lasted longer than two hours two biscuits were given to each child. The shelter I was assigned to as 'escape hatch boy' was used by the very junior children.

On one occasion the raid was very noisy so the teacher diverted the young children by getting them to sing loudly. She also instructed us two senior boys to sing but we thought that singing the songs the younger children sang was beneath our dignity. It was no surprise that we were promptly reported to Mr Farthing for disobedience and we were hauled up before him and asked why we had refused to sing. Obviously, Mr Farthing's 'medicine' (the cane) hovered over us, as we endeavoured to put up a plausible case in our defence. I cannot remember now just what we each had to say but whatever it was we did escape the cane.

Gerald Read

At school the teachers had to march all the children down the footpath by the allotments to the air raid shelter when the siren went off. The teachers insisted on 'an orderly fashion'. We walked along - all us little 'uns with our gas mask boxes banging against our little legs. But we got out of lessons!

The boys at Sarisbury Secondary Modern school were very good at growing vegetables. They dug up half their school field and kept the school kitchens in vegetables all year.

John Williams

"We were machine-gunned when we went back to the main school"

Titchfield was quite an exciting place to grow up in during World War 2, but maybe not so for children whose fathers had to go off to War. When the War started I was nearly six, so I had been at Titchfield County Junior School for almost one year. The headmistress was Miss Sarr. If there was a siren sounded we went into the school air raid shelters. I think different classes went to different shelters. Once inside it was a bit frightening for young children, but there was some compensation in that we had a tin of broken biscuits to eat. On one occasion we were machine-gunned when we went back to the main school. I believe what happened was that a Spitfire was chasing a German plane over the school at low level and firing at it.

At the bottom of the school playing field was a fence where small lizards sat in the sun. We used to try and catch them but usually they shed their tails and got away. The old school in West Street was occupied by Canadian troops during the War.

Spitfire chase

My sister went to Gosport Girls' Grammar School, which was evacuated to Eastleigh and she was billeted out. I was never sure why Eastleigh was chosen because it was quite a strategic target for the Germans as it had the main factory for building Spitfires nearby as well as being an important railway maintenance area. There was some talk of us younger children being evacuated to maybe Canada but I don't think my parents agreed and I don't recall any others going either.

Because of its position halfway between Portsmouth and Southampton, a lot of German bombers flew over the village so that a lot of stray bombs fell in the surrounding area. Some of the bombers mistook Mr Swatton's and Mr Lupton's greenhouses opposite our house in Southampton Road for factories. As a result there were many craters. On a couple of occasions due to explosions nearby, we had our front windows broken and the ceiling came down, plus the porch in the front was damaged.

We had a fairly deep ditch outside our house. During one raid, my father and the man next door, Mr Rich, thought they saw a parachutist coming down so they grabbed their rifles, as they were both in the Home Guard. Luckily they soon realised it was a land mine floating down so they quickly jumped in the ditch and the land mine went off over St. Margaret's Lane area.

I was quite keen on sport at Titchfield Junior School. We had only female teachers at the time and they were not too interested in football or cricket. I managed to persuade the caretaker to put up some goal posts and we organised some sort of kick-about, but the lady teachers had their own idea of the offside rule! We didn't have proper football shirts, just coloured bands. You wore a red band if you played on the right and a green one if you played on the left. If a person wearing a red band strayed to the left side he was offside. I don't think this rule has been adopted! We used to jump on the bus and go to play against other schools such as Locks Heath, but I think we had to organise our own games.

June Pellatt

I went to Titchfield Primary School. When the sirens went off the caretaker and teachers took us to the shelter. We all marched ever so orderly and then we said our times tables in the shelter. We had broken biscuits for ha'penny (0.2p) and watery cocoa for penny (0.4p). We stayed there until the 'all clear' went.

Pamela Fullick

I went to the village school and was issued with a gas mask. I didn't like school at first and used to play on the stile in the school lane until the caretaker came along, Mrs Lambe, and carried me up to the school where I had to stay in the library after school for a while. I was then in more trouble when I arrived home. We didn't have school dinners then and had to go home to dinner and were sometimes caught in air raids when German planes came low and you could see the pilot grinning at you. A teacher always grabbed you and pushed you under the desks because we didn't have shelters then. When they put shelters in the school grounds the teachers would take a tin of broken biscuits there in an air raid and everyone would try to sit the closest to her. The headmistress was Miss Sarr and she came with her two nieces from Guernsey when the Germans occupied it. They were given a house at No 1 Bellfield Road.

Rita Prior

"I hated putting on my gas mask"

I remember the air raid shelters being put up in the school playground at the start of the War. Before the shelters we had to practise putting on our gas masks and sitting under tables in the lobbies. I hated putting on my gas mask, but dutifully carried it backwards and forwards to school for the rest of my school days. We were not allowed home from school if there was an air raid on, unless accompanied by an adult.

Children in gas masks

When Sarisbury Senior school was damaged in an air raid in 1940 some of the pupils came to Titchfield for a while. One of them, Hensley Hurden, lived at Catisfield and used to accompany us home at lunchtime. I enjoyed my time at school, especially mental arithmetic and spelling when we used to stand around the classroom and answer questions. Also reading out loud was done this way. I can't remember learning to read it just came naturally to me. I was told that mum used to hide the newspapers as I could read the headlines as soon as I started school.

I went to senior school at Brook Lane, Sarisbury, catching the school bus at 8.30 a.m. in Titchfield Square. This time was also disrupted with the War. We all carried our gas masks each day and identity cards. I remember wearing a gold bracelet, not expensive, with my name and identity on, EDJD 1215. I still have my school reports to this day.

Margaret Groves

Life at Wykeham House School, Fareham, went on pretty much the same. The library was made into an air raid shelter and we had to go there when there was an air raid, being counted in, but that didn't happen that often. We had our gas masks, which were a bit frightening so they later made them into more child friendly ones, like Mickey Mouse. I would catch the bus to school and back from the Fisherman's Rest pub.

Micky Mouse respirator

Mr Booth looked after the Abbey. He lived in the house where the garden centre is. It was run as an orchard, but Mr Smith, who was the landlord of the pub, kept pigs there.

Celebrations and Leisure

Douglas Elkins

The Lee-on-the-Solent golf course was fully open and used during the War. At the club house an assortment of 'would be' caddies would gather on Saturday and Sunday afternoons in the hope of being asked to carry a member's clubs. For we boys the going rate for 18 holes was two shillings and sixpence (half a crown) actually 12p in real terms.

I caddied for Mr Downing who ran the then garage at Elmore, Lee-on-the-Solent and made sure I was there weekends and evenings whenever I was asked. My two and sixpence per round then became three shillings, an increase of 20%. Similarly when not caddying, the next best activity was to search the golf course for lost golf balls. The professional, a Mr John, always insisted we brought the found balls to him for which he would give us only a penny or two. It was not long before we found we could get better rewards from the members who might be interested in what we had to offer.

Pam Fullick

We lived on the estate and we had to make our own fun. In the summer holidays we walked through the river to the beach with our sandwiches and drink, where we spent all day. In the winter we went to the beach with the mothers winkling. We had three copses to play in. All the various games we played never cost any money.

As a teenager my cousin, Paula Weaver, was still at school but we could go to places if she slept at my house so that her dad wouldn't expect her in at 10 o'clock. The Parish Rooms were for the people. We learnt to dance in the Parish Rooms, as the Community Centre was used by the Territorial Army (TA) as their HQ. Mr Beavis taught us to dance.

As we got older there were things we could join such as the youth club and a Red Cross class run by Miss Maddocks (later married as Mrs Judy Stokes). Also in the Parish Rooms we could see films once a week and when we were a bit older there was a dance we called the village hop. As we reached our teens dancing and cinema were our interests. We also followed Titchfield football team. They were called The Wanderers.

Rita Prior

Ball games and skipping were very popular. We used to play mothers and fathers. We had leaves for plates - really make-believe. I used to read a lot. I was always in trouble for reading too much. Our house was full of books. During wartime they collected books for the troops. I think I took books to school and I remember getting a shield after taking 50 books. Many lovely books went.

Food and Farming

Donald Upshall

There was rationing, but being out in the country there were lots of chicken farmers and there was always a supply of chickens and eggs. We were lucky because city people couldn't do that.

Douglas Elkins

Steam threshing rig

Farm work was still open to us as well and this too took a turn for the better in the form of Tom Cage whose farm was along Woodcote Lane - due east of Peel Common. One job was the threshing of wheat. Farmers in those days brought in a contractor to thresh his grain and the firm for this was W. M. Wheatley & Son from Wickham, Hampshire. Their steam engine, drawing the threshing tackle and baler, would turn up and set up their stall, as it were.

My job was to rake away the never-ending stream of shucks, which streamed out of the thresher. At first quite easy but as the day wore on the sheer volume demanded frantic efforts to clear the heap of shuck from the machine. The day was from 7.00 am until 5.00 pm with a lunch break at noon. There is a small needle like spike on every ear of corn and these fly everywhere all day long. Mr Gage would laugh when at 5.00 pm I took off my shirt to shake out these little needle spikes. My body had received thousands of mini pricks over eight hours of raking. The pay was three pence per hour the grand sum of two shillings (10p) for a day's work.

Some of us discovered another source of grub in the form of the 'British Restaurant'. British Restaurants were set up in towns by the Government so that workers and bombed out people could access a standard hot meal, so supporting the War effort. The Fareham BR consisted of a couple of joined Nissan huts built upon the back gardens of properties in Westborn Road. The dinner cost 10d (4p) and the dessert cost 3d (1.2p) so for one shilling and a penny it was excellent, and all off ration.

A British Restaurant in London

George Watts

I remember how there were no gaunt faces during WW2 in Titchfield. There were 600 or more market gardeners in the area. His family had strawberry fields at St Margaret's Lane where they were allowed to grow a quarter of an acre of strawberries as a cash crop. To keep vegetables free of disease they had to be grown in a different bed so the strawberries were rotated with potatoes and other vegetables. Most houses in Titchfield had generous gardens and people would swap the produce they grown.

George's dad was good at trapping wild rabbits. Men who were serving in the forces were paid and the army pay was more generous than an agricultural labourer's so soldiers' wives and families were better off. There was also the opportunity to rise through the ranks and be promoted.

Gerald Read

People had pigs up on the Common but we didn't keep our pig all to ourselves. The policeman always came around when the butcher was slaughtering them. And the butcher always had a bit to keep under the counter for his favourite customers! You had to hand some over but you could keep the rest. We had 100 or more rabbits. The rabbits tasted very good in a stew with veg. A lot of things were rationed during the War: bacon, sugar, tea, meat, cheese, preserves, butter, margarine, lard, sweets and clothing to name but a few.

John Williams

My father ran a family business in South Street with a couple of shops and three or four vans mainly delivering general goods and paraffin to the surrounding areas. He had set rounds on different days in different areas. If for any reason my mum had a message for my father or if he had forgotten his sandwiches for lunch, my mother sent me out on my bike to find him. Because I knew his rounds I knew roughly where he would be, but I used to follow the oil patches left on the road. He had 100-gallon oil tanks in the van connected to a tap at the rear to fill the measuring cans but invariably the tap dripped a bit after filling.

He sold a lot of rationed goods. Everybody had a ration book and the coupons had to be collected. One of my jobs, together with my sister, was to count the coupons on a Monday night into their various categories to be taken to the Ministry of Food offices the next day.

On Saturday mornings I used to queue up for my mum outside St John's for cakes. It was interesting because there was always a house martin nesting on the wall above the queue. On the way home I sometimes looked over the bridge of the main road at the fish in the River Meon. Somehow one day, I managed to drop the shopping basket so that the week's ration of cakes went floating down the river! I also shopped for meat at Lankester & Crooks.

I didn't eat a lot of sweets. My father brought our ration home on Saturday evenings, and I remember when I went to school in Fareham some of the boys bought wax balls or sticks to chew, or medical type sweets.

Kate Scott

I think the photo is posed because I remember them saying it was a photographer from the newspaper. Great granny used to tell the story that, during the War, there was a dogfight over the Solent. A parachutist came down near the ladies so they made him take his boots off so he did not run away and marched him up to the NAFFI that was in what is now The Earl of Southampton's day room.

The Posbrook women

Mrs Singleton and great granny took a boot and took it round the pubs, collecting money for people who had been bombed out. One of the women hoeing the field is Flo Churcher, she lived in West Street. In 1985 we were going on a coach trip when she got off quickly to tell me that "There is a dunny on the coach" (*toilet*).

The woman with a beret on is my great granny, Maude Bowman, nee Carse, and Mrs Bedford is the one with a hat on. She was Jono Jones's mother, from Bellfield. Second from the end is Mrs Singleton, sister to Mrs Bowman. They didn't work for Steve Harris, but a company in Portsmouth. Their aprons are sacking but my great granny's is leather. They would gather the potatoes up in to their apron like a bag.

Because great granny worked on the land they were well off for food, as a few potatoes would 'slip' into pockets! Great grandfather had a chicken farm. He said, "chicken farms are the future." They also had a pig in WW2.

Lesley Downs

When I was 14 on 28th December 1939 I came to work on this farm. I was only a boy. I did bits and pieces. It was called Meon Farm then. First of all I drove a horse with a plough. I ploughed, harrowed and rolled the land. We grew spuds, cabbages, sprouts, and corn - all market garden stuff. The ground went right up to Hill Head. Extra food was needed because of the War .

I used to drive horses, up and down the lines. When I was old enough to drive a car or lorry, I used to go with Steve Harris to serve the shops in Portsmouth and Southampton. I later took over the Portsmouth job as an extra. I used to drive to the shops on a Tuesday or Friday unless we had lots of stuff then I did extra days.

I had to collect the money and bring it back into the office. The girl used to check it up. I remember one day, as usual, I would throw the money in and get on with the work. I said "Everything OK," and she said "No it is £28 short". With that the phone rang and the customer said

Horse ploughing

the lad had forgotten to pick the money up. I was really worried at the time but didn't get in trouble. Then things changed. Steve Harris was on his own as his brother left. The brothers went their separate ways but remained good friends.

Steve and Jim Harris

I did Portsmouth deliveries as well as the wholesalers. It worked out. Then Mr Harris said to me one day, "I am going to build some houses down there." I said, "Do what?" "Oh yes," he said, "for people who come to work for me so they have somewhere to live." I thought I would like to live there, up on the main road. Then he came up and said, "Would you like to live up here?" My wife worked here. She came from Bournemouth. Then we went out together. She worked hard, picking strawberries, and she also fed us all well. People worked very long hours in the summer until dusk. I used to cart the strawberries. The farm is really my life but I am a Portsmouth Football Club supporter.

I drove the lorry and a tractor and was still harrowing, rolling etc until quite recently. Nowadays, I let my son think he is telling me what to do. We have a really good father-son relationship but he is the farm manager now. Oh yes, I've had a tractor in a ditch and also pulled lots of other people out of the ditch who went too fast.

Herbert was a prisoner of war (POW) who worked on the farm at the end of the War. He is now part of the family. He sends us biscuits every Christmas. There were six POWs.

Linda Felton

My aunt Betty loved dancing and during the War years there were lots of soldiers to dance with. She worked in the army canteen and loved it. Later when she was married they occupied one of the cottages in Thatcher's Wood where the soldiers had been housed.

Margaret Groves

I can't remember us ever being short of food, because mum being district midwife was always being thanked with food parcels. There was always plenty of fruit and vegetables available. I remember also always having plenty of meat from somewhere!

Paul Cousins

Paul's aunt lived next door to him and had Land Army girls lodging with her. They were a uniformed force and were drafted into the area to help on the land. They wore green corduroy britches tucked into their socks with green jerseys and hats that looked a bit like western cowboy hats. German prisoners of war were also made to work on the land and some of them stayed after the War to marry local girls. They included one called Irwin Shroeder and another called Kirk.

Pam Fullick

My dad was in a reserved occupation for the Admiralty at Collingwood. He was a good provider and used to shoot rabbits and game for meat and grow vegetables. He kept chickens too and in the right season would go prawning, cockling and winkling. We had to go strawberry picking to make a few shillings. I was given two weeks extra off from school to go potato picking.

We knew where to go scrumping for apples, pears and plums. We picked blackberries and sold some for a few coppers. We also picked primroses in the spring and tied them in bunches and sold them.

In the autumn we went to the chestnut copse at Chilling but often got chased by Mr Mortimer, the owner, with a shotgun. In the summer I went shrimping with my dad. He made me a small net to push along the seabed. The men took their clothes off and put twice as many old ones on to go into the sea, even a hat. I just wore a bathing suit, woollen, which came down to my knees when it got wet. In the winter we went winkling with the mothers. That was a cold job.

Sunday tea was a plate with a pin for the winkles and a plate of bread and butter. We used to get a little bit of butter and cheese but hardly any meat during the War. My dad shot rabbits but we had to spit out bits of shot in the rabbit.

Paula Weaver

Mrs Gann had a fish and chip shop and she also made ice cream. We bought five scoops of ice cream in a dish. We had to rush up the road to get it home before it melted. We went up to the bake house to get the bread. During the War the loaves looked as though they were two loaves, but we fought because there were only two crusts. We also used to love the skin off the custard and the skin off the rice pudding. We used to go up to Mr Wolf's by the Abbey to get our dairy products and often would get chased by the geese.

Rita Prior

Children were allowed time off school to help on the land, fruit picking and potato picking in particular. They used to have cards, which were signed by the headmaster, Mr Skilton, and their employers. I hated powdered egg. We kept chickens. You had to be registered to get corn for chickens.

Work

Paula Weaver

Mr Williams was our teacher. His family also had a sweet shop and a hardware shop opposite in South Street. He used to come round selling oil, paraffin, candles, kindling etc, thus he was called 'Oily Williams'. There were lots of shops, at least 30 or more. The village was self-contained. It provided everything including numerous public houses.

Rita Prior

"My wages were £1 per week minus four pence insurance"

Rita and colleagues at Lankester & Crook

I left school in December 1944. I stayed at home for a while then one day the grocer called and mentioned that Lankester & Crook Ltd was looking for a cashier. I went for an interview on the Monday and started work on the Wednesday. My wages were £1 per week minus four pence insurance. This remained the same for at least for two years. The War in Europe ended in May and I remember forgetting to return the weekly set of books to head office on that day. I was in trouble!

A register was kept of all customers' names and addresses from ration books. Points and coupons were used for tinned goods and had to be counted. For some things books were marked (crossed off). Rationing became worse after the War. At one time bread was rationed. The small bread coupons were horrid to count. Bread rationing did not last long.

I worked at Lankester & Crook Ltd for 11 years.

Victor Chase

I had the opportunity of an apprenticeship at Boniface and Cousins garage in Fareham. This was because my elder brother already worked there.

Church, Chapel and Religion

June Pellatt

By the wall of the churchyard is a gravestone where there are the graves of three children. Mrs Hinton, their mother, sent them out shopping with errands that meant that they would return at different times. She killed them all and was sent to Knowle Asylum.

Hinton children's headstone

Margaret Noyce

My mother was very Victorian, without doubt, church, Sunday School, no discussion. As I grew older I went to the service for older children and then finally to church with my mother, who always went to the 6 o'clock service. My father never walked inside a church.

War and Fighting

June Pellatt

We used to live half way down South Street, facing the doctor's. My dad had bought a new radio, which didn't need an accumulator as it was an electric one. All the neighbours came over to listen to it and I couldn't understand why all the ladies were crying. It was a party but then I was told that War had started. I was only six at the time.

Rita Prior

I remember when War broke out; we were watching the men digging out an underground shelter. Mum came out and said we were at War. It didn't mean much to us children really.

Donald Upshall

When the War broke out I was 13 years old - old enough to know what was going on. We had a taxi service at the side of the car repair garage. The first day war broke out, Sunday 3rd September 1939, my father said, "You can go for the ride" on the front seat, next to the taxi driver. He had to send a car to fetch some people we knew from West Wykeham, near Croydon, and I remember driving up the A3. We passed a garage and on a board they had chalked up, 'War Declared'. We were actually at war.

War had only just been declared an hour ago but the siren went and, of course, being the first alarm, the ARP wardens were riding their bikes through the streets, blowing their whistles and saying, "Everybody take cover!" Nobody knew what was happening as the War had only just been declared. I remember thinking, "What is going on?" There was a hell of a big panic! We found the address where we had to pick these people up. The people had cooked lunch, but when we got there they threw the lunch away as they just wanted to get back down to Titchfield. It was a false alarm but we didn't know at the time. Nobody knew what was going on.

Jean Faulds

At the beginning of the war in 1939, my dad, Albert Godbehere, being in the TA, was called up immediately. During the War he was taken prisoner at Boulogne and for five years he was a prisoner of war in Germany.

Shortly after the War began, the private school on West Hill was taken over by the Government and it was turned into a nurse's home. The nurses had to travel to Cold East Hospital to care for the wounded soldiers when they were brought back from France. We used to clean the nurses' rooms and prepare food for their return from their shifts at the hospital.

Huts were built in the woods at Meon and the Army moved in, with a big ack-ack gun and searchlight. After the War ended these huts were let out to young married couples with a single-decker bus service, which carried passengers to and from work and the shops.

Dances used to be held in the upstairs room of the Queen's Head public house during the War and we danced to a man playing a piano accordion.

Another school taken over by the military was the school that sat halfway up West Street. This was used for the army headquarters. The No. 12 Commando was one of the troops stationed in the village. They were billeted with families who had a spare bedroom. My mum was persuaded to take in two of the commando men, Peter Faulds and Jock Allen. They were very helpful to my mother when the night air raids started. They would get us four girls into the Anderson shelter in our back garden.

When the Commandos were parading and marching in the Square the children of the village used to join in - creating chaos for the well-organised troops.

George Watts

The council built new houses at the top of West Street and our family moved in to number 72. As it was a large house, we had people billeted with us. This proved to be a useful source of income. The first people were four very sad French soldiers who had been evacuated from Dunkirk. They were quickly sent to Scotland for training and returned to France to fight with the Free French. Later the family had some commandos and then an RAF airman staying with them. The Government paid for people's board and my mother was given their ration books. The boarders were actually fed at their base so the ration books were useful to supplement the family's rations. After the War the family had an RAF airman and his family staying with them as RAF Titchfield was being run down.

Andrew Mills

My father was in the Royal Engineers during the War and ended up in the Argyll and Sutherland Highlanders - a southerner in a Scots regiment! He was lucky not to have been drafted into the 'Hampshires' as they lost most of their men in North Africa. He found himself, a lot of the time, at home in charge of searchlights and artillery. He was manning a searchlight in Heath Road, just off Church Road in Locks Heath. There was a house there owned by Mrs Louard, a fairly wealthy family, and my mother was in service there. The searchlight was in a small recreation field at the end of the garden and that's where my mother met my father. They used to talk over the fence.

A TS operate a searchlight

My father was also on a searchlight at Bursledon the other side of the railway bridge on a rise above the railway line, a little bit south of Manor Farm. My father's got a couple of stories of Spitfires flying under the bridge there, just showing off. He also tells of Messerschmitts flying at mast height up the river then zooming up over the bridge to knock out the light. He could remember a plane coming so close he could see the pilot's eyes and he remembered being shot at with the bullets going just over his head and hitting the shed behind. There was a pot-bellied stove in there that just exploded when a canon shell hit it. I can't imagine what that must have been like.

Ben Waterfall

We lived in No. 46 Bellfield, which was off Coach Hill (now 36 Coach Hill) and I was born there in 1940. We had an Anderson shelter in the garden and when there was an air raid I would get into the shelter first and mother would hand my brother Mick to me until she got in. Then she would sit there shaking. We didn't know what was going on.

I remember one time the siren went and there were all these streaks of light across the sky up Park Gate way. They used to drop incendiary bombs to light up the area so that the bombers had something to aim at. So mum said "Get under the bed" and we got under the bed a bit quick.

Mike Ferris

During the early part of the War not everyone was given an air raid shelter and our family and our neighbours had to share the Anderson shelter which was dug into the garden of our neighbours in No. 80 Bellfield. To reach it we had to clamber over a wire fence and run up their garden path. I recall very clearly asking my mum if I could stay outside and watch the pretty lights that could be seen over Portsmouth. This of course was Portsmouth being bombed and the sky was ablaze with gunfire and the bombs exploding.

Gerald Read

Thank heavens we had the air raid shelter to rush out to. It was a wet and cold place. Mum never knew whether to dig the kids out of bed and then we would catch cold in the shelter. She used to wait until the ack-ack guns went off, then we'd shift!

When the flying bombs hit Park Gate Towers the air raid warden, Mr Bungey, was on duty outside Arthur Hale's bike shop waving his hands about. "Get under cover!" he said, "Get under cover! There's doodlebugs coming over." and getting all irate. My dad said, "I ain't worried about that, when they are still goin' it's when the buggers' engines stops I worries! I'll take cover when they stops and it all goes quiet!" Boom!

The billeting officer was bossy. Mrs Brown said she wouldn't take any soldiers in her house, but he threatened her with a charge and she had to! Still I reckon there was some romances. We didn't lose too many of our girls to them GIs.

Paul Cousins

Paul remembers that there was a large air raid shelter on what is now the grassed open space at the corner of West Street and South Street. It was large enough to accommodate about 40 people and, inside, lining the walls, it had wooden benches on which most would sit. Others would try to sleep in bunks.

This shelter was available to Paul and his family. However his mother very much disliked the smell of Jeyes Fluid that filled the air inside. So instead they chose to remain at home during air raids and would gather under a steel-reinforced table. Paul was the exception. Being the youngest, he enjoyed the comfort of a tin bath, in which he would lie on a feather mattress. Snug in this makeshift cot, he was given the added protection of the cupboard under the stairs, where he often slept soundly.

The main targets of the air raids were Portsmouth and Southampton but, occasionally, something would hit Titchfield. A large landmine fell into mud just north of the A27, behind the site occupied by Priory

Garage. It didn't explode on impact and so later received the attention of a bomb disposal team. Paul also remembers being woken by a loud explosion when a shell landed in the Square. Fortunately, no one was injured and damage to property was small. Flying shrapnel dented some doors, but Paul and other children were amused to collect fragments of it the next morning.

Donald Upshall

"Then right behind them came the dive-bombers - we actually saw them come in"

My first experience of seeing the Germans was around 1940 when I was with my father driving into Southampton over the old Northam bridge. The skys were alight as the Germans had fired incendiaries, setting the balloons on fire. Then right behind them came the dive-bombers - we actually saw them come in. The Supermarine factory was what they were after as that was where they made Spitfires. They absolutely wrecked it and killed a lot of people. We were in Southampton and we were far enough away so we weren't involved in the bombing but we could hear it and see it going on. They built the Spitfires in the Supermarine factory and then took them up to Eastleigh and flew them from there. In those days, they took them on a trailer. The Germans knew the Spitfires were the top fighters. They were definitely after the factory, and obliterated it in one raid. It was dreadful. It all happened so quickly.

Battle of Britain 75th anniversary

Then, because the Supermarine factory wasn't usable, they commandeered any buildings over a certain size all over Hampshire to make aircraft parts. The Priory Garage on the A27 was commandeered. It was just a filling station, but it was extended and toilets put in for the ladies who worked there.

In 1941 I remember hearing the first German bomber. It was in the clouds. You could hear the drone of the engine but you couldn't see it. Suddenly it came out of the clouds and you could see the swastika and then it disappeared again in the clouds. There was no gunfire and people think it was lost. It was quite an experience then!

After that I remember when the bombers did start coming over at night, especially in the summer. When you were in bed you used to dread hearing the siren. Once the siren went you knew the Germans were coming. First of all you would hear the siren going down in Portchester, then Fareham and then in Titchfield blaring out. Then you would hear the anti-aircraft coming out but sometimes they went the other way. That was in the '40s. I remember 1941 one of the German bombers dropped three bombs, down by the meadows, where the bird sanctuary is down by the river. We heard them in the night, in the dark and you could see the craters the next day. I think they dropped them to get back to France, as it would be faster without the bombs.

Early on in the War they put four 3.7 anti-aircraft guns in the Meon Road, past Steve Harris' Farm at Thatcher's Copse. It was a proper site with an army crew to defend it. They had what they called a 'predictor' - a range finder. It wasn't electronic and wasn't very accurate but it was all part of the equipment. The troops built a lot of Nissen huts and after the War a lot of people lived in them as temporary housing while they waited for a pre-fab house. The site was called Greenwoods after the army moved out.

When the guns were firing you could hear the shrapnel coming down on the roofs of houses from all different sizes of explosive shells. Of course if anyone was out in it they would be in trouble but it was very rare that they got hit. We picked up some shrapnel near our garage when I was young.

Kitty Potter

I was ordered to do War work and went in St Margaret's Lane making parts for the Royal Air Force. My sister Lily, who had a hole in her heart, worked in the office there.

Victor Chase

When I was 14, I went to work repairing Spitfires at the Hamble. I met Douglas Bader. I mended the seat harness in his plane and I was the only one that didn't get his autograph. By the time I finished working on his plane security said, "No more autographs". The Mark 1 and 2 Spitfires had a tail that was bolted on. They had a little hatchway and because I was small, I was only a nipper, I had to get up inside and put the bolts through and my mate could put his hand through and tighten

Douglas Bader

them up. Fifty-four bolts there were, round the tail. We also repaired the outside of the Spitfires with metal plates when they were damaged, and we worked in the cockpit to change the seats and repair the canopy.

Paula Weaver

When War began dad was called up and posted to Blandford in Dorset in the Royal Artillery where he worked on the ack-ack guns. He was discharged in 1948.

Mum was a great one for moving her bedroom furniture around. When dad came home on leave, sometimes it could be late at night or early hours of the morning, so as not to wake us up he used to creep in and never put the lights on. He often stubbed his toe on the wardrobe and could never find the bed! You can imagine then we were all awake! Poor dad, he took it all as a big joke.

We saw a German plane shot down and saw the German running away. They dropped a land mine in Triangle Lane in Mr Harris' field. There was a big hole - a crater - opposite the rec. by the school. We always called it the rec. But it was really the recreation ground.

I can remember being in our shelter in the garden and watching the Spitfires flying above us after the German planes. The next day when we came out of the shelter we used to pick up the bits of shrapnel from the shells.

There used to be an artillery gun in the field at the back of the estate and there was also one in Brownwich Lane in the fields and soldiers in tents. When mum and some of the other women on the Bellfield Road went to work on the land they had to pass the soldiers' camp. The soldiers would tell our mums to send the children over at dinnertime and they would give us a meal. It was great, they used to give us sauce for the chips and whatever else they had, I think it was egg, chips and beans. They had these big bottles of sauce and big tins of jam I'd never seen before. It was like a banquet.

We always knew when Portsmouth or Southampton was bombed. The sky over both cities used to be all lit up with a big red glow in the sky. We could see it from our garden. It would be Portsmouth and Gosport one night and then it would be Southampton. The planes came right overhead then. Eventually the beach was barbed wired off in case of invasion. They built Nissen huts at Greenwoods for the army and ATS and they had heavy ack-ack guns all in the fields and lanes around our houses.

There was a big Canadian Army camp on the Titchfield to Stubbington road, which the children were drawn to because the soldiers gave us chocolate and chewing gum because our sweets were on ration. They had huge tanks and on D-Day we all went down to the village streets to wave them off.

We had a few bomb craters around the area, one opposite the village school, one in Triangle Lane. One was caused by a doodlebug which came down on Bay Tree cottage in Meon Road while my dad was picking peas in the field opposite. It was 11 o'clock at night but there was visibility because it was double summer time. *(This lasted 1941 -1945)*. We saw a German plane shot down. The pilot baled out in the field next to our estate and was arrested. We used to go out after a night raid and pick up shrapnel for souvenirs. We can remember seeing the dog fights above our heads in the Battle of Britain and thought it was one big adventure.

Pam Fullick

We did see the dog fights above us in the Battle of Britain and we did line the village to wave goodbye to the Canadian soldiers in their big tanks as they left to go to the D-Day invasion.

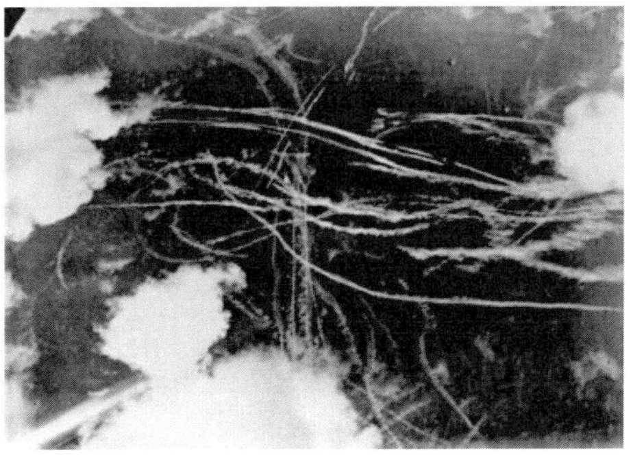

Trails left after a 'dog fight'

My mum wouldn't go down the shelter so she sat indoors doing her needlework. We got all the stories when we were down the shelter.

Leslie Downs

I was 14 when War broke out and registered at 17 but because I was working on the farm I didn't do national service. I was in the Home Guard. The tunic they gave me was too big. It was laughable. We were based and trained in the Drill Hall, which was owned by the TA. Later it became Titchfield Community Centre. We did a bit of exercise in the night. There were Bofors guns up the road. In 1940, Steve, who owned the farm, and I were delivering vegetables in Portsmouth when they started to bomb. We just got out in time along the old A27.

When there was a warning we told everyone to get into their air raid shelters. I was living in Bellfield during the War. It wasn't too bad. We thought it was exciting. We were between Portsmouth and Southampton, so Titchfield missed most of the War. War was a bit of excitement for us. There was a lot of camaraderie and people helped each other.

Margaret Noyce

We had neighbours who had relatives in Canada. When the War was on it was decided I should be evacuated to Canada. I went on a ship called the SS Volendam, which was torpedoed just after we left Liverpool harbour. We were eventually rescued. I came back home and just got on with life.

Quite recently I met up with other Volendam survivors and now we meet regularly.

The torpedoed SS Volendam

Douglas Elkins

One day when I was walking back to school along the field footpath to Rome Farm Cottages an air raid began without the warning siren. This was high level bombing unlike the much lower flying we were familiar with. Afterwards people said this was an Italian aircraft. As the bombs blew up I decided to run back home to our Anderson shelter. Once it was clear that no airplanes and no bomb or shell explosions could be heard I set off to school again. When I reached Marks Road, I met all of the schoolchildren streaming out from school. Apparently two of the bombs had landed in the Tips copse at the bottom of the playground. The explosions had blown out all of the school windows. Our joy at not being at school was short-lived however because all of the windows were replaced over the weekend, so it was classes as usual on the following Monday.

Later in the War, my brother Frederick, together with two other boys, Frank Hobbs and Robert Fullick, joined the Home Guard. Robert Fullick was killed by an accidental discharge of a rifle when he was on duty with his uncle at the church tower. His grave is marked by a War Graves Commission headstone in the Crofton Old Church cemetery.

Fairey Swordfish

The Home Guard had a peculiar way of awarding rank. Someone who was, for example, a works foreman, a transport supervisor or an overseer would be ranked non-commissioned officer (NCO). People such as bank managers and businessmen held commissions. Alfred Munday, who was a grocer, tobacco wholesaler and a retailer with several shops was therefore deemed officer quality and rejoiced in the rank of Captain.

As the War went on, the facilities at HMS Daedalus expanded and became a target for Luftwaffe bombers, often at low level in daylight. Aircraft were parked around the perimeter and serviced by Royal Navy (RN) mechanics. When an aircraft carrier came into Portsmouth harbour its aircraft were flown to Lee-on-the-Solent for servicing. This was while the ship was serviced in the docks. The aircraft were flown back on board once the ship was back out of the harbour. Many types of plane came to Lee-on-the-Solent including the famous Fairey Swordfish torpedo bomber biplane that outlived several of its replacements. The successful American Grumman Avenger torpedo bomber also came and remained in service up until the 1960s, as well as the Grumman Wildcat carrier-based fighter which was also used by the Royal Navy where it was known as the Martlet. The RN mechanics gave us the cartridges used to fire up the aircraft engines. We tipped the cordite from these onto newspaper and ignited it for fun. Not being in a confined space it did not explode but just burned slowly and brightly.

HMS Collingwood had been built before the War and a balloon barrage was installed in the field opposite the main gate. The army brought a searchlight to a field roughly where the Peel Common sewage treatment plant main entrance now stands. This came at dusk and left each morning. The generator for the light stood beside the road a distance of 100 yards from the beam source.

A Free French battleship was anchored off the slipway in Portsmouth. During air raids the anti-aircraft armament on it would immediately fire on enemy aircraft. Once the battle of Normandy began, landing craft returning to the Hardway slipway sometimes brought back German prisoners of war (POW). The POWs walked in an orderly column up towards the road. Some had been severely shell-shocked and were seen tottering about as if they were drunk.

Margaret Groves

I would go out with my father, on his ARP duties, kitted out with my own tin helmet. We would sit on a gate opposite the house and watch for bombing. One night there was an incendiary bomb dropped in the field by the river. There was a whoosh and then the explosion, which frightened me so much that from that time onwards I never went out as an ARP warden again.

Much later there was a doodlebug that flew over the cottage. We could hear it droning and leant out of the bedroom window watching it. It landed on Bay Tree Cottage, Meon, demolishing half of the cottage. There was an old couple living there but they escaped uninjured.

Peter Trott as ARP Warden
Titchfield Spirit 2014

We used to play in the Abbey a lot and during the air raids would hide in there. One day we were playing in the field opposite the cottage. I was with Tommy Wolfe and Alan Abrahams. A German plane flew over and was firing at us. The boys rushed me into the hedge and we could hear my father calling me, but the boys kept me in the hedge until the plane flew over. The scarf I had on at the time, a red and white check, had holes in it from that day onwards, I kept it for a long time.

Bessie Traves

In early 1942, after my husband Cyril was promoted to Chief Petty Officer, he joined the destroyer HMS Petard, which was being built in Newcastle. In June 1942 HMS Petard was deployed to the Mediterranean (via South Africa).

HMS Petard 1943

Douglas Elkins

My father worked in HMS Vernon, Portsmouth, now Gunwharf shopping complex. HMS Vernon was the base for the Admiralty Mine Design Department (MDD) headed by Professor Haldane. Once hostilities began, enemy mines, which had been swept, were brought to MDD for examination. The focus of interest was the fuse mechanisms and the booby trap devices. There were explosions, occasionally causing considerable damage. A 60 feet high static seawater tank was at ground level beside the quay and this was used to test mines. One night during a heavy raid on Portsmouth the tank was peppered with shrapnel causing a huge number of holes out of which the water spurted like a huge watering can. The next day when my father returned from work, he said that tomorrow the whole MDD would be loaded onto a train and taken to Loch Long, Scotland and their work would continue there. He didn't return until hostilities had diminished towards the end of the War.

Dorothy Francis

Dorothy and husband Den

I was born in Yorkshire and volunteered for the Women's Auxiliary Air Force (WAAF) on the 16th October 1941. I went to Gloucester for two days to get my uniform, then to Morecombe for two weeks 'square bashing' - that means drill. I then went to Titchfield Balloon Centre where they made lots of barrage balloons. I was a batwoman there, looking after an officer. Five months later I was posted to RAF Madley in Herefordshire where I was a waitress in the officers' mess. While there I was given seven days leave to go home to Castleford to get married.

In 1944 I was posted to West Camp, RAF Cranwell, Lincolnshire, as a waitress in the officers' mess. I was discharged on the 18th October 1945.

John Maginnis

Lord Mountbatten with No. 6 Commando

My father John (Mac) Maginnis served with the Royal Ulster Regiment (RUR) in Belfast and then joined the Commandos along with many other men. They trained in Scotland in harsh conditions and were then posted across the country. Mac was in No. 12 Commando and when the troop numbers got low due to losses he went to No. 6 Commando. They took part in many operations such as Operation Archery, Operation Myrmidon and Operation Overlord.

Whilst being stationed in Titchfield, Mac and two other Commandos, Sam Brodison and Billy Eager from Ireland, met three sisters from the village Rose, Trixie and Molly Laxton (my mum). They all married and created a large Irish/Titchfield family.

Mac and the others were billeted in the junior school prior to D-Day and left from Warsash.

Antony Norris

On Saturdays my mother used to take me to visit her mother for the day and we'd go shopping in Commercial Road or in Southsea. On Saturday 24th August 1940, having had lunch, we walked out early in bright, warm sunshine. I particularly remember seeing young children playing on the pavement in Buckingham Street, just around the corner from my grandparent's house.

Later, we were in Lyons café having a mid-afternoon snack when the air raid sirens sounded. On leaving Lyons, we were directed to the Landport Drapery Bazaar at the junction of Commercial Road and Arundel Street. Here we were told to take shelter in the carpet department in the basement. Later in the afternoon there were sounds of heavy gunfire, bombs falling and the sound of a succession of loud explosions. The raid was brief but seemingly violent. It was the first time that I had been close to where bombs were landing and exploding.

It was not until sometime later that the crowd was allowed out onto the street. There was a lot of smoke outside and there were police in helmets and fire and emergency services. It was also clear that there were no buses running. My mother enquired about the extent of bomb damage and was told that Lake Road had been badly hit. We tried to walk to Hertford Street by several routes but were prevented from going further by the police. Finally we managed to find that the route via Church Street was open. We got to the house mid-evening. Some of the windows on the ground floor had been blown in. The Spickernell's factory close by and the houses around the corner in Buckingham Street had been destroyed. Some of the children I had seen playing in Buckingham Street that afternoon had been killed.

June Pellatt

Lady Jackson was tall and elegant and lived just outside the village at Posbrook House on Posbrook Lane. We went to deliver some paper and tins there for the War effort. I went with a neighbour to see where a doodlebug had dropped on a house past the Harris' farm, further down Posbrook Lane. I had my cousin in a pushchair, when a German plane came over. Two British ones were chasing it and I could see the markings on the planes and it frightened me to death. My cousin was screaming and the pushchair was folding up. Panic stations! Mr Love, who was Lady Jackson's gardener, came out and pushed me and my cousin to the ground to save us. I can still taste the dirt in my mouth. Mr Love walked us to the copse and then my mum came up to find us.

My dad was in the Home Guard with his friend Mr Gregory. They were on patrol when they got panicky and shouted "Halt! Who goes there?" It was only a cow! The top man in the Home Guard was Mr Phillips who had been in WW1. He had four daughters who were in the WAAFs and Auxiliary Territorial Service (ATS).

Tony Traves

My dad Cyril Traves was Senior Petty Officer on HMS Petard, one of the three destroyers sent to find a U boat in the Mediterranean Sea. It was a dark and rough sea and there are differing accounts as to what happened. HMS Petard hit the submarine with a depth charge and Traves was sent to the wheelhouse, as he was coxswain, to helm the ship. The most important thing was to get all the Germans out of the water as they had abandoned the submarine.

Enigma code machine

Usually there would be a nominated boarding party but Gordon Cannal took some men to salvage what they could from the sinking submarine. The water started to rush in to the sub and Gordon called to the remaining two British sailors to get out. They did not make it and were awarded posthumous medals. One was a 1st lieutenant and one a naval seaman. Tommy Brown, who was only 16, was also awarded a medal.

Some of the material they salvaged from the sinking submarine was of huge importance. It was a codebook, which was sent to Bletchley Park and used to help crack the Enigma Code used by the Nazis to encode their messages so that the Allies could not anticipate their moves.

Jennie Hill (1906-1981)

Jennie's account is a transcript from her diary for a month in winter 1940/41 when she worked as a WAAF at RAF Titchfield, courtesy the Hampshire Records Office.

Corporal Jennie Hill

29/12/40 - Feeling very dull and gloomy after Bill's departure yesterday morning. The old-days have gone forever. Did not go home as I was on night duty.
30/12/40 - Fetched Group Captain Curtis from Hill Head as usual at 08.50. Nothing doing, got coffee etc. ready to take with me to see Bob. Had a nice chat. Strange to eat my supper alone at the old place.
31/12/40 - A quiet day. Cannot get over Bill's family. No-one now to do anything for me any more. Took C.O home at normal time 6.10 and was on night duty.
1/1/1941 - Met Bill this evening on his way back from Bournemouth, had coffee and cakes and he produced a meat pie. We went out on a side lane in the car to eat it together. Then as late, drove him to Portsmouth to spend the night with his mother.
2/1 - Bill due up at Woking at 12.00. Wonder when if ever I shall see him again. A quiet day - feeling sad and lonely and fed up with little to do.
3/1 - Only fetched the C.O. in a.m. and took him back at night when he told me he would not want the car until Monday 6/1. Told flight, who advised me to take 24 hours leave, so I will do so in a.m.
4/1 - Pass OK so I left at 1.00 and went into Fareham to see 'Private Lives of Elizabeth and Essex' a very good picture in colour. Bought some kippers to take home with my milk. They all v. surprised to see me. Saw Mrs Rassain. Enjoyed my evening. Talked over the doings of the week. Mother v. sympathetic over Bill's going and knows how I must miss him and his thoughtfulness and kindness to me always
5/1 - All went to church. Had our New Year celebration with roast lamb,

Battle of Britain 75th anniversary

potatoes and Brussel sprouts, Xmas pudding and sauce v.g.i. Then packed up my stores to bring back for the week. Did not want to return.
6/1 - Fetched the C.O. No work all day. Wrote Bill a long letter. Very cold. Feeling fed up and wonder if I'd do better service in civvy life again.
7/1 - A fall of snow in the night, made the roads slippery V. cold. No work. Everyone advised me not to take the Sniper [car] out tonight, so rung up Jock to say wasn't coming.
8/1 - Still cold, but road conditions improved. No work again, on duty tonight. Cooked my supper as usual, coffee for the duty driver.
9/1 - Was very annoyed, as had been promised the Fareham run and somebody else did it, so not able to get Bill's fountain pen. Went to see Jock this evening and had a nice talk by his coke fire.
10/1 - Jane Winton posted this a.m. Am very sorry she's gone. Siren sounded 18.05 and C.O. said he'd stay on as reason to believe there was trouble. Portsmouth had the Blitz, first bomb put out all the electricity so no light or heating for us.
11/1 - P'mouth had a bad time. Candles to dress by for me and cold water. No heat, perishing cold. Had a very busy day, driving Gilder and C.O. Latimer at different times. 932 Squadron moving to Portchester D flight HQ because of DA Bombs. Asked Latimer's permission to make up some hot coffee in the old kitchen, so in evening did so and C.O. went home later. Also filled up my hot water bottle. Longing to get home tomorrow for bath and warmth.
12/1 - Fetched C.O. and drove him to Portsmouth to see to his business and the damage to 932 HQ. Hit a Jowett car in Merton Rd. not much damage but furious, got home late and enjoyed a bath.
13/1 - Fetched C.O. No work, but wrote Bill a letter of 15 pages - No light again, still very cold - cooked my supper on a small spirit stove given to me by mother.
14/1 - At midday the lights came on and such a cheer went up from everyone, by night the heating was on - it was bliss to be warm again.
15/1 - My cold still bad and everyone suffering from the same complaint.
16/1 - Couldn't go to Winchester as battery dead flat - Sparshott and Capt. Warren saw to it and Cpl. Wolven is getting me a new battery.

RAF Tichfield, No 12 Balloon Command, WAAF's

17/1 - Had long letter from Bill. In p.m. - drove the C.O. to Portchester to the old castle grounds to have the awards of bravery presented by the S.O.S. Quite impressive.

18/1 - Had a photo of himself from Bill, not a v.g. one, also one from Jock. Had 24 hour leave granted me, as staff car going into dock today and tomorrow. Gave Ted Charlton a lift to Fareham and did some shopping for mother. Back to camp to make the promised gingerbread for the officers' mess. Ted returned before it was done - He might be called up - It was strange being in the kitchen again. Went home and they v. glad.

19/1 - Packed up the fountain pen to send to Bill from us all. It was lovely being home. Got up at 8.0 and got breakfast, then went to church; had remains of Xmas pudding for dinner v.g. - 2 p.m. packed and got foodstuff together. Raid in the evening. Bombs dropped and S'oton down in flames.

20/1 - Fetched the C.O, Wrote a long letter to Bill. No job for today. Took C.O. home, on night duty so cooked my supper on my little electric stove as usual.

21/1 - Fetched C.O. - no job in a.m. but fetched a Major Jackson to the camp and took him back after. Got leave to go to Winchester. C.O. returned late, so rushed off but alas never saw Jock, he'd gone.

22/1 - Wrote a letter to Jock explaining things. No job today except to take him home. On night duty.

23/1 - Took F/L Latimer to Middle Wallop H.Q. and to a battery HQ. Stopped at F/L Halfords house as he had gastric flu. Had lunch there in the nursery with 3 small children. Coffee in drawing room.

24/1 - Did not have to fetch the C.O. as he spent the afternoon in camp owing to the practice invasion stunt. Washed the staff car with a bucket and sponge and now trying to stand by for any emergency.

Kate Scott

There was a raid on Dieppe. The Canadian commando troops were camped at the back of Barry's Meadow. Some were billeted in West Street. It was a suicide mission, something to do with dogs.

There were 5,000 troops at West Hill Park School. George Fairbanks was there and he used to walk down to the Bugle as it was a hotel. Gran said it was the place for officers and was the 'place to go' as they had a back room for dancing. You used to have

Canadian POW's Dieppe 1942

to go through two blackout curtains so you did not let out the light. You could get nylons there too. There was the Coach and Horses pub, they had a room too, and the Wheatsheaf pub.

Flo Rogers was gran's bridesmaid and her mum was a dressmaker. She used to save scraps from the dresses she made and put them on their clothes so they always looked 'posh' as they went to the dances at the bases.

Paul Catcheside

I never got much out of my father, Gerald Joseph Catcheside, about his War experience until I asked him whether he had ever brought down a German plane. He said that he hadn't but he had brought down an English one. Years after he had died I thought, "Let's see if we can find anything in the National Archive". So I got hold of the regimental squadron diaries together with my father's service record and found the following: 'Mark Hood's grandfather was flying high in an RAF Whitley Bomber which collided with a cable from a balloon of the Gosport Barrage. His plane was damaged but he managed to fly to HMS Raven in Eastleigh and crash land.'

Gerald Catcheside

The entry in the squadron diary refers to an incident on the following day but as they were working at night that may account for the discrepancy about the date. I think this was the incident, which my father spoke of.

Armstrong Whitworth Whitley Bomber

My dad, a Yorkshire man, worked at Hampshire County Insane Asylum, Knowle, and lived in Fontley cottages. He enlisted on 13th Feb 1939, which struck me as interesting because the War didn't start until September 1939. Five weeks after signing up, the Portsmouth HQ was

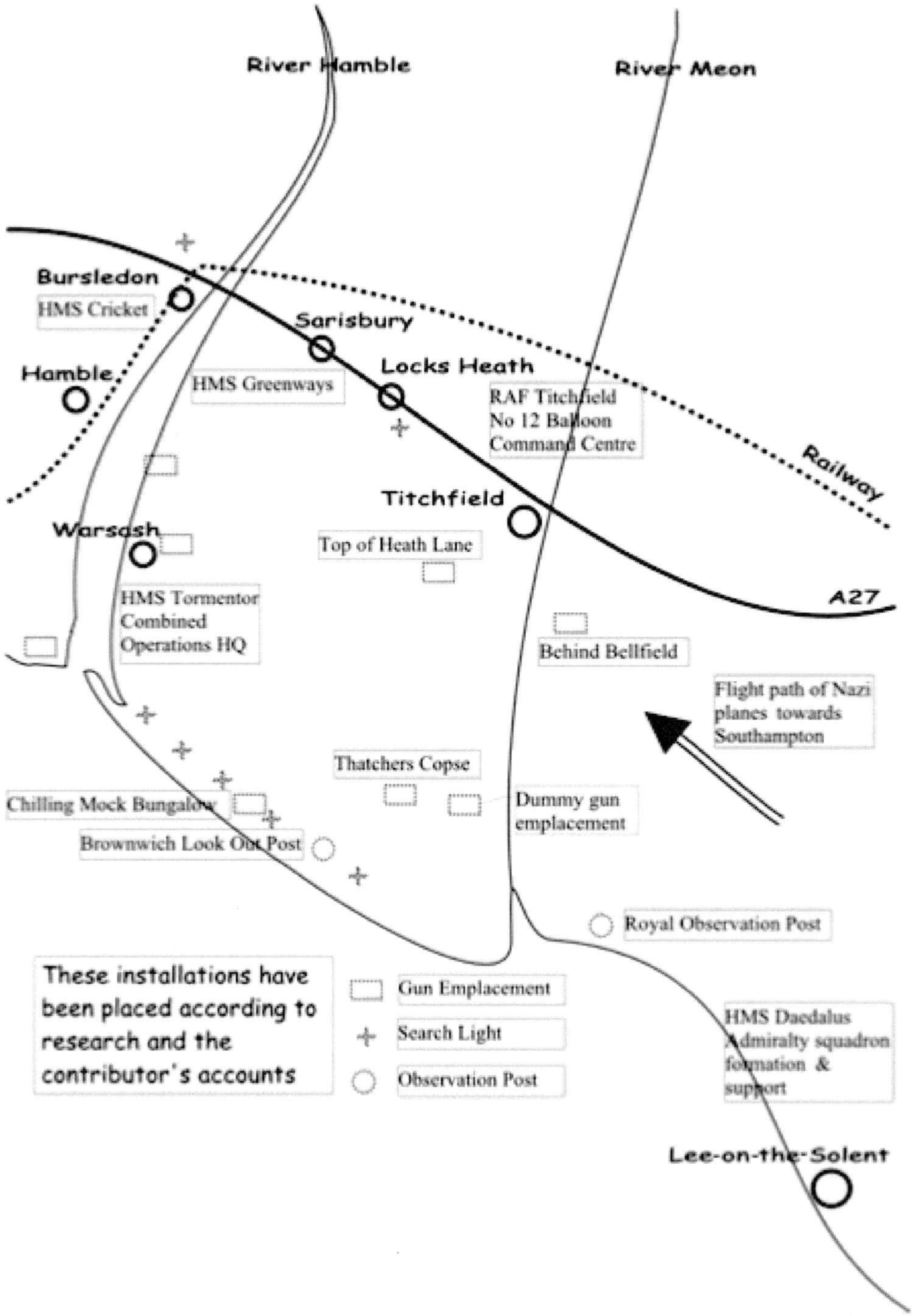

WW2 military bases in Titchfield area

opened for drill and training and dad cycled into Portsmouth two evenings per week for basic military drill. Two months later, Titchfield Balloon Command was opened and this meant a shorter journey of about two miles. He was then moved from Titchfield to near St Vincent's in Gosport (probably in San Diego Road). In the meantime mum moved back to her mother's in Worcester with her young son Robin and she stayed there until after dad's demob in December 1945.

The Balloon Squadron around here was divided into three units Portsmouth, Gosport and north of Portsmouth. They began training at Portsmouth then they very quickly equipped the field at Titchfield and they would do drill and things there. The Balloon Squadron headquarters was Cardington, Bedfordshire, a place originally built for the big German airships, (Zeppelins) which flew between Germany and the UK before the War.

There was a phoney War at first and the balloonists used that to get the knowledge of what they were dealing with. It was a case of 'learn as you go'. Part of the learning was not to fly balloons in winds in excess of 35 mph and the squadron diaries contain lots of details of storms. A lot of the negotiations with the Army were to get lost balloons back. In the Squadron diary you can see that No 33 Balloon was lost and later recovered wrecked at Haslar bridge.

WAAF balloon crews, RAF Cardington

There was an attack at Gosport, I think by mistake, because they were trying to get in low for Portsmouth. A balloon team contained a dozen men. One team was wiped out plus a couple of other casualties.

The main blitz in Portsmouth was after my father left. He went to Cardiff and I think they were stiffening the units there with the experience my father had gained in this area. When the Africa front was developing and becoming successful they tried to continue using barrage balloons in the same way. Women took over the balloon barrages here and men were shipped overseas. My dad was in Port Said and later in Israel.
In 1944 my dad came back to the UK and things got quite nasty with the

V1 bombs starting in June of that year, and the V2s in September, being aimed at the local population. After the War in Europe ended, my dad was involved in shutting down balloon stations and moving equipment where it was needed and accounting for it generally.

Donald Upshall

I went into the RAF, in February 1942, as an apprentice. I wasn't quite 16. My father took me up to London to Marylebone via Waterloo Station. We did two years training and got home about six times a year. When I was coming home through Waterloo 75% to 85% of the people were in uniform, people from all over the Commonwealth. When I was training near Aylesbury, Buckinghamshire, we didn't see much action apart from the blackout but we weren't bombed there. All the cities were bombed, London, Portsmouth and Southampton.

At the end of the training I volunteered for aircrew training and was posted to a fighter squadron. I was only 18. I packed more into 1944 than I did in the rest of my life! Our entry passed out in 1944 and I went to various airfields and had to go on a driving course. I remember, we went to North Wales driving old Austin 10 cars and we also had a week driving RAF Bedford lorries. The reason for that was when we were being driven out of Dunkirk, France, in 1940 a lot of vehicles were disabled as no one could drive them. So what they did was make sure we could all drive. They would say, "Jump into that and drive," but of course unless you had been taught, you couldn't drive.

de Havilland Mosquito

We knew that D-Day was coming, as the country was so full of Americans, Australians and people from all over the Commonwealth. Travelling was restricted. I 'd just got back from a week's leave and my father's funeral. I was on a night fighter squadron. They were called Mosquitoes, a well-known wartime plane fitted with radar to spot the enemy planes. Their job was to protect ships. A plane came in from night patrol over France, and the pilot said, "It's on". They had seen, as dawn broke, a mass of ships going to France. Imagine the wake in the water as they all moved towards France.

Joseph Waldron (aged 9) a pupil at Titchfield Primary School

I am proud of my great granddad, Edward Joseph Beech because, in 1939 at the outbreak of WW2, he was already a regular soldier in the Royal Artillery. He fought in all the major campaigns such as Dunkirk, El Alamein, Libya and the Battle of El Agheila, Tripoli, Tunisia and the Battle of Mareth, Salerno, Naples, D-Day, Caen and the push into Germany. During the North African campaign he fought under the leadership of Field Marshal Bernard Montgomery (Monty) as a Desert Rat. We have many interesting items from my great granddad, such as his diaries, photographs and medals.

Edward Beech in the desert

I am also very proud of my great grandma, Marjorie Beech, who worked in the munitions factory in Gosport throughout the War.

Andrew Mills

During the War, when she was in her thirties, Auntie Vi found a pilot in the fields off Posbrook Lane. She saw him in the field gathering up his parachute. She went over to him and could see he was only about 18 or so, and he was in tears. He had had enough. She brought him back to her house in Bellfield, sat him down, gave him a cup of tea and probably took his parachute away for the silk! They sent someone to get the policeman, who arrived to find them sitting drinking tea and showing each other pictures of their families.

I did think a lot about my parents losing six years of their lives to the War. I feel very sorry that they had to do that.

Douglas Elkins

Leading up to D-Day, I saw thousands of troops assembled along the coast together with equipment of every conceivable kind. Lee-on-the-Solent High Street had Sherman tanks nose to tail as the number increased. When the tanks were loaded with ammunition the shells were delivered in a triangular wooden pack containing three shells each. The soldiers needed to rid themselves of the wooden packing and we were able to take as much as we possibly could. This brand new timber was put to many good uses lasting many years to come.

George Watts

First Aid Post 1941

My mother worked in the Parish Rooms, which was the First Aid Centre for the village. She joked that the only first aid she had to carry out was minor injuries caused when people were rushing to get to shelters and slipped or scraped their knees as they dodged shrapnel. The only real emergency she had to deal with was a man who had the unfortunate experience of being the only person whose house in Titchfield was bombed. He lived in a bungalow below the Harris' farm in Posbrook Lane when a V1 bomb or 'doodlebug' ran out of fuel and dropped just outside his house. He was 'patched up' at the First Aid post and taken away to hospital in an ambulance.

Heinkel bombers

I remember three German planes being shot down in the area. The Heinkel bomber had three airmen: pilot, navigator and gunner and the Home Guard caught them. The bomber that came down in the area was thought to be trying to return home as they jettisoned bombs but was hit by the ack-ack guns. Much to the local boys' disappointment, the RAF guarded the area below Posbrook Farm and cleared the site in three days, so opportunities to collect shrapnel trophies were denied to them.

Southampton was an important port and it was blitzed and set alight. The glow as it burned could be seen from the top of Coach Hill. RAF Titchfield was the Balloon Command Centre for Southampton and Portsmouth and housed many Women's Auxiliary Air Force personnel

(WAAFs). I remember the trouble that always occurred at the dances that were held there; an explosive mix of alcohol and young people during a vicious war.

The young men from Bellfield were renowned for being tough and fighting so the RAF sent for a Southern Champion boxer who challenged a local man with the time-honoured phrase, "Come outside." A short time later the local man came in rolling up his sleeves with a big grin on his face.

West Hill Park School was requisitioned as a sports centre for RAF Titchfield. The Americans in the area were better equipped. They organised competitions between the two forces including a steeplechase or cross-country race. The Americans sent their favourite man, smartly kitted and confident and a RAF fellow came in his blue shorts and RAF shirt. They set off, followed by George and all his friends on their bikes. At first the American pulled away and, as they emerged out of the copse on Hunts Pond Road, the RAF man was in the lead but the American caught up. This happened again at Common Lane and then St Margaret's Lane. Eventually the American man staggered and collapsed as the RAF man ran past and won, much to the jubilation of the boys. The worried Americans put their man in a car and drove him back to base.

My grandfather had served in the military and was employed as a storeman at RAF Titchfield. Unfortunately he hit his head at work. He managed to walk back to West Street where he told his wife, "I've hit my head on one of those bloody boxes." He was put to bed but died a week later. I think that he may have had a stroke, which caused him to fall.

Gerald Read

I knew the balloon was going up 'cos there were American troops all around, belting through the village with their tanks! They chipped the kerbstones in the Square with their metal tracks. And there were troops and guns an' everything all up in Bere Forest. You know, over by Wickham. And them Americans brought over all

Canadian D-Day landings Juno beach

them strange boats, like boxes. They could take a platoon of men over to France. They didn't look as if they could cross the Channel.

After they sank that other ship, SS City of Benares, with all them kids on who were being evacuated, mum said we had to stay in Titchfield. She didn't let me and my brother go on the ship to Canada, to her sister's.

John Williams

When the V1 (doodlebugs) started attacking it was rather frightening listening for the noise of their Ramjet engines and when it stopped you knew there would soon be a large explosion. One night my father saw a doodlebug, in fact he thought there were lots of them, but it was just one being chased by a fighter firing tracer bullets. He grabbed me out of bed and carried me down the stairs, my head hitting some of the banisters, to our indoor shelter.

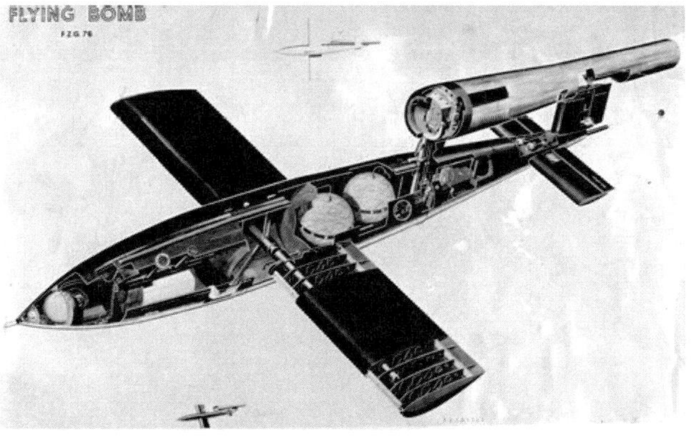

Cutaway of V1 bomb

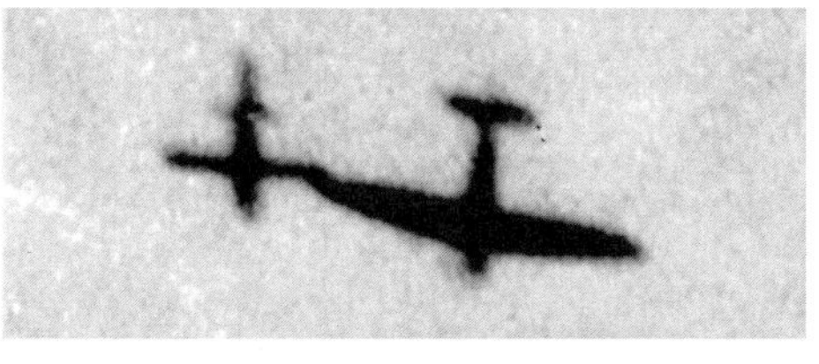
Spitfire 'tipping' a V1

In the living room we had a Morrison shelter, which was of steel construction the top of which acted as a large table. During bad air raids I slept in it often hitting my head on the very hard edges! In the early part of the War, we had an Anderson shelter in the garden, which was made from curved, corrugated iron covered in earth. I don't think we used it much because it filled up with water but the frogs loved it! At odd times when we didn't have a shelter we went down the road to the primary school shelters. In front of the shelters was a long ditch. I remember that Margaret, the girl next door, fell in this ditch and ruined her new siren suit. Siren suits were like the tracksuits of today. They were made popular by Winston Churchill - easy to slip on in an emergency. These were one-piece suits so they were warm and cosy, with no draughts. They were usually made from old clothes especially coats.

Southampton and Portsmouth were both badly bombed during the War. My father quite often had to go to Southampton on business on a

Wednesday, and on occasions took me with him, so I saw some of the devastation caused by the bombing, whole streets in ruins.

The garage just down the road was Priory Garage and to help the War effort it was used to assemble Spitfire tail planes. I believe there was also some Spitfire assembly work in St Margaret's Lane. There were not many private cars around so not much petrol was sold. The glass domes on top of the petrol pumps advertising Shell, Esso etc were taken down and Mr Maltby, the garage owner, stored them near his house. Whilst playing hide and seek with the Maltby girls I somehow managed to tread into one of the globes, badly cutting into my shin. My mother took me to the local doctor, Dr Windermer, who put three stitches in my leg. Nowadays there would have been many more stitches and so as it is, I have been quite badly scarred for life.

Sisman and Goatchers' garage (on left) Southampton Hill

I used to call in to Sisman and Goatcher's garage at the bottom of Southampton Hill and watch them at work and my father used to take his vans there. Because of petrol rationing there were some rather unusual lorries using the roads. Some of the old steam-engined brewery lorries were used and some other lorries had a trailer behind producing some sort of gas to use instead of petrol.

I was quite keen on aircraft spotting and of course it is a very good time and place for that. Being wartime of course it was mainly English and German military aircraft flying above Portsmouth, Southampton and along the Solent.

A German bomber crashed in the fields by the River Meon towards Meon shore. Quite a few children clambered round it although it was guarded by the army; one of the attractions was the Perspex windscreens because there was quite a craze for making Perspex finger rings.

When I got a bike later on I used to ride to Lee-on-the-Solent to watch the Fleet Air Arm planes at HMS Daedalus, also the Walruses and Sea Otters taking off and landing in the sea.

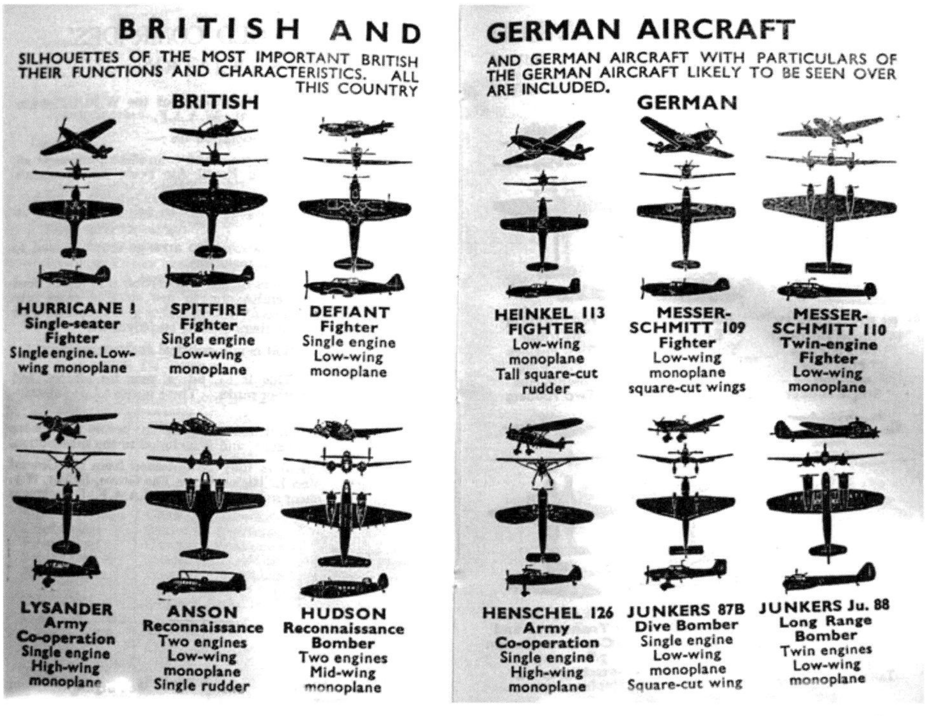

Insert from RAF Diary 1940

The Balloon Barrage later became Plessey's, not sure what it is now. This was the maintenance station for balloons along the south coast. The balloons were large and gas-filled. They were held by cable to special lorries. They flew at about 5,000 feet. They were positioned around vital towns and ports where they were very effective against low flying aircraft and parachutists. Many were positioned around London and proved effective against the doodlebugs. We lived just down the road from the Balloon Barrage and the odd balloon escaped from its mooring and floated past our house trailing its steel cable. The Navy had slightly smaller balloons mounted on their ships to protect them and we could see them from our house flying above Portsmouth together with the normal balloons.

We had one or two RAF personnel billeted with us during the War.

Titchfield had its own unit of Home Guard, 14th Hampshire Regiment, mostly older men, some of whom had served in WW 1 and others that were on essential duties. They met in the Drill Hall. At first they didn't have uniforms or weapons just armbands with LDV - for Local Defence Volunteers. The only weapons they had were old pikes (long spears). Thus equipped they set up in vantage sites on the lookout from water towers on local farmers' land along the Meon Shore Road. There was a scare on one occasion when some bodies were washed up on the shore, which turned out to be from some ship sunk in the Channel. The Home Guard were on the lookout for German invaders landing on Meon shore. When they had their exercises, we boys hid in the trees at the top of

Southampton Hill watching the Home Guard come up the hill. They couldn't see us, so if we had been snipers we could just have popped them off. My dad was a Quarter Master Sergeant so I was quite proud of him.

Titchfield had quite an active fire service of volunteers, one of which was my uncle Alf. He had been in WW1. He told me tales of when the village had a horse-drawn appliance. The horse was kept in a field down by the river behind the church, so they had to catch the horse first, take it back to the fire station and connect it up! It was always exciting, when the siren went, to see all the local firemen dash up the road on bikes and jump on lorries. By now, of course, they had a proper fire engine and they had very good response times.

My uncle Will was in business with my dad but he also had to work on the railway during the War, which was considered an essential job. In the build up to D-Day, Titchfield and the surrounding area was very important and busy. Military vehicles, lorries, tanks, DUKWs were all along the sides of the roads especially along the A27, parked up ready to go to various departure points along the south coast. More gun battery stations were set up at various places. I remember one in the woods on the road to Meon shore that had quite a number of anti-aircraft guns. Down the road from us in Mr Hills' strawberry field was a Bofors gun and searchlight. The soldiers let us wind the handle of the Bofors gun to rotate it round and up and down. The Solent was an amazing sight full of all sorts of shipping, so that it almost looked as if you could walk across to Ryde, on the Isle of Wight. There were so many ships, some 5,000 or so. Meon shore and all along that area was out of bounds to most people, but my father had special dispensation to deliver essential goods for cooking and lighting, namely paraffin, to the beach huts.

Control handles on Bofors gun

There were various campaigns during the War for which they put out posters like: 'Careless Talk Costs Lives', 'Dig for Victory', 'Look Out in the Blackout'. I got involved in 'Save Paper' and won a gold medal for collecting 100 books. Actually the gold medal was a cardboard replica. Thinking back, amongst the 100 books there were probably some quite valuable ones because my grandfather used to go to house sales in old houses and buy up books.

I did wear a uniform towards the end of the War because, after the boy scouts, I joined the Army Cadet Force at Prices School in Fareham. Maybe I was lucky in that none of my immediate family had to go and fight abroad.

Kate Scott

"Gran's sister had small hands and had to pick out human remains when they were repairing the Spitfires"

At Brownwich and Chilling beaches they loaded the tanks for the D-Day invasion.

Tank crews parked at Titchfield

Gran and the other girls worked in the Spitfire factory - now BA Systems. They were picked up from the ferry. Gran's sister had small hands and had to pick out human remains when they were repairing the Spitfires. Bob Chase had a garage on Titchfield Hill on the A27. He used to make bits for the Spitfires. In the late '40s the doodlebugs started to come over. Gran used to will them over when they were making a noise. One landed behind West Hill Park School.

My grandfather, Stan Sentance, was a reservist and he left Southampton on a ferry to Le Harve and drove to Dunkirk. He was told to drain all the oil out of his lorry and leave the engine running so the Germans could not use it.

He was in the Bedfords, assigned to Oakhampton. They left in 1941 and sailed to Canada on the old Arcadia, a Greek ship. After Halifax, Canada, they refuelled at Cape Town and then sailed to Columbo, Ceylon (Sri Lanka). Then on to India and to Singapore, which fell just after they got there, 15th February 1942. He was taken to Changi prisoner of war camp. He didn't go on the railway in Burma but he would never talk about his life.

I have all the surviving letters between my grandparents. My grandfather's regiment had never seen live fire. They were put into a large house with so many men crammed into it that my grandfather had to sit on a plate rack. My granny did not get notification that he was alive until 23rd July 1943. She wrote to him every week and described what was going on in Titchfield. At first she was only allowed so many words. My dad wanted to write but his handwriting was so bad he wasn't allowed to. In later letters she wrote, "I long to hear from you to know that you are alive".

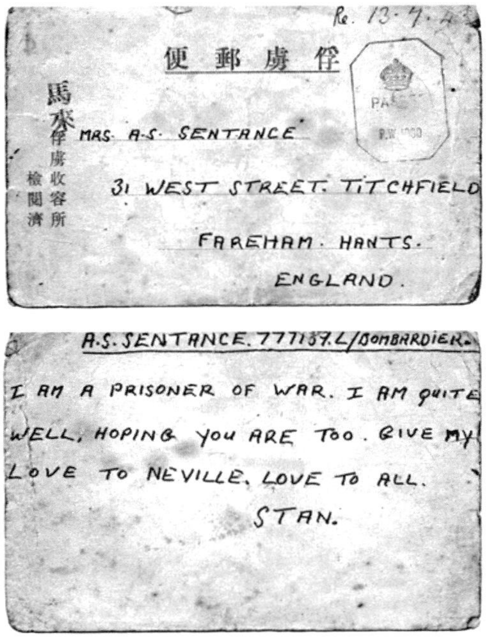

Stan's postcard after 17 months

He was liberated in August 1945 and he was sent to Japan where the Red Cross assigned ladies to help. He was only five stone. He could have flown home but he didn't want to as he wanted to put on some weight before he got home. When the ship got to Gibraltar there was a party with some girl singers. He did not know what they were singing as in Singapore he had had a perforated eardrum, which left him deaf in that ear. He had very bad dreams and wrote that he wasn't the man he used to be, as he got angry sometimes.

He asked my granny to put out his civilian clothes for him but he told her not to come and meet him. He caught a taxi back. When he got back he ripped the banner down the family had put up. Granny used to give him a tot of brandy for his 'shakes'. May Watts, who used to work at Knowle hospital, was worried about him. Today I think it would be called Post Traumatic Stress Disorder. All the family, who lived in Ivy Cottage, West Street, came to see him. He went to work at Fort Grange and then at HMS Daedalus.

Margaret Groves

When I was six I had a tricycle with a truck on the back. I was going along Atkins Lane, which had a farm at the top. The little truck broke and there were Canadian soldiers in camouflage along the hedge with their vehicles and tanks. They had a fire going and came over and mended my truck and gave me a large piece of fruitcake. I appreciated this, as we never had cakes or sweets. I always

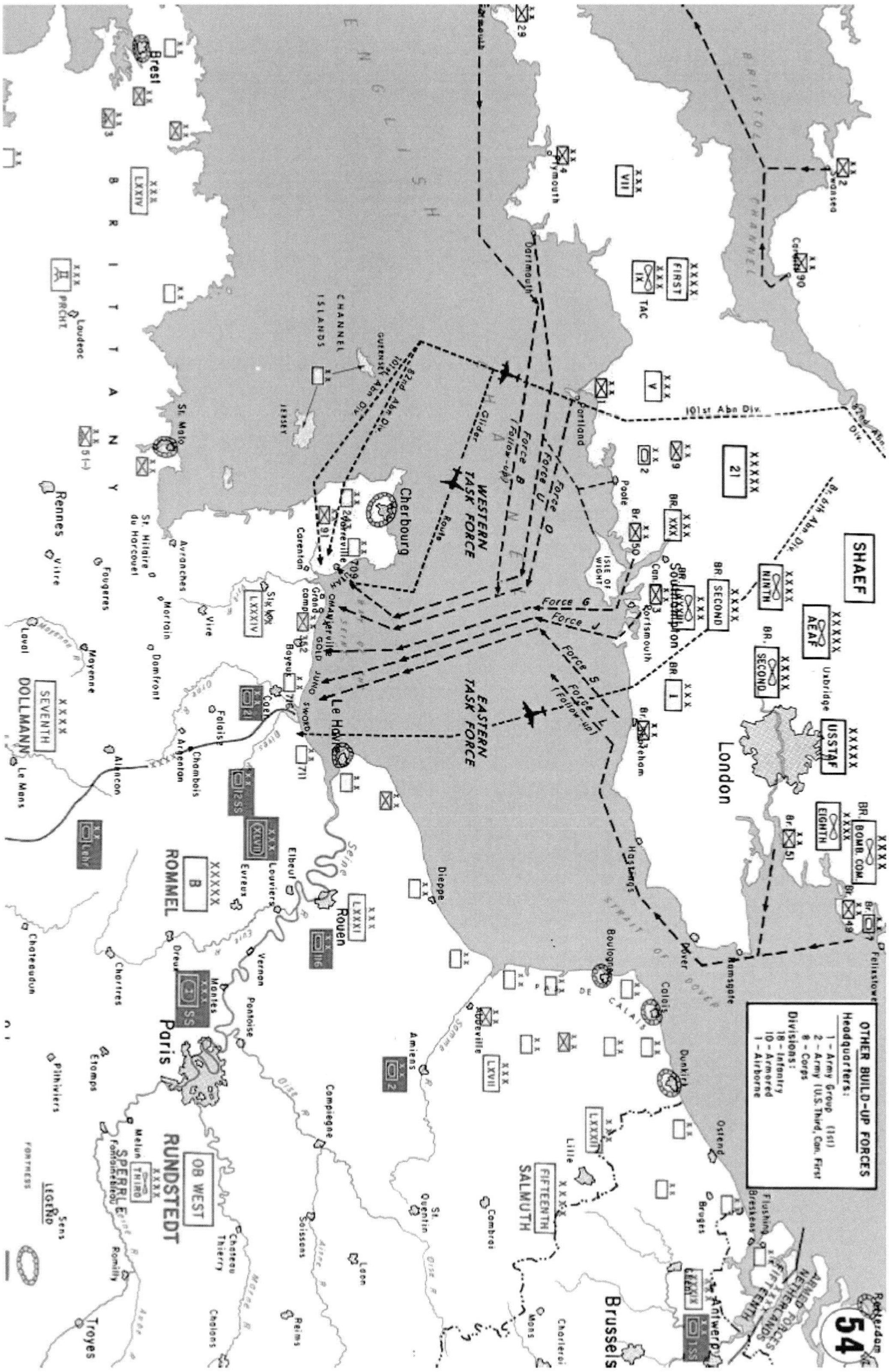

Allied invasion plan for D-Day

remember one of them said to the other, "You're not going to give her that f.....ing cake." I said "I know what that means!!" They moved off the next day, I think this would have been in 1941.

We used to sleep on the floor in the lounge to keep warm and also when the air raids became more frequent. The Anderson shelter in the garden flooded all the time so we had a Morrison shelter indoors, but before we had the Morrison we used to go next door into No. 2 to use their shelter, which was the only one in the terrace.

Linda Felton

During WW2 the family had to use the air raid shelter in the neighbour's garden. They would all huddle together, terrified when the doodlebugs went over in case they dropped on them. One night whilst hurrying to the shelter grandmother tripped over the wire fence. The children thought this was very funny. My mother remembered playing on the bank when a German plane went over and showered them in bullets.

My uncle, Frank Albert Biddle, was named after his two uncles Frank and Albert who were killed in WW1. He was a gunner in the Royal Artillery during WW2. Soldier No. 5498756. He was captured in Boulogne along with others from Titchfield when they were hiding in a house after their gun was blown up. There were only a few survivors after the attack. They were all forced to march to Thorn Podgorz in Poland, a prisoner of war camp. Frank was POW No. 6841. During the journey he had amoebic dysentery and frostbite. His two friends, one called Johnny Mann, saved his life by carrying him. They stopped at Belsen and were fed there.

The band that never was

The photo is a German propaganda image of Frank Biddle (bottom right) and mates dressed in uniforms that were not their own, playing instruments for a fictitious band. This was to show that the allied POW's were being well treated.

Frank worked on a local farm and often sneaked out of camp at night to meet his Polish girlfriend, but the romance didn't last. German doctors had operated on him to remove his appendix. Two Polish children visited him in secret at the hospital, which was run by Polish nuns. Prisoners often swapped food for cigarettes, so that they could use the lighted cigarette end to kill lice on their skin and clothes. The camp was liberated by the Russians who stole their Red Cross food parcels from them.

Frank came home from the War with TB and was sent to a sanatorium in Aldershot where his new love and fiancée Betty visited him. They were later married in Titchfield Church and Frank gave her a brooch in the shape of an ear of corn, which he had found in the camp and brought home. Their daughter Sandra was born in 1946 and son Roy in 1959. He still lives in Bellfield.

Paul Cousins

Paul also has vivid recollections of the preparations for D-Day in May and June 1944. The Congregational chapel, which was next to his family's garden, had a schoolroom, which was used as a canteen for the troops. It was organised by the Women's Royal Voluntary Service (WRVS), with Lady Chalmers in charge. She and her husband (who later became Admiral Chalmers) lived in Guessens, the large house on Coach Hill, where Paul's mother worked as a maid. The main entrance to the canteen was along the passage that now leads to Paul's current home. The troops were English, Irish, Scottish, American and Canadian. Paul used to make a point of playing in the garden to ensure a good supply of candies from the Americans.

In the final days before D-Day the No. 12 Commandos, who were to spearhead the attack, were billeted in the old school - now Gaylords Antiques. They were called 'the famous 12ths'. There were other camps nearby - at Greenwoods on land now called Chillings and the Royal Artillery took over Hollam House. Some of the 12ths came back after the War and married local girls. Paul remembers that they included Billy Eagar, Mac Maginnis, George Templeman and Ted Gosling but he thinks that they have no surviving relatives still living in Titchfield.

Rita Prior

Cousin Sylvia could always get some gum or chocolate from the Americans and Canadians. I can see aunt Amy with tears in her eyes watching the tanks and army trucks and lorries full of troops passing our house. One plucked a rose and tucked it in his cap. She was wondering how many would return.

Sheila Hignell

There was a big army camp in Thatcher's Copse. We were lucky because if there was going to be an attack someone ran up from the camp and told us to get into the air raid shelter.

I remember a doodlebug falling on Bay Tree cottage. Mum walked over with us in the evening to see the terrible damage to what was a lovely house. Luckily no one was killed.

Mike Ferris

There were at least two aircraft crashes in Titchfield. One of these was in the field opposite Road Copse on House's Farm on Posbrook Road. I believe this was a bomber but the area was quickly sealed off and I only saw it from a distance. The other was a Bristol Beaufighter, which crashed in Brownwich Lane on Charlie West's nursery. Charlie had a worked out sandpit on his land and this night fighter had crash-landed and finished up teetering over the edge of the pit.

Bristol Beaufighter

My grandfather had a nursery on the opposite side of Brownwich Lane from Charlie West's nursery and he had anti-aircraft guns there. The soldiers manning these used to help out by working on the land.

The only actual bombs I remember landing in Titchfield were, in fact, parachute land mines, which were probably jettisoned from the planes. These were more powerful than most bombs and one landed on Chant's nursery, next to Hewitt's Farm at Meon. I remember seeing the shattered conifer trees, which were little more than matchwood, and the greenhouses which were destroyed by the blast.

My aunt had moved from Gosport to live in a wooden bungalow in Brownwich Lane because it was thought to be safer away from the bombing. However a parachute mine landed within feet of her 'safe' bungalow, blowing a large crater in the lane and flattening her bungalow. There were no casualties from this incident.

A doodlebug exploded, landing on the house of nurse Bailey, in the Meon Road.

Again I believe no one was injured but what I remember is seeing her bed hanging from the part of her house, which was still standing. Rosie Bennett, who lived on the Posbrook Road, was riding her bike nearby and was blown off by the blast. She was found lying in the road completely unhurt with her bike wheels still spinning screaming, "I'm dead! I'm dead."

It seems incredible that the massive American tanks ever managed to drive through the village without destroying some of the houses. The only damage I ever saw was to the granite kerbs immediately next to the Coach & Horses pub where the tank tracks chipped them. Those damaged kerbs were still visible until the Mews houses were built. We used to run alongside the American trucks crying out, "Any gum chum?" and the American soldiers were very generous. Besides gum they threw all sorts of unheard of goodies like chocolate bars and tinned food such as spam.

During this build-up period, the army billeting officers used to come around armed with a list detailing how many rooms you had in your house and how many lived there. If you had any spare capacity at all, you were asked to provide accommodation for soldiers for a number of days prior to D-Day. We had two soldiers sleeping on the floor in our house.

Bren gun carrier in use in France

In the troop build up before D-Day, the field on Heath Lane was filled with troops and included amongst their equipment were Bren gun carriers. These were like a mini tank mounted with a single Bren machine gun. The soldiers used to give us rides on them around that field.

Leslie Ellis

In 1940 Leslie was called up and joined the Royal Army Medical Corp as a medical officer. Early in 1941 he was stationed at the British Military Hospital in Sialkot. He then went to Northern India which, following partition in 1947, became Pakistan. Leslie then went as the medical officer to the Worcestershire Regiment as they were doing field exercises near Jhelum in the Pabbi Hills.

Leslie's unit moved on to Singapore and was captured in February 1942 when the Japanese invaded. Conditions were atrocious but, on Easter Sunday, Leslie was among the first party to leave Singapore. He went by boat to Saigon, where

The D Day landings in Normandy, on the Channel coast of France

most of the men worked in the docks as slave labour. He, however, was sent on to Hanoi until 1943. The next move was as M.O. to the people working on the Burma-Siam railway which was being built. The conditions were grim; there was starvation, illness and brutality.

Leslie remained there until the atomic bombs were dropped on Japan in August 1945. Leslie said he is still uncertain about the morality of the atomic bomb but within days after they were dropped, the War was over. He returned to India and had three and a half years of a major's back pay waiting for him.

Sylvie Whittaker

I rode to work by bicycle, up hill and down dale, taking all the back roads from Blackpool where I was billeted in a semi-detached house out of town. The high hedges were green and fresh and the birds were flying down the lanes.

I worked for the Ministry of Pensions, Norcross. The girls in our office were sitting about in summer dresses drinking tea or coffee from flasks, and were bored. We seldom mentioned family members being away, we kept the chat light where possible, talking about weekend plans and rationing difficulties of getting butter or getting a decent piece of meat to roast.

The whole place was made up of large offices where hundreds of typists waited for incoming data from towns which had been bombed, ship's crew lost at sea, together with soldiers and airmen lost. Pension slips were dispatched against appropriate data for dependents of those men injured or killed. The slips were only about six inches by four inches, listing name, number, which unit they were in, and what had happened to them - killed - wounded - missing, believed killed. Whilst in one sense we were pleased to be reasonably quiet, we sometimes truly wondered whether it was worth being there at all - nothing much ever happened for us. We seemed to be so numerous - a whole office doing practically nothing. So there was a war on - we weren't informed or asked about anything, we felt we were practically redundant.

Sylvie Whitaker

The news on the sixth of June 1944 was a revelation - our troops had landed in France and the Americans had joined them - at last things were on the move. 'D' Day was under way and its legacy became very obvious to us. After a day or so, the slips of paper began to be more than just a trickle. On the bottom of each slip was another set of details - next of kin - National Insurance number, dependent relatives. One of these slips had an address I hadn't come across before. It said 'Hants' for county so I queried this from the head typist. She had to go to another office and found out that this meant Hampshire. We were northerners so hadn't recognised the abbreviation. The address was 'Titchfield', and the soldier was in the Hampshire Rifles. His relative was listed as 'dependent: wife plus two children'. Just cold details.

My job was to copy this scrappy bit of information down and list it so that the wife could get her widow's pension. The arrival of this news to her would have been by hand - a telegram boy. We tried not to think further than typing the details - she would never know of our despair and sympathy for her. Skimpy bits of cheap paper detailing the loss of a good man who would be badly missed.

From being practically unemployed, the little scraps of paper came faster and piled up in the in-tray, overwhelming us all. We felt guilty going home. If we didn't have children to care for we worked overtime. The head typist was a hard-faced woman, dressed mostly in dark colours. She stalked between the rows of girls but her dedication to office procedure was surely more valuable to the families receiving this devastating information than any amount of weeping by the workforce of young girls. We cried lots. "I see you are in tears again. There is no help given in a shower of tears. Much better to get the forms filled as quickly as possible. Put in extra hours if you feel so bad!"

Donald Upshall

After D-Day, the RAF squadrons moved down to Middle Wallop, near Salisbury, and you gradually worked your way down to Southampton dock. We ended up in a transit camp, just outside Salisbury. And there were Americans and you were all together. We went down to Southampton docks and when we got down there we boarded a Liberty ship. The Americans built them - they were all welded and they produced so many a week as we needed them to get the supplies across the Atlantic. They were mass-produced and you did not launch them like the liners, stern first, but sideways. They were especially built to bring stuff across for the War effort. We boarded this ship in Southampton dock and we sailed out and anchored just off Calshot as we were in a queue because there were so many ships going across. We were on the ship for a few days and I was talking to these Americans. One came from Seattle, but I could almost see Lee-on-the-Solent. I said "I live just over there" and he said, "Well I live 6,000 miles away!" It was amazing really.

Typhoon rearming

I always remember that these ships were manned by American Merchant Navy and we had to do sentry duty. I remember this man tapping me on the shoulder, he must have been about 50 and he must have thought I was only a youngster. He gave me this beef sandwich because they made their own bread. I think it was the best meal I ever tasted in my life because the other rations we had were wartime rations, which you had to carry with you. They were horrible things - you just existed. I often wonder what his name was. Little things like that you do remember. After that we were queuing up to get unloaded.

When we were in the Southampton docks it did cross my mind to pop home to see my mother but it was just as well I didn't as you never knew when you would suddenly sail and then you would be in serious trouble. There were even some Australians and they were 12,000 miles away from home. There were so many people from all over the world.

MkIV Stirlings, Operation Market Garden

Then we were all moved to various airfields and we were reposted to a Typhoon squadron. It was one of the fastest aircraft in the world, at that time. We went over to France in September '44, pushing up to Germany. We landed at Omaha beach but of course there was nothing going on, you could certainly notice all the wrecked tanks. I remember we were in this RAF convoy, we'd landed, and we went through Caen and it was completely flattened. The Americans bombed in the day and we bombed it in the night. We were told to keep inside the lorries, as some of the French men did not like it because they thought we over-did the bombing. It was just one of those things during the War. Then I was sent back to England. After that I was I was on a Stirling bomber squadron, they did some bombing raids and gradually the War came to an end with all the victory parades.

I remember being on a train from Waterloo, to Southampton, I was standing next to a chap and he said, "I know you. You're Don Upshall aren't you? I'm Fred Pack." This chap was a sergeant. It was a family who lived at Bellfield. In those days he had just come back from the Isle of Man. He had been training as an air gunner in a bomber squadron. He was killed in a flying accident and his name is on the War Memorial in Titchfield.

Judy Stokes

Judy Stokes had a fascinating career during and just after the War, helping to mend the minds and bodies of men who had sustained disfiguring injuries . 'What an honour to work with Sir Harold Gillies', Judy Stokes' talk, was given in September 2014 in St Peter's Chapter Rooms to the Women's Breakfast Group.

I was at school in 1939 when War broke out. My older sister had joined the Red Cross and once a month we had a practice. They needed people to use as 'patients' so I was taken along. I learnt a lot from this, for example don't have the knots too tight, talk to the patient. Our stretchers were made of a wire mesh and when you got up you looked like a waffle, they later padded them.

Judy Stokes

Then the age for joining the Red Cross was bought down to 16 so I joined up and became a member, taking my turn at day duty. When it was night duty we slept under the stage of the Parish Rooms. I made the tea and enjoyed the fellowship and was learning all the time.

When I was 18 my call-up papers came through and I was sent to a factory making drill braces. The bits had been made and we just had to assemble them; it was like an egg whisk. I kept asking to become a Voluntary Aid Detachment (VAD) worker but every time the answer was "No".

Eventually we realised something important was happening as there were troops everywhere along the south coast and large lorries that needed the trees cutting back to get through. I was given a temporary release for a week to find a post. If I didn't find one, I had to go back to the factory. Three days later I was in an auxiliary hospital at Liphook. The men were either recovering or waiting for discharge as unable to return to the front. There were men with such injuries as being deafened by an explosion but one man had an unexplained rash. Then it was realised that it was scarlet fever, which he had caught from his children when he was home on leave. Needless to say he was quickly put into isolation.

I was sent to Winchester for reassessment and then subjected to the 'chamber of horrors'. These were photographs of men who had been terribly injured and scarred. Some girls fainted and some had to leave the room. I was one of two girls who were interested and unaffected so I went to Park Prewett hospital in Basingstoke. There were 800 beds in villas, which were better than Nissen huts. The main house had been taken over by a London hospital, St Mary's, Paddington. I carried out all the usual routine such as blanket baths, feeding and shaving the men as many did not have hands. These were men from the Tank Corps and if they had to get out of a burning tank it meant putting their hands on the top of the open turret to haul themselves out. By the time a man had done that the rest of the crew would be dead and his hands were burnt so badly they became claws and it was necessary to amputate them.

The doctor in charge of plastic surgery was Sir Harold Gillies who was a pioneering surgeon. He was keen that as well as having to mend the men's bodies they should try to build up the men's minds. He encouraged the staff to fraternise with the patients to keep up their spirits. He wasn't like the other doctors, as he would come round the wards and talk, socially, to the patients. I even saw him open a door for a ward maid, "After you my dear." he said. He was a New Zealander and my pin-up boy.

He pioneered new procedures such as a pedicle. It was difficult to get skin to graft, especially onto the face and jaw. Sir Harold would cut round three sides of a rectangle on the man's forearm to form a flap, and then sew it to the jaw with the circulation intact keeping the skin alive. The poor man had to stay with his arm against his face for a very long time and had to be plastered in place to stop it from moving. We had to do everything such as feeding and washing because he could not move.

We also had a man from Fareham, who had lost all his toes to frostbite so Sir Harold took body tissue and sewed it into a bag of skin and sewed this onto the man's feet. I remember this man being in a wheelchair and then standing up, saying, "Look Nurse, I can stand." Another man had lost his eyelids so Sir Harold took a little flap of skin from behind his ear and sewed it onto the eye, the hair became his eyelashes. It is very difficult to sleep without eye lids. When the Allies went into Europe we saw terrible atrocities such as men from the concentration camps with noses and ears cut off.

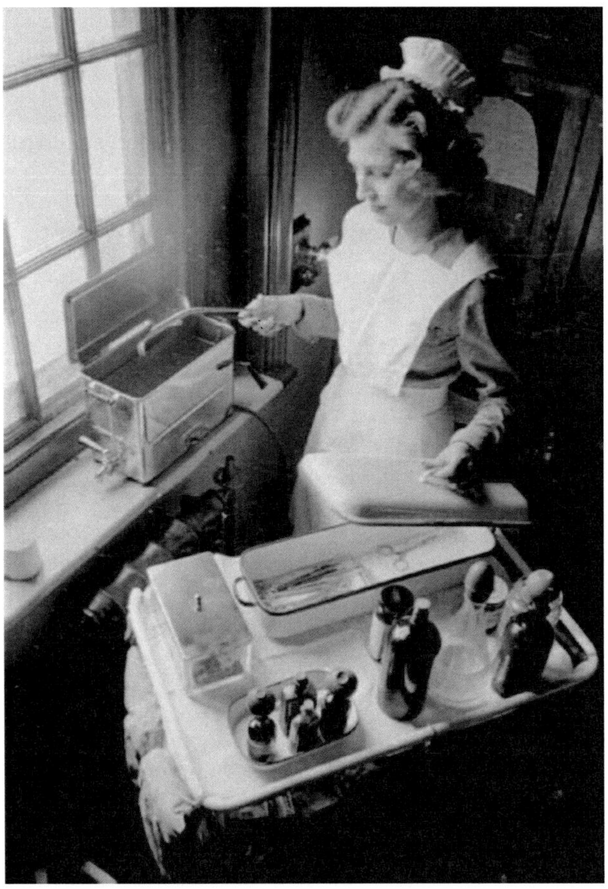

A nurse Park Prewett Hospital 1941

Sir Harold said that one nurse would be assigned to a man; she would prep. him and stay with him in the operation and then, when he was back on the ward, she was to build a special relationship with him. When they came round from the operation men would ask, "I didn't talk did I?" It was just as well I had worked in a factory and I had learnt how the other half lived as I had learnt some new words there! The staff had to be so careful in those days as there was not any penicillin or surgical gloves to keep infection down. Sir Harold was a great artist and he hung his pictures on the walls of the wards, as it could get very boring staring at walls day after day.

The people of Basingstoke were so good; they invited the men for lunch or tea to get them used to being looked at. The Canadians donated a pavilion for entertainments. There were things like the Entertainments National Service Association (ENSA), the forces entertainment group. Again it got the men used to being with other people. Sadly some people could not get used to them and we saw men whose marriages and engagements had broken up.

The nurses and VADs lived in the old admission block with only curtains between a bed, little dressing table and a long wooden box which we called our 'coffin'. There was not a wardrobe so everything had to go in there. It had been a hospital for people with mental illness so they had three baths with only curtains between them. The tap was a mobile one so we had to ask the other girl to pass it though the curtains. The dining room was enormous but it was not open at night so we had to cook the food ourselves. It fell to the lowest of the low, in this case me, to cook.

Everyone just joined in, we all took our turn although I felt I was a little cog in a very big machine but I felt it was worthwhile. I didn't see the disfigurement but the personality of the man. I respected the courage of the men.

Judy's Badge of Honour

When I was able to return home, I became a dental nurse. I was able to undertake Red Cross duties, first aid, Darby and Joan Club, assist at foot clinics and blood donor sessions, For five years I was a cadet officer for the Titchfield girls unit. We met at the Parish Rooms at first but when an adult group was started we were joined by the boys' group who had their meetings elsewhere. Red Cross HQ took over the old school on West Hill (now Gaylords) and we were able to share lectures and demonstrations and work together at sports events and wherever first aid might be needed including, of course, the carnival. Steve Harris very kindly provided us with a lorry or tractor and trailer for us to join in. His daughter Joan was one of the cadets.

I have continued with my Red Cross work and I have a badge for 70 years service.

War's End

Paul Cousin

I remember the celebrations at the end of the War, when Lady Chalmers and Miss Parry, the chief ARP warden, headed the parade.

Gerald Read

We had a bonfire, yes, in the Square to celebrate VE-Day. No more 'lights out!' No more listening for the air raid siren and the bombs falling on Portsmouth Naval Dockyard, or watching the glow as Southampton burned!

Donald Upshall

VE-day was in 1945 and everybody celebrated. Rationing still went on for years after that but at least you knew you wouldn't get bombed! There was petrol rationing and we had clothing coupons. After that my career in the RAF ended because my father had died and I had to take over the running of the garage. I was going to make the RAF my lifetime career. There were some good opportunities because after that there was the Cold War and they were building up the RAF squadrons again.

Kate Scott

Liberation of Changi POW's 1945

On 15th August 1945, VJ-Day, my great grandfather, John Thomas Carse, who lived at 29 West Street, put his favourite armchair out on the road and set fire to it. He had heard the news on the radio of the Japanese surrender. His son-in-law, Arthur Stanley Sentance, of 31 West Street was a POW in Changi, Singapore. There was also another POW in Japan who came from further up West Street. Everyone came out of their houses to celebrate and they lit a bonfire on the street opposite the pub, the Old House at Home.

John (also known as Jock) had survived WW1 on the minesweepers, but was too old to serve in WW2 and he later died in 1959. My great aunt Marleen (John Thomas Carse's youngest daughter) was there. She now lives in Coach Hill.

Mike Ferris

The main event for VJ-Day celebrations was organised by returning servicemen. It involved a large bonfire right in the centre of Titchfield Square, unbelievable as it now sounds. Prominent amongst these men were Albert Godbehere from middle Bellfield, who also started a boxing club, Johner Jones from Posbrook Farm, Tosh Bartley and Stan Sentance from West Street. We kids collected any material we could and this was stored until VJ-Day, in the corner against the wall of the then Lankester & Crook butcher's shop. The sight of the bonfire in the centre of the Square was very exciting although I don't recall there being any fireworks.

What made it memorable in particular though was when a bunch of the men from the Bugle pub decided to make it more exciting by adding a barrel of tar to the flames. During those times, road repairs were carried out by rolling stone chippings in hot tar and someone had spotted that the council had placed some barrels of tar on the corner of Ranvilles Lane at the top of Titchfield Hill ready for road repairs. A gang of them, including Ern Privett who worked at the gasworks, nicked a barrel and rolled it down the hill to the Square. The ultimate result was that rivulets of molten tar were running over the road and everyone had to step back to avoid them.

Churchill waves to the crowds in Whitehall on VE-Day

World War Two terms explained

Ack Ack guns	Nickname for anti-aircraft guns
Air Raid Patrol, ARP	During Blackout, checking no lights showing
Allied Powers	Britain, France, USA and Soviet Union opposing Germany and the Axis Powers
Anschluss	Hitler's desire for political union with Austria which led to its annexation
ANZAC	Australian and New Zealand Army Corps
Appeasement	Efforts of British Prime Minister Neville Chamberlain to avoid war with belligerent Germany
Axis Powers	Germany, Italy, and Japan opposing Britain and the Allied Powers
Battle of Britain	Britain's RAF resistance against the German Luftwaffe attempts to destroy it in late 1940
Beadle	Person who checked up if your child was at school
Black market	Selling things unavailable due to rationing or scarcity
Blackout	Cover on windows so enemy planes didn't see lights
Blitzkrieg	Hitler's invasion strategy, sudden with overwhelming force, literally 'lightening war'
Blitz	Shortened from above, a term used for the major bombing of British cities in late 1940 and early 1941
Bombed out	City or building destroyed by bombs
British Restaurant	Somewhere bombed out families could get a meal
Called-up	Notice that you are to join the military services
Chindits	British and Gurkha troops who worked behind Japanese lines in Burma
Civvies	Non-uniform clothes
Concentration camp	Prison where people were held without trial, like the Jews in Germany
Conchy	Conscientious objector, someone who wouldn't fight on ethical grounds
Convoy	Naval escorted merchant ships supplying food and armaments, often attacked by German submarines
D-Day	1944 invasion of German-occupied France, beginning of the push which ended the War in Europe
Demob	Demobilisation, release from the armed services
Doodlebug	German rocket fired at British cities
Dried egg	Method of preserving /transporting eggs
Dripping	Fat saved from cooked meat, used instead of butter
Dunkirk	Evacuation of the British Army from northern France following German invasion of Belgium
El-Alamein	Britain's decisive victory over German forces leading to securing of North Africa
Evacuee	Child moved from urban life to 'safety' of rural areas

Faggots	Internal organs of pig rolled up with bread crumbs and herbs, and eaten hot
Final Solution	German plans to systematically exterminate the Jewish population of occupied lands
Gerry	British nickname for a German
Gestapo	Feared German secret police
GI's	American service personnel
Gurkhas	Soldiers from Nepal
Holocaust	Genocide of Jewish people in concentration camps
Home Guard	Volunteer force who defended 5,000 miles of British coastline against German invasion
Hiroshima	Also Nagasaki were the two Japanese cities where the Allies dropped atomic bombs forcing surrender
D-Day beach	Five invasion beaches between Cherbourg and Le Havre: Utah, Omaha, Gold, Juno and Sword
Lebensraum	'Living space' Hitler's justification for invasion of Germany's neighbours
Luftwaffe	German air force under Hermann Goring
Liberty ships	American ships built at great speed
Little Ships	700 private boats used for Dunkirk evacuation, which rescued 338,000 British and French soldiers
Maginot Line	French eastern defensive line
Manhattan Project	American programme to develop the atomic bomb
Marshall Plan	Post-war strategy to redevelop Germany
Mein Kampf	Hitler's autobiographical political manifesto
Molotov cocktail	Petrol bomb - home-made incendiary device
Mulberry Harbour	Dock in kit-form, towed to France for D-Day
Operation Overlord	Code name for the British invasion of France June 1944
Oslo Meal	Quick nutritious meal, a bit like a 'Ploughmans'
POW	Prisoner of war, someone surrendered or taken during wartime, frequently put to work by captors
Reserv'd Occupation	Job considered too important for the person to be called up into military service
Shrapnel	Pieces of metal from exploded bomb
Siren	Audible warning of imminent attack
S.S.	German elite paramilitary unit
U-Boats	German submarines
VE Day	Victory in Europe day, 8 May 1945
Vichy France	Southern France governed in collaboration with Germany
VJ Day	Victory in Japan day, 15 August 1945
Whale meat	Eaten when other meats in short supply
WRNS	Women's Royal Naval Service
WVS	Women's Voluntary Service

Part Three Bonus Pictures

Balloon ready for deployment in Gosport

Landing Craft Infantry, D-Day crossing

Supermarine factory, Woolston

British Commandos, Operation Plunder

Mk 1 Spitfire K9795

D Day preparations, Southampton

Liberty Ship construction days 2, 10 and 24

Royal Naval training for D-Day

George VI in Gosport

Hyde Park anti aircraft battery

View of tracer shells /Spitfire gun film

WAAFs working on balloon duty

HMS Hood 1917

Significant Dates

1938 - German Chancellor Adolf Hitler annexes Austria
- British and French allow Hitler to annex part of Czechoslovakia
- British Prime Minister Neville Chamberlain negotiates with Hitler over Czechoslovakia and declares "Peace for our time"
- Kristelnacht, Hitler arrests 30,000 Jews and 7,000 Jewish businesses are destroyed

1939 - Hitler invades the rest of Czechoslovakia
- Spanish Civil War ends with dictator General Franco in charge
- Hitler invades Poland - Britain and France declare war on Germany

1940 - Germany blockades British waters with U Boat submarines and begins bombing raids on Britain
- Ration Books introduced in Britain
- German Blitzkrieg overwhelms Belgium, Holland and France. Allies retreat through Dunkirk
- Neville Chamberlain resigns and Winston Churchill becomes prime minister
- Battle of Britain, Germans fail to gain air superiority over England
- Germany invades the Channel Islands (British territory)

1941 -The Blitz, German terror bombing of British cities
- Japan attacks Pearl Harbour so the Americans join the Allies

1942 - Singapore falls to the Japanese

1943 - Germany's first defeat at Stalingrad by the Russians
- Allied success in north Africa leads to attack through Italy

1944 - D-Day, Allies invade northern France and liberate Paris

1945 - Auschwitz liberated. It, with other German concentration camps, had murdered six million Jews
- Russians push westwards and reach Berlin first. Hitler commits suicide
- Germany surrenders - Victory in Europe Day, VE Day
- America drops two atomic bombs on Japan forcing it to surrender
- Victory in Japan Day, VJ Day - the War is over
- The War has killed 60 million people: 22 million combatants and 38 million civilians

Part Four 1946 - 1964

Childhood and Families

Jean Faulds

When my dad returned from being a prisoner of War he opened a wet-fish shop in one of the empty shops by the chapel and he also became caretaker of the Drill Hall in which he organised dances for the villagers.

Some of the commandos returned to Titchfield after the War finished and married some of the village girls and I was one of those girls. I married Peter who had been billeted in our house. When the War finished, I left home in Titchfield with my new husband and moved to Birmingham to find work and to set up a home. However, even today, 65 years later, I continue to return to the village twice a year to holiday with my sisters and their families.

Andrew Mills

I was born in Titchfield Common in 1947 in a cottage next to the Sir Joseph Paxton public house. There were eight railway cottages there in Sydney Terrace. They were truly condemned when we moved into them and they were knocked down about eight years later. At the back of the cottages there was a path, and a shed and the outside toilets. My father used to have to bury the contents of the toilet bucket each week at the top of the garden and we grew the most incredible rhubarb!

Titchfield Common, Sir Joseph Paxton pub

It was pretty primitive and I think we only had one standpipe tap and a black cooking range. Next to the houses there was a laundry and next to that there was an air raid shelter for about 25 people. I used to play in there. When the cottages were knocked down they found there was a lake underneath them. We moved to the top of Hunts Pond Road.

There were seven other families in the cottages and some of the families were distantly related to me. One family was the Wheatears (pronounced 'Whitcher'). The reason we had so many relatives was because my great grandmother, Mrs Wheatear, had ten children. They lived in a small house on

West Street, Titchfield (one of the end-on ones, not the ones facing the road). Clary, the only boy, stayed at home and the rest of the siblings got married, including my grandmother. When they had grown up, my great grandmother left her husband and Clary for a couple of years and joined the circus. There was no animosity as she returned later. Many of the family lived on Bellfield; they weren't rich people.

I remember the horrible smell of tobacco and ale in the Joseph Paxton pub. I was sent there to get cigarettes. Oh it was a horrible place then!

At the end of our street there was the recreation ground and they had local fetes there. Our neighbour, who was a cousin of mine, Betty Wheatear (later Brind), was in the egg and spoon race. She was running backwards and forwards when she fainted during the race. It sticks in my memory.

The Brewery Tap

There was also a brewery in the village in Bridge Street and a pub called the Brewery Tap. That's where my father got caught by a policeman. There were no cars about so he would cycle down Coach Hill with his hands off the handlebars and swing round the corner at the bottom. One day a policeman jumped out and caught him.

On the corner of Abshot Road there was a gypsy caravan camp and a lot of the kids would come to my school from there. Just down the road, on the way to Hook on the right hand side, there was a house that looked like it was built from an Anderson shelter. The people who lived there were called Randall and their son David used to come to our school. This house fascinated me. It was a really nice house, I don't know if it's still there.

If you carry on along the Hook road there are gravel pits and you can continue to Warsash. There were stories of kids firing air rifles and throwing stones at the gravel trucks and getting chased by the workmen. A couple of my friends used to make pipe bombs and were always blowing things up. The best trick was burying a pipe bomb in the beach and watching the shingle fly up. There were reports on the radio and in the newspapers about explosions and things. They never thought the reports were about them until one day they suddenly realised that they had been scaring the local community and didn't know it.

Bessie Traves

My elder brothers Jim and Steve Harris started their own business farming and market gardening at Meon. At times I helped Steve's wife look after their growing family.

Although we couldn't afford to have the bells rung for our wedding, on the occasion of our Diamond Wedding anniversary, our family arranged for a peal of bells to celebrate our 60 years together. I have two children, four grandchildren and five great grandchildren.

I had a stroke ten years ago, which unfortunately left me with a speech difficulty. Up until then I had served on a number of community committees, which I had to give up. I am still a member of Titchfield WI and usually attend the monthly meeting. I was one of the original cooks for the Day Centre Lunch Club for a number of years.

The bells rang for Bessie and Cyrils' diamond wedding

During my life in Titchfield, I have seen the area undergo great change from a mainly rural, agricultural and strawberry growing area, to semi-suburbia.

John Ekins

In the '40s and '50s when I was a child, Catisfield was much more of a discrete settlement than it now appears as it was separated from Fareham by farms and open fields. Catisfield itself was a collection of a few mainly large houses with a number of terraced cottages. It had a post office and a church, St Columba. In the early '50s there was only a very sparse bus service to Fareham run by Glider coaches. Our address then was just Elm Cottage, Catisfield. Highlands Road connected to what is now Catisfield Lane and then to the A27 opposite Ranvilles Lane. This was the starting point of the Titchfield bypass, constructed in the early '30s.

Our connection with Catisfield and with Titchfield began in 1916 when my grandfather Arthur Ekins moved to Elm Cottage, renting it from the Catisfield House estate. He had returned from India, where he had been building railways, to join the Royal Engineers and then served in France.

My parents were married in St Peter's Church in Titchfield in August 1940 on my mother's 21st birthday. Her parents evidently did not approve of the match. Three years later I was baptised there and in 1965 St Peter's is where Judy and I were married.

Past times are quite difficult to recall and in looking back over 70 years it is apparent how much change there has been. When my recollections start, the experience of the War loomed large and we still had food rationing, power shortages and it was the dawn of the modern welfare state. There was much hope of better times, but fear of the atomic bomb and the spread of communism.

June Pellatt

Greenwoods was an ex-army camp, just below Harris' farm on Posbrook Lane. People who had been bombed out or made homeless lived there.

People only had two hundredweight (2 cwt, or 101 kg) of coal and there were only two buses a week to Fareham.

Mary Parrett

The article below was first published in St Peter's Church magazine in October 2014, entitled 'Hitler Youth to Church of England Priest'. Mary Parrett, who grew up on Meon-Bye Farm, Titchfield, had her memories stirred by George Gebauer's autobiography (available through Amazon) as she recalls German prisoners of war working on the farm in the immediate post-War years.

Mary and Sheila with the POWs

I have just read the autobiography of the Rev. George Gebauer entitled 'Hitler Youth to Church of England Priest'. The very title suggests an extremely interesting story. His story tells of his early years in Berlin and indoctrination into the Hitler Youth movement, conscription into the German Army and fighting Allied troops.

He was captured by the Americans after D-Day and eventually came to a POW camp near Romsey. While working on a farm at Botley he met his future wife. He later became a British subject and was ordained into the Church of England in 1973. Reading George's story brought back so many memories of my growing up at Meon Bye Farm.

In 1946/47 we had a number of German POWs living and working on the farm; they apparently integrated well. I remember them as being very kind and courteous. The photo shows a group at the end of their stay. Standing next to dad (Steve Harris) is Erwin Schroeder, a POW who married Jean, a local girl, and worked on the farm until he retired. He died in 2007 and because Rev. Bill Day was on holiday, George Gebauer took a very fitting and moving funeral service. The tall chap at the back, Herbert Bartsch, became a friend of the family and visited us almost every year. He lived in Titchfield and calls it his second home.

Mike Ferris

"PC Lockyer would quite literally give you a clip round the ear"

Bellfield houses, phase 3, were all painted white at the time - rather unusual for council houses. They were built largely by ex-servicemen returning to civilian life and I spent many happy hours helping the bricklayers who used to give me a pay packet with one shilling (5p) in it each week.

We were fortunate to possess a proper bathroom but many people only had a tin bath. Whichever method of bathing you had, it still required a supply of hot water and I knew of no one who possessed that on tap. Our own particular method required heating a large copper boiler, which was in the corner of the kitchen, and then carrying the hot water in a bucket to the bathroom. This, of course, used some of our coal allowance and was obviously not a daily occurrence! Few people had wash hand basins, so generally washing and shaving was done in the kitchen sink using hot water from a kettle.

The principal village coalman was Bill Pitman who lived on Coach Hill. I don't think I ever saw him when his face wasn't black with coal dust, even after washing. Coal was severely rationed and most people would save up their ration allowance, which I think was something like about ten

Bill Pitman delivering coal

bags a year, until the autumn and hope that they could make it last through the winter. This was only made remotely possible if some other form of fuel such as logs could be found to supplement it.

The coal merchants collected coal from the wharf in Fareham Creek where coastal colliers delivered it. Alternatively there was a depot at Fareham railway station. The merchants used to carry a set of scales on their wagons and weigh the coal in to one hundred weight (1 cwt, or 50.8 kg) bags. They then carried it on their shoulders to the coal cellar in the house - hence Bill Pitman's colour. At Fareham Creek, beneath the viaduct arches, there was a pub called The Coal Exchange. This was one of the pubs owned by Fielders Brewery in Bridge Street, Titchfield. Fielders owned about nine pubs in the area including the Queen's Head and the Sir Joseph Paxton at Locksheath.

Shoeing a horse

During wartime, and for a period afterwards, much of the farm work still involved horses and there were many around the area. My grandfather owned a working horse and, from about the age of ten onwards, I was allowed to collect the horse from the blacksmith's shop after re-shoeing, and lead him on foot back to Brownwich Lane. The last two working horses in the village were owned by an old ploughman named George Watts who lived in West Street. He used to be hired by the smallholders, who didn't have any horses of their own, to carry out the annual heavy ploughing.

The showing of horses in competition was very popular until well after the War and to see them being taken in their full finery and gleaming brasses was a fine sight.

Almost every boy went scrumping for apples at one time or another. The secret was not to be caught by the owners, or if you were, to give a false name and run. Anyone who was caught would be handed to PC Lockyer, who would, quite literally, give a clip round the ear and a lecture. The worst part however was that he invariably told your parents and that was the real punishment because, certainly in our house, dad's leather belt would come in to play. The favourite apple to scrump was called a Russet. They were delicious, and finding this particular type was quite rare so if you did find such a tree it was kept a secret.

Johner Jones was one of the returning servicemen involved in the VJ Day celebrations and eventually the Bonfire Boys; he lived in number 1 Great Posbrook Farm Cottages and his wife worked on the farm, and eventually for my grandfather.

Austin Atlantic

During the War, our vicar was Rev Spurgen; our policeman PC Lockyer and our doctor Dr Windermer. When Dr Ellis appeared in the village in 1947 to take over he was the first of the new people to arrive. I clearly remember his arrival as he was in, not only the first new car I had ever seen, but also a car which wasn't painted black. It was a rare model Austin Atlantic if I remember correctly, and certainly was the first white car in the area.

Greenwoods was a woodland on Triangle Lane, now known as Thatcher's Copse. During the War this housed a large Royal Artillery army camp and the concrete gun emplacements were close to the seaward side of this wood. They housed heavy guns for coastal protection as well as anti-aircraft. When this camp was abandoned after the War, parts of it were taken over by homeless squatters until the council took it over to provide temporary accommodation whilst Bellfield phase 3 was constructed. There was even a public bus service to it along the Posbrook Lane.

Paul Catcheside

My dad was demobbed on 31st December 1945 and was billeted at Hollam House on the Titchfield Road, with his wife, two boys and me as a baby. He got his pre-war job back immediately as Finance Officer at Knowle Hospital and carried on from there.

1947 Hawker P.1040 prototype

My mother was part of a family of ten and every year most of her family would come down for a seaside holiday. All of my aunts and uncles were down one year. I would have been 18 months old then so it was about 1947. We were sitting down to tea and a jet fighter flew over. Everyone got up because they were all interested and they all went out to have a look at it. Tomatoes were quite unusual at that time and there had been a half a tomato on every plate. When they came back in I was found under the table steadily polishing off all the tomatoes.

Eventually a council house was built at Hammond Road (off Gudge Heath Lane) and we moved in there, where my youngest brother was born. I would have been about two.

After my dad died, I found his release book among his papers. In this he was recommended for a commission. It said he was: 'A loyal and intelligent airman with good personality and a pleasing disposition. He has a good concept of supervising work of others and a sound knowledge of office administration. A superior type in every way.' He never did become an officer; he was a self-effacing kind of guy.

Rita Prior

"Our heating was by paraffin stoves"

Notable events were the whirlwind, which hit Titchfield blowing down the tall chimney at the tannery and damaging many houses. I think that was in 1946 but it may have been the year before. One of the plate glass windows was also broken. A chimney collapsed through the roof of number two South Street, the home of our manager Mr Ralph Bates.

Titchfield including the tannery chimney

In 1947 we had a very cold winter with snow and slippery roads. The shop where I worked was often closed early. When the thaw came, we had baths and buckets in the shop to collect the water coming through the roof along a beam. Our heating was by paraffin stoves, how different from today.

Miss Read, who lived in Church Street, came across to tell us of the death of King George VI. Shop windows were blacked out as a mark of respect.

Pudge with dad Rod

Lorna, Jim and Pudge

Pudge Moore

Bet and Rod Veck, my mum and dad, lived at Greenwoods. I was born there on 16th September 1952. Dad rode his bike to fetch the midwife, Nurse Gardner, who lived next to the Fisherman's Rest in Mill Lane, Titchfield. Then rode back to Greenwoods where mum was left with my sister Lorna. Soon I was born.

It's worth mentioning that they had no running water and an outside loo, but both my parents loved living there.

Tony Dugan

I have memories of playing in a disused wartime shelter in Portsmouth. One time I was woken up in the night to walk from Hilsea to North End/Kingston Cross with mum, uncle and aunt for what I now know was VJ Day celebrations. There was a mass of bonfires in the streets with people singing and using anything to make a noise.

In the winter of 1947, the worst winter on record, snow seemed to be continuous and my school was closed for a week or two. Shortly afterwards I was informed by my aunt that mum and myself would be going to the 'sticks' to live. My father was serving in the Middle East and was about to come home. I was puzzled by the word 'sticks' - this turned out to mean countryside and a little village, Titchfield. I had lived in Titchfield Common/Locks Heath area before being taken to Portsmouth.

My father was about to retire from a career in the RAF after 28 years, being a boy entrant straight from school aged 14 or 15. He arrived from the Middle East with, for my benefit so he told me, several small jars containing the dead carcasses of strange insects including large spiders (today's Customs and Excise!!). This would lead to an interest in butterflies of which there were many at the time. My interest extended to collecting them. The trick was to catch them with a net, put them in a jam jar layered at the bottom with crushed laurel leaves. This provides a cyanide K.O. blow, which enabled the abdomen to be laid into a special professional strip of wood with the wings pinned out. I had quite a collection at one time.

School friends would encourage me into egg collecting from bird nests. Here again birds were in huge numbers and varieties at the time. For my sins I can say only one egg of a particular bird was kept - no need for duplicates. The egg taken would have the customary pin hole made each end and now what seemed a breath-taking skill to blow the yolk out. Most annoying when this went wrong. I also had quite a collection at the time.

Thankfully both the above would be out of the question, perhaps illegal today and rightfully so. But in the '40s a much different time. Today I encourage both birds and butterflies in the garden by planting the right type of plants and hedging.

Note: Tony is right to warn us off these hobbies that were common at the time. It is now illegal to possess the egg of any wild bird, and many butterflies have direct legal protection. Tony's time was different, get out your digital camera and no-one gets hurt.

My early days in Titchfield had all the ingredients of the television series *The Darling Buds of May*. Dear old dad had arrived in the countryside along with an appetite to belong. He set out in the 'Good Life' way before the television series became popular. Planting the garden with trees: apple, pear, plum, peach, cherry, greengage. "Greengage, what's that?" I asked. Answer, a green plum. "What's the point!!" I replied. So we had a mini orchard only that in a year or two's time the birds would eat all the soft fruit while we were waiting for ripening to our taste.

The Darling Buds of May

Of course like everyone in the village, it was almost compulsory to keep chickens for the egg production and, come Christmas, a guaranteed meal. Therefore pens were put up with six brown chickens. Now I thought all chickens were brown, but dad had purchased an additional six coloured a sort of speckled grey. They must have been the aristocracy of the poultry world. Like everyone, as Christmas got closer, the question was, who was going to throttle one (break its neck) - my granddad came to the rescue. We also kept two rabbits. A vegetable plot was made but the white cabbage butterfly would soon lay its eggs and the resulting caterpillars would decimate the plants leaving nothing for the kitchen table.

I remember some older boys tied a dead adder from a tree branch to give younger children a fright. Another time there was a haystack in the field at the back of Bellfield, which was being taken apart. Now I had heard the story of the 'Pied Piper of Hamelin' but I had never seen so many rats. The older boys were swinging them around by their tails and throwing them to anyone daft enough to get too close.

So the countryside was going to be the new place to settle. Titchfield was pure countryside compared with today. We don't need to worry about the loss of adders and lizards but I miss the array of birds and butterflies we used to see.

Mary Burner and her brother Robert Chase, The Chase Family

My father used to play hockey for Fareham and Gosport. He was also a member of Fareham Round Table and supported the Bonfire Boys. The business regularly used to put a float in the Titchfield Carnival procession.

David (centre front) in the hockey team

My mother Joey settled down in Titchfield, and then father was called up to War in 1945, rather late but he had not been called up earlier as he was in a reserved occupation. The army sent him to Yorkshire for training with the Royal Engineers and he ended up in Egypt with the rank of Staff Sergeant. Allegedly he drew the plans and designs for a theatre where plays and shows were to be put on for the troops. He also designed and built, with his team, the prisoner of war area. We have a cigarette case, which was made by POWs for him from their melted down metal mugs. It is a beautiful design with a scene of camels, trees and the sphinx, with leather inlay and his name etched into the metal. He seems to have been a nice chap and was liked. We still have many letters my parents wrote to each other during his time away from the village, all his in his minute, neat handwriting.

David and Joey

My mother tried to keep the building business going when most of the men in the village went to War. The women needed to make money to pay rents and buy food by working where they could locally. However, rents were not being paid which had a knock-on effect on the building business. Mother was really struggling to pay the men and trying to get money in. She didn't like it and we have some letters she wrote to father declaring her dislike of the War, him being away and she running a business she knew nothing about - her fears and worries. She busied herself and, as she wasn't working during the War, she trained and ran the local Red Cross and did first aid training for the ARP. There is a photo of her in 1941 in the green Titchfield History book. See page 84.

We always knew mother as a busy lady and she was on many committees, a governor at the local primary school, and chair of the local NSPCC. Our mother was a caring and loving person, but could have a temper. She was honest, hard working and seemed a popular lady. During the time of her State Registered Nursing exams, she had caught rheumatic fever, which damaged her heart. Very sadly she had a stroke in her early forties, due to this heart damage, and this really affected the rest of her life - and obviously ours. She was determined and she was not going to give in once she got over the awful shock of it all. Life changed for all of us. My father was her main carer as she lost the use of her left arm. He had to cope with trying to run the business, look after two young people and his wife. He did this in his calm, gentle and loving way.

Very sadly, also at that time, the building firm collapsed as many building businesses did. But father was able to retain quite a few of the properties, which we still have. David, my father, became an NHBRC building inspector in south Hampshire.

My grandfather, my father and my brother (Robert David Chase) and I were all born in the house at 31 East Street and our son, Robert William Burner, has known the house since his birth but has lived here since he was four years old. All the grandchildren have some memories of their grandparents and this house at various ages, but Damien Chase, who is the eldest of Robert's children, has many fond memories of spending time with his grandma and granddad in the garden or having meals or trips out with them.

We have a walnut tree in the garden, which was planted by my great grandfather. Because squirrels love walnuts they have become planted all over the place. We dug some walnut saplings up recently and gave one to the owners of the Old Lodge and planted another in a secret location in the village. In Old Lodge they have a beautiful piece written and framed in their hall, about the connection of the Chases and Old Lodge, so the walnut tree has brought that connection up to date! Charles Aitkenhead who owned Old Lodge at one time, framed the plans father did for him, he was so impressed.

Attached to 31 East Street is a cottage, No. 29. Here, as recorded in the 1911 census, the Richards family was living - Mrs. Richards and her children, two daughters and a son, plus a lodger. When we were growing up the Misses Richards, Elsie and Gertie, played a large part in our memories. They were two little ladies who were seamstresses and made dresses for many people in the village. They were churchgoers and had their own place in the pews; they cleaned the church and delivered the parish magazines. They enjoyed card games and used to have their friend, Mrs Sandy from Mill Street, to join in. Sometimes I would join them, which I am sure they loved! We have many of their belongings still but their treadle Singer sewing machine was stolen from the courtyard after their deaths.

Growing up in the '50s, we had electricity and a telephone (our number was Titchfield 2166, although we have printed business papers from earlier with 166 on). Our toilet was indoors and we had a bath, which was heated by a wall immersion heater. We had an electric cooker and fridge. However, at the same time, Elsie and Gertie next door had an outside toilet, they cooked on a range with an oven and top plate that was blacked (cleaned) every day and the fire laid every morning. As well as the range they had a paraffin cooker. They had a cold tap so had to boil their water for washing. They had commodes in their bedrooms, which were emptied every morning. They had an electric light but mainly used candles. The abiding image I have is of the two sisters in their chairs sitting either side of the range with a roaring fire going, their faces lit by the fire while they listened to *Mrs. Dale's Diary* on the radio and then *The Archers*.

Their cottage is now part of No.31 East Street where I live.

Over the years the Chase family have been deeply involved in village life, they have looked after paperwork and wills, countersigned official documents, been a character witness in a court case and been treasurer of the Foresters Friendly Society in the village. The men have been held in high esteem.

The Chase family have been here for years and we're not going anywhere just yet!

School

Andrew Mills

After War began, Mr Farthing, the head teacher at school, recruited several 'senior' boys aged ten years to form the school fire brigade. A stirrup pump and umpteen buckets of water appeared and duties were allocated. Several boys had to carry water from the playground standpipe. Several were needed to do the pumping, because it demanded energy output too great for one boy. Some had to lay the hose out, and finally, the most sought after job, the 'squirter'. On being given a warning, boys ran around looking for evidence of the fire's location, revealed by smoke pouring out. The most favourite place for the inferno was the anthracite store where Mr Farthing had already ignited his smouldering smoke bomb.

Most of the children from Titchfield went to Sarisbury Secondary Modern School or Fareham Grammar School. I met many of my cousins at Sarisbury and I was probably related to about a third of the kids in the class. We had a reunion recently, which was nice because a few of us still keep in touch.

One thing we did at Sarisbury School was to doctor all of the hammers in the hall piano with drawing pins. Someone kept watch at the door while the rest of us did it. Nothing was said and we all gathered for assembly the next day. We had a maths teacher, Laurel Green, he was a nice old boy so we had a soft spot for him. He was also the piano teacher and, because he was so familiar with the instrument, he didn't even think to touch the keys, he just launched straight into playing it. What came out was a perfect honky-tonk and the whole school, as one, burst out laughing - even the other teachers. All except Laurel, who was most indignant. We were dragged into the head's office but he was laughing while he was telling us off. "You'll pay for any damage to the piano of course," he said.

Another trick was to wait 'til everyone was in assembly and quiet, then roll a marble along the parquet floor down to the front where it would go 'dank' onto the front of the stage.

Sheila Hignell

I went to Titchfield Primary School in 1946. The school was very overcrowded. I look back and I can think how terrible the punishment was particularly of naughty boys. The headmaster caned them in front of the whole class. Teachers in Titchfield did their best in very difficult times with 50 to a class.

We then changed schools when we were nine and were far behind the other children at our new school. For us it was very exciting because people just didn't leave Titchfield. I expect there were some people who had never left the village.

Paula Weaver

Celebrations and Leisure

Paula Weaver

I joined anything to get a uniform. I joined the Red Cross when I was old enough, probably 18. I joined the TA and got my own uniform and I was so proud of it. I used to love walking down to catch the bus to Fort Fareham to train. I had a great time during the four years I was in the TA.

Andrew Mills

I spent most of my summers at Brownwich. I would spend all of my time in the water and the family would pick cockles and winkles. There was nothing there except the gravel beach and cliffs and the WW2 buildings. There was a pillbox in the cliff and a look out on top of the cliff. My family would ride our bikes down there past a tree, which had been hit by lightning. My father would take an old army tent and we would stay there all day.

The big thing for me was the house on the cliff because I was delivered by a midwife called Nurse Gardner who lived there. When she delivered me, my father had cycled all the way there to fetch her at two o'clock in the morning. I was born at 5.30 a.m.

Brownwich shore

Ben Waterfall

I can remember the first carnival after the War because I was in it with my brother Mick. Mothers used to get National Dried Milk. It came in a big tin and you mixed up the feed for babies. We also had little bottles of concentrated orange juice in flat type medicine bottles. In Fareham there was a place called the Food Office, a Government place, up towards Westbury Manor in West Street. Mother used to go there to get National Dried Milk so she got some posters from them. Dad tidied up an old pram a bit. It was one of the Marmet prams, so you could get two children in it. I was quite chubby and my brother Mick was quite skinny - my dad said he was like a matchstick with the wood scraped off. I was coming up to six and Mick was two or three. We sat in the pram and we both had bottles and were sucking on dummies. We had the posters all round the pram saying 'Get National Dried Milk' and we had labels on us. Mick was the 'before' and I was the 'after'. My cousin Beryl was dressed up as a nurse and pushed us round the carnival route.

The post-war carnival

The carnival was always on the first Monday in November. In those days once the carnival was over they would start raising money for the next one - they had whist drives, beetle drives, all sorts of things going on to raise a little bit of money. They used to have rings (hoopla) competitions and make money that way and there were dances all the year round at the Drill Hall (now the Community Centre).

On carnival day they used to have huge bonfires and some fireworks and a good time was had by all. In the carnival there was always plenty of music, sometimes five or six military bands. They used to play all of the time - coming down Coach Hill. As soon as one was out of earshot the next one would come along. Dad did that pram up to use through the late '40s to the early '50s. One year they tarted it up and I wore a sea scout's uniform and I pushed the pram myself as HMS Amethyst in the Yangtse incident.

Note: HMS Amethyst was caught up in the Chinese Civil War in April 1949 on her way up the Yangtse River to defend the British Embassy in Nanking. She came under fire from the communist army losing 22 of the crew. It was ten weeks before Amethyst managed its dramatic escape under the cover of darkness.

There is a bungalow at the bottom of Coach Hill and they had an effigy of Hitler standing on the pavement and that went on the bonfire. Everybody

TITCHFIELD BONFIRE SOCIETY, 1946

THERE WILL ALWAYS BE AN ENGLAND AND THERE WI[illegible]ISH CUSTOMS.

[illegible] AND SEE ONE ON

MONDAY, NOV. 4TH

when the above Society revive their Old November Custom,

commencing in the Square at 2.45 with the Crowning of a CARNIVAL QUEEN who will lead

THE CARNIVAL PROCESSION

from the BREWERY MEADOW, (kindly lent by J. R. Fielder & Son,) led by the

SOUTHAMPTON ALBION PRIZE BAND.

Supported by the Band of Prices School, by kind permission of Major Hilton, and the Fareham Red Cross Cadets 2560 Unit Band.

The Procession will take the following Route, Bridge Street, South Street, West Street down Coach Hill to the Square where a halt will be made for public inspection. Off again via East Street, Mill Street, Soton Road down Soton Hill to the Meadow.

To be followed in the Evening at 7 p.m. over the same route by a

GRAND TORCHLIGHT PROCESSION

A HUGE BONFIRE will be lit in the Recreation Ground.

If available a Fun Fair will be in attendance.

A Dance will be held at the Drill Hall and a Whist Drive in the Parish Room to end the day

A Cash Prize of £5 will be drawn for by the Carnival Queen at the Dance on Nov. 4th. Tickets 6d. each can be had from the Committee.

The following CLASSES & PRIZES will be open to all comers.
The Prizes being given by the Society and Various Donors.

	1st	2nd	3rd	
TABLEAU CARS -	£2	25/-	15/-	Presented by Mr. R. S. Mortimer
TRADE CARS -	"	"	"	£2 presented by Mr. F. Ingram
SIDE SHOWS -	"	"	"	£2 presented by Mr. A. H. Frewing
HEAVY HORSE TURNOUT	"	"	"	Presented by Mr. F. Dyke
LIGHT HORSE "	"	"	"	" Messrs. N. & S. Harris
LIGHT TRAP, BROUGHAM or WAGGONETTE	25/-	15/-		
MOUNTED COSTUME	£1	15/-		
WALKING COSTUME " " (Ladies)	£1	15/-	10/-	£1 presented by Mr. G. Pink 10/- " Mr. R. B. Wicks
" " (Gents)	"	"	"	
" " (Girls)	"	"	"	10/- " by Mr. F. Ingram
" " (Boys)	"	"	"	
DECORATED CYCLES	15/-	10/-		25/- " by Mr. & Mrs. J. Bailey
DECORATED PRAMS	15/-	10/-		25/- " by Mr. S. Flowers
Best DECORATED HOUSE	£1			Presented by Mr. A. H. Frewing
Ditto BUSINESS PREMISES	£1			
Ditto COTTAGE	£1			" by Mr. F. Dyke

N.B.—Will anyone requiring a vehicle, book one before Oct. 26th. If unable to obtain same communicate with Sec., 17 South Street.

Additional Reserve Prizes will be awarded at Judges discretion.

Judging of Vehicles, Cycles and Mounted Entries to take place in the Brewery Meadow before 3 p.m. Officials and competitors only admitted; Walking Costumes and Prams to be judged in the Square.

SPECIAL REQUEST.—To Prevent Accidents with Horses or Burning of Decorations and Clothing we respectfully ask that all Fireworks be let off in the Recreation Ground, not in the Streets. The Co-operation of the Police is sought in this matter. Thank You!

NOTICE.—The Three Objects of the Society are :—

1. To provide Music and Fun for the People of Titchfield and District.
2. To give Prizes for the best efforts of all interested in making a Good Procession.
3. Any Surplus after paying all Expenses and keeping small balance in hand to be devoted to such Charities, decided by the Committee.

TOPICAL TITCHFIELD TITBITS by our TACTLESS TITTLE TATTLER who says that :

Mingled with the Procession will be found Rookies, Bookies, Publicans and Sinners, Gamblers, Ramblers, Losers and Winners.

The Knock-out Match between Bowlers and Fielders ended in a Draw.

The Bowlers drawing towards their Woods. The Fielders Drawing out of their Woods. Top Score of the Match was by "Charlie" who Tapped a 36 on to the Stand with one stroke of his mallet.

The United Services Club with "Our Jimmy" as 'Coach' have taken their PLAYERS off the Shelf, sorted out their STARS, added a few new ones from the SENIOR SERVICE and will Challenge all comers in the Smokers' Handicap. ALL HOLDERS barred, ALL PLAYERS WEIGHTS to be equal. All members are asked if they WOOD BINE themselves to the Club for two Seasons.

The Ringers Contest is to be held in the West End. This has brought up the Old and Bitter argument "Is Thirteen Unlucky"? ALF says no cos if you hang one on, two more are bound to follow. We've heard of Boxing Rings, Ear Rings, Wedding Rings and Rings round the Moon, but we still don't get it. Give us a 4½ to take away ARTHUR and we'll go home and work it out

The Sunshine Opera Coy. will render that Pathetic Ballad "Say it with Flowers." Opening at 12 with One Blast from the Bugle, and two from SIDNEY as he drops a Case on his Pet Corn. The music is set to 4 Beats in the Bar and Two in the Lounge. NOTICE. If any member of the Coal Club is short of supplies, see Harry and George Sunday dinner time when they can have a few 'TONS' of "Large Blacks" in exchange for a few "Small Browns."

A Nasty Accident took place at Head Quarters. We hear that our Worthy Host decided to murder a few of his Pals one night. With a BIG WOODEN Sword BUCKLED to his Side, Three Arrows in his hand, he shook his Feathers and put the first one 'Over the Bar' up them Stairs, into his own Bed. This nearly caused a riot, but HUTCH calmed the crowd with a fine rendering of "Thats why DARKIES Were Born." A.LA B.B.C.

Fred now believes in that Old Saying 'Crime Never Pays,' its better to let your Customers do it.

A Visit to the Wheatsheafe Cinema should not be missed.

This Week's Programme includes some fine Desert Scenes. With your Back to the Bar you have a lovely view of the Pyramids. After taking four Pints of "Coopers Special" you begin to understand why a Camel can go for Days without Water, and a Man only a few Hours without Beer. After mopping Nine Pints one of the Regulars swears he saw a Camel Slip through the Knee of an Idol, Trip over the Last Straw and break his neck.

Now Ladies and Gents, as the Sands of 'Time Please' are running low we must say Good Night Everybody.

"GOD SAVE THE KING."

Chairman, Mr. W. BURGESS. Vice-Chairman, Mr. H. E. St. JOHN.

Committee - Messrs. S. Harris. R. Powell, W. Brown, T. Kill, F. Ingram, T. Bennett, E. Bowman, E. G. Watts, A. Kirby, H. Hart, E. Smith (Sec.) D. Mortimer, F. Tift, A. Hebditch, C. Traves.

Hon. Treas. Mr. F. BUSH. Hon. Sec. Mr. E. H. MATTHEWS.

A supplementary list of prize givers and donations will be published later, and additional Committee.

H. B. DUFFETT, PRINTER, HIGH STREET, FAREHAM.

looked forward to the big carnival posters going up as they would include a skit on what had happened through the year. Everyone would stand around and read it and although no names were mentioned we could tell who it was.

Bessie Traves

In 1946 my husband Cyril was one of the founding members of the re-formed Titchfield Bonfire Boys Society and he went on to be their secretary for a good many years. As the society progressed, members' wives became involved in organising the children's tea parties but at this stage the wives were not members themselves. The tea parties were the children's reward for taking part in the carnival. The cakes were provided through St John's bakery. We, the wives, also cooked a meal as a treat for the over '70s of the village and they were also given an evening's entertainment and community singing. One member's wife made the dresses for the carnival queen and her attendants for a great number of years.

The post-war carnival

John Ekins

"The carnival was the high point of the autumn calendar"

I moved to Catisfield in 1946 when I was three but my earliest recollection of Titchfield was being taken to the VJ Day celebrations the year before. All I can remember is a happy jostling crowd and flags in the Square.

As a child I would spend many happy hours playing around the river and water meadows between Fishers Hill and the bypass. I had a friend whose uncle ran the mill, then still used for milling. With little regard for health or safety we delighted in scampering around the grain silos at the top of the building.

My friend's mum made a delicious fruit dough cake made with dough from St John's bakery in the Square. Titchfield village is where our doctors were, where we shopped, worshipped and each autumn enjoyed the carnival.

The carnival was a high point in the autumn calendar. It was a source of great delight and was an unmissable event. It attracted large crowds from around the area not only to the carnival but also to the fair, fireworks and bonfire. We would walk down to the afternoon procession and marvel at the military bands and the floats and wait eagerly for it to pass on each of its circuits. In the evening things could be quite rowdy with fireworks being thrown amongst the crowd. On carnival evening the village would be packed and even in Catisfield we felt the effect. Throngs would pass through on their way to Titchfield. Our streets would be full of parked cars and late into the night we would hear the sound of the fair.

John Williams

"There was not much entertainment so we made our own"

We played cricket and football on the recreation ground with piles of coats for goal posts or wickets. We organised our own cricket team and called ourselves Titchfield Colts and played against Warsash and Locksheath. On Saturdays we watched Titchfield Wanderers play football. Later on when we were a bit bigger, I used to go to watch Pompey with my cousin, Alan, on the bus. After the War Pompey was a very good team.

There was not much in the way of entertainment so we just made our own. Radio was about the only thing we had. They did have film shows in the Drill Hall later on with westerns and silly films.

John Rousell and his sister, Margaret Mugford

We lived in Gosport while my father served out his 25 years in the RAF at Titchfield where he worked on Vampire jets. It would have been about 1950 when, at primary school age, we both went to the Christmas parties held on the RAF station, travelling there on a small military coach, which was either blue or khaki brown. Most of the children came from married quarters on the camp and knew each other very well so we were really outsiders. I remember a long table set out with many treats to eat and lots of paper chain decorations. Father Christmas came and gave presents to each child. My sister was quite shy and seemed a bit overawed. It now feels so long ago.

Louis Stamp

The picture is of Titchfield Amateur Boxing Club (TABC) boys. I think it was taken about 1956/7. There's Dereck Hoile, Danny Shawyer, Tommy and Bobby Elliot, our first national champion, a young Micky Elmes and a few others.

Titchfield Amateur Boxing Club boys

June Pellatt

We had funfairs near the gasworks on East Street. To raise money for the carnival, we had smoking concerts (so called because of the cigarette smoke that filled the air) when we went round pubs and anyone who could sing or play an instrument provided the entertainment.

Mike Ferris

The large barrage balloon hangars were used for a variety of activities after the War. One of these was hosting Titchfield Carnival Dance where the carnival queen was chosen. This was a very large and keenly fought competition and was decided during a series of eliminating dances attended by many hundreds of people. Titchfield carnival's revival after the War was triggered by the VJ Day celebrations.

Paula Weaver

There were three dances before carnival day, then one on the night of the carnival at the Community Centre. We had to get permission from school to stay off to see the carnival.

The Bonfire Boys who were the group who raised funds for the carnival were good at making money. They went off to other carnivals to see what they could be doing. Pam Fullick's dad was a Bonfire Boy.

The carnival in West Street

I remember there used to be up to 48 carnival floats. Uncle Jon made a helicopter once; it was fantastic. People made their own costumes and dresses. It was great, the carnival! You couldn't move until the carnival had finished - the police were in charge. All the floats used to have writing on to say what the floats were about - you could get a laugh from those. The carnival was always on a Monday so you had Saturday and Sunday to work on your float ready for Monday. No one knew what you were doing. It was a closely guarded secret.

When the travellers (we used to call them gypsies) came with the fair we used to go into their caravans and clean their brass. They gave us money for doing this. We had a funfair at Frog Lane. We wore 'kiss me quick' hats for carnival day. We didn't have time to change so went to the dance as we were.

Sheila Hignell

Carnival was the biggest day of the year to us. Every year the Bonfire Boys did a dinner with entertainment for the elderly people in Titchfield after the carnival.

Alan Brind

"He wasn't accepted in the village until he married a Titchfield girl"

Junior School football champions

The photo shows the 1957-1958 Football League Champions. Teachers (left) Mr Wilkins (right) Mr Wilkie. (Top row from left to right) Derek Kettle, Dave Wort, Ted Richards, John Waterfall, Ian Ord, Roddie Frampton. (Bottom row left to right) John Collins, Keith Bowers, John Armon, Dave Greenland and Ron Grey. Best team Titchfield Junior School ever had. Goal record for season: 79 for and 9 against.

My dad lived in Stubbington, but played in the Titchfield Warriors Football team. He had to be collected and taken home by car on match days because the Titchfield lads would beat him up. He wasn't accepted in the village until he married a Titchfield girl!

Kevin Ford

I think my dad would have played against this team [Titchfield] back then. He played for Sarisbury I can remember him telling me about playing against Titchfield, it was the local derby. He told me the old Titchfield women on the touchline would trip you up and give you a clout if you got to close to them - happy days.

Food and Farming

Andrew Mills

Alf Pannell loading strawberries

We were strawberry growers with about an acre of land called Earl's Charity - it's what is now the Hunts Pond Road Recreation Ground. Strawberry picking was backbreaking work, but the fruit tasted great. You can't get a good strawberry now unless they have been grown in the traditional way. The varieties, the method of growing, and being bred for transport and shelf life, mean that they don't taste right. Ray Colverson picked up our strawberries in his lorry and took them to Swanwick station. From there they were taken to Bournemouth mostly, or London, and sold in the markets.

Some of the strawberries were grown under cloches and were available in April. The first week they could fetch a price of one pound a pound (£2.20/kilo), which was a lot of money in 1955. They went down a lot after that, to less than threepence (1.2p) a punnet by the end of the season. This wasn't my father's main occupation, as you needed to be a big grower to make any money out of it. An acre of strawberries gave us a little bit extra and meant that we could go on holidays or have some other little niceties that we wouldn't have had otherwise.

Sheila Hignell

My mother was always there. German prisoners of war came to live on the farm in 1946. They were good workers and courteous. They had first been stationed on Portsdown Hill. Dad got extra petrol allowance to collect them. He then made accommodation for them on the farm in a converted barn. Their rations were meagre so mum used to cook them a big pot of potatoes. One of them still comes back to village to this day. He was the first POW to learn to drive a car. They all went back to Germany in 1947 except the three who married English women.

We were lucky we always had food, hens and geese. There was lots of bartering.

Lesley Downs

I have worked on the Harris family farm since I was 15. I am now 88. I still go to 'work' every morning and get the tractor out and check the place. My son Eric is our farm manager. He was born on the farm and he has never worked anywhere else.

Lesley Downs and Steve Harris

Linda Felton

My father Ronald Tunbridge came to Titchfield in 1950 with his mate John Austin. They were army friends and John invited Ron to stay with his family when they were on leave. Ron met John's sister Joy and they married in Titchfield Church in October 1950. I was born in 1951. My father was a Londoner and as an 'outsider' was nicknamed 'London' for a while.

Sister Valeria

"Mr Roberts would harangue us about doing our bit for Britain"

"It's August 1946 (and '47), and Talbot Heath School, Bournemouth, has organised a harvest camp for about twenty girls who would enjoy some hard work for Britain's post-War effort as well as enjoy all the fun of camping." This was an advertisement I saw at school. I went on both these occasions, to the farm owned by Mr Roberts, near Titchfield, Hampshire.

We arrived, plus cycles, at Fareham station and then were transported to our campsite on a sloping field near the farm. The school staff that accompanied us cooked wonderful meals, which were served in a kind of Nissen hut. Both staff and girls slept in canvas tents so there was all the excitement of settling down in all weathers. I seem to remember that those two Augusts were mostly fine, bar one very wet and windy night when we thought the tent would collapse on top of us. The efficient loos, also under canvas, were at the bottom of the field, and the journey had to be negotiated carefully in the dark.

Every morning, we would assemble round the Union Jack in the farmyard, and Mr Roberts would harangue us about doing our bit for Britain, which was still suffering quite badly the effects of war, rationing and the like. Then we would be given our work, which varied from lifting potatoes, a rather back-breaking and muddy job, to weeding - again back-breaking, to layering strawberry plants, even more back-breaking and exceedingly fiddly. The best of all was picking raspberries. No we were not supposed to eat them! We would each have six punnets on a string, which we tied round the waist, and we'd pick like mad until all six were full. Then we would go back for more. I really enjoyed the challenge and competition of this lighter job!

Meals in the Nissen hut were a combination of a picnic and a feast, and we were assigned our turn in clearing and washing-up. After supper we would sit round a blazing campfire and join in Guide songs (I wasn't a Guide) and rounds and there would be a lot of laughter. As we had only torches in our tents, we went to bed early and rose early, as was befitting for our 'War work'.

Sometimes we had a free afternoon on a Saturday, so we would joyfully cycle into the village of Titchfield, to spend some pocket money. I regret to say I never went into the church, but we would look at some of those lovely old cottages, and I am sure we bought postcards and stamps, so perhaps the post office was then open on Saturday afternoons. Our main objective was a tearoom where we would have a very un-camp-like tea, which was a highlight for all of us. On a Sunday (we were in camp for a fortnight) we could have visitors, so my parents drove from Bournemouth on both occasions, once bringing my birthday cake, which would be big enough to share.

Our staff members were very efficient at dealing with injuries, which were mostly minor. One morning I had a wasp on my bread, which was the same colour as the marmalade, so, once in the frightening 'cavern' of my mouth, it retaliated by stinging me inside my mouth, which swelled alarmingly and made my face very lop-sided. I don't remember what the treatment was, but it was successful and I returned home with a normal face!

I shall always be grateful for this glimpse of hard work in the countryside, and for the companionship and enjoyment of our camps. Thank you farmer Roberts of Titchfield!

Strawberry Growing - Debbie West

Debbie and Nick are the 3rd generation West family strawberry growers and Debbie has put together a short history of the industry.

In and around the Titchfield, Locks Heath, Swanwick, Sarisbury and Warsash area there is a long strawberry growing history. In the 1880s what was once known as Titchfield Common was divided up into small plots of about three acres or less where families were encouraged to make some kind of living. Thanks to the mild climate and gravelly soil, conditions were excellent for drainage thus making the land warm up quickly, which was ideal for growing strawberries. It was not long before strawberry growing became a thriving industry in the area.

Bob and Janet West 2nd generation

Most plots of land locally had strawberries planted on them. Families would spend hours out in the fields, hoeing, weeding and bedding down plants with straw just before the strawberries were ready to pick. Rain or shine, every day they would be looking after their crops so that they would produce perfect fruit for everyone to enjoy. When the strawberry season was at its peak in the summertime growers would employ casual labour, men, woman, young school leavers and travelling families who used to come to the area to help pick the strawberries ready for market.

At the end of the season any fruit that was left on the fields would be picked for making jam. Some would go to a local jam factory that was built in Hunts Pond Road (in the 1880s) which did not prove to be a success for long. Later on, around the mid-1900s, Robertson's Jam Company would take them to make strawberry jam, which meant we could all enjoy the taste of strawberries all year round. Many local people also loved picking the fruit from the fields so that they could make their own jam, teaching their children and grandchildren

Strawberry picking

the tricks of making it set perfectly. At the end of the season all casual labour would cease. The growers would then set light to their fields to be sure that there were no pests or disease left in the soil, preparing the land to start all over again. You could tell when it was the end of the season as there would be grey clouds of smoke in the area and a very sweet burning smell.

Soil testing

The strawberry industry became very competitive as Hampshire and Kent would compete to get their fruit to the London Covent Garden Market. Hampshire usually won, as the weather conditions were generally warmer. This would govern the price as the market paid top prices for early fruit as it was in great demand. Hampshire could be as much as a fortnight in front, which gave them a head start on the high prices. As the season progressed and the market became flooded with fruit, prices would soon fall. It was every man for himself, as growers would strive to pick every last strawberry to enable them to make a living for their families. The most common varieties of strawberries grown were Cambridge Favourite and Red Gauntlet. In this area there are two public houses named after strawberries 'The Sir Joseph Paxton' in Hunts Pond Road and 'The Talisman' at Park Gate.

Pickers relax on the beach 1960

The transportation of strawberries was all important, as they are perishable items. The fruit looks at its best when it is freshly picked so it was essential to get it to the markets as quickly and safely as possible. In the late 1860s some growers would take their fruit by horse and cart to markets in Southampton and Portsmouth. They would have to leave in the early hours of the morning, to arrive at the markets on time ready for the day's selling. Fareham and Botley were the nearest train stations in the area at the time where a few growers would send the fruit by train.

The Strawberry Special

It was when they constructed a new railway station in Swanwick in 1888 that the strawberry industry began to reach an all time high. In the early 1900s the railway station played a very important part in the transportation of strawberries by laying on a train which could have up to 20 carriages, which later became known as the 'Strawberry Specials.' It would leave Swanwick every evening during the season, full to over flowing with freshly picked strawberries. Their destination would be Covent Garden in London, also Leeds, Liverpool, Scotland and in time many other cities across the country.

In the evenings, roads around Swanwick station came to a standstill with horses and carts filled with fruit waiting to be carefully loaded onto the train. This was fitted with special slatted shelves to ensure minimum movement in transit so as not to damage the fruit. In one evening alone there could be as many as 100,000 baskets loaded. It was rumoured that some of the older growers had said that on a hot summer's evening during the peak of the season all you could smell around the district was sweet strawberries. In the year 1913 it was estimated that over 3,000 tons of strawberries passed through Swanwick station.

Pick your own, PYO

At the turn of the century growers came together and formed what was known as the Swanwick Fruit Growers Association. In 1913 the Swanwick & District Basket Factory was also founded by local growers of the Association, who became shareholders of the company. The factory was set up to manufacture baskets and punnets. Punnets in those days were commonly nicknamed 'chips' as they were made of thin shaven pieces of poplar tree that were shaped into punnets. Later on the factory also sold many other sundries connected with the growing industry.

In the 1950s the 'chip' punnet was replaced by cardboard as this was a cheaper material. These were being produced by other companies. They themselves were later replaced by white plastic punnets in the early 1970s and by around the late 1990s you could also get clear plastic punnets with lids. As more competition evolved it saw the decline of the Swanwick & District Basket Factory, which sadly closed its doors in 1990.

Growing under polythene tunnels

Very little changed apart from the horse and cart being replaced over the years by steam engines, small petrol vans and lorries. Up to the late 1960s many thousands of tonnes of fruit had passed through Swanwick station, then it was announced that the 'Strawberry Special' trains were to be axed! Once again about 40 of the area's growers united to form the Growers Fruit Freight (backed by the National Farmers Union) which organised transportation facilities for fruit. Strawberries were then picked into punnets that were in wooden Dutch trays. This made it quicker and easier to load. The fruit would then be loaded onto large container lorries on land at Swanwick station, (and in later years fields in Fleet End Road, Warsash), these would then be delivered by road to London where they would be distributed all around the country.

Grow bag cultivation under glass

In the early days there was never a shortage of pickers but by the late 1980s many people had full-time jobs, which meant casual labour was less readily available and growers had started to sell off plots of land for building. Sadly this led to a decline in the industry. So therefore it wasn't long before the Growers Fruit Freight ceased running. Slowly there became fewer and fewer growers.

A lot of things changed, a few growers carried on growing traditionally in the ground, as P.Y.O. (Pick Your Own) was very popular, others grew in polythene tunnels or glasshouses, with the plants in peat bags at shoulder height, still to this day trying to produce early fruit to ensure better prices. Markets around the country now see strawberries arriving from all over the world. Very few of our local strawberries are sent to the markets these days as most of them grown in this area are now sold directly to the loyal local customers and those who travel far and wide for the 'perfick' famously-known Titchfield strawberry. In and around the surrounding area there were once 80 producers. That diminished to just a handful by the millennium. Thankfully that handful still produce in Titchfield to this day.

Titchfield strawberries

Work

Andrew Mills

I remember the smell of the tannery - it must have still been going when I was a kid, but I think it must have closed shortly after that.

Workers at Funtley brick works

After the War, when my father came out of the army, he wanted to become a carpenter but could not afford the bus fares to get to the training on the other side of town. He took work as a clay digger at Funtley brickworks and, together with his mate, dug 20 tons of clay a week. He got £4 per week for that. The strawberries he grew supplemented this until he eventually got a job in the Gibbons Foundry in Fareham. They were very good to their workers and they had a good social club and everything. Sadly, Mr Gibbons died but his wife carried on the business. They paid a wage that was always above average so from that point on my father earned reasonable money.

My grandfather and grandmother were school caretakers at Sarisbury Secondary School, and my mother was chief cook supervisor for four schools in the area.

I have never actually lived in the village of Titchfield, but I remember some of the people who were there including Mrs Macfarlane who lived on the East Street side of Everett's in the Square.

Lyons Maid ice cream van

Lyons Maid Ice Creams had a depot in East Street opposite the Wheatsheaf pub. An old coaching yard was turned into a massive refrigerator cold store at -18°C and the yard was always full of vans. These were loaded at night ready for delivery the following day. I worked there evenings and weekends during my college days in Southampton. There were stories about a ghostly horse and carriage coming through the gateway. I have always been an atheist and didn't believe this stuff but some of them did. This fascinated me, but it scared the hell out of these guys. When you opened the big fridge door the cold air would come out and condense and spread across the yard like mist and it would swirl if you walked through it. At three o'clock in the morning it would give them the jitters.

It was quite dangerous work as everything was rock hard and you could only be in the fridge for half an hour at a time. There were alarms at floor level so if you fell over and banged yourself you could set one off. The warm air entering the fridge from the door would form into icicles of snow on the ceiling and one day one of these fell onto this chap. He thought someone had tapped him on the shoulder and there was no one there. He ran out of the cold store and across the yard at full pelt and out of the gate and was never heard of again. We knew what had happened to him because he was shouting at the top of his voice as he went but actually it happened to everyone.

Annette DeVoil

Annette sent us this account of her father's, Lieutenant D.J. DeVoil, bomb disposal work in 1946 written by Major A.B. Hartley MBE

Lt. D.J. DeVoil

An interesting bomb we had to deal with at this period was near Bursledon, in Hampshire. It was one that had been abandoned earlier but it was later reviewed by the Home Office, who now requested its removal. For the subaltern in charge of the job, Lieutenant D. J. DeVoil, it was his first bomb, and naturally he gave it a great deal of personal attention.

The bomb was accurately located and the sub-soil strata checked. It was about thirty feet down, but at sixteen feet there was a layer of running sand. This had to be sealed off; otherwise the unstable sand would cause the shaft to collapse. DeVoil decided to drive Larssen interlocking-piles to 22 feet for a shaft 16 feet by 16. Having excavated that, a smaller shaft could be driven inside the larger down to the bomb.

Bomb locating

The platoon sergeant, Sergeant John, had been working on steel piling-shafts almost continuously since his release from prison in Germany and the duty of setting out and driving the piles was delegated to him. He had had no wartime experience of Bomb Direction Indicator (B.D.I.) work. Another unit was anxious to get some of its non-commissioned officers (N.C.Os) trained in the use of steel piling and had asked me to let a Corporal Thom attend at this site so he could learn from the sergeant. Unlike John, this corporal was an experienced bomb disposal N.C.O. A good many of the men on the site were Germans - working now under a recently released prisoner from Germany. The whole situation was a little paradoxical.

The piling and excavation went ahead quite successfully. We knew the bomb was a 1,000kg. S.C. (Sprengbombe Cylindrisch 1000, nicknamed a Hermann after Hermann Goering the Luftwaff commander) because of bits of fin found as the digging progressed, and I was not particularly worried because this type almost invariably had a 25- or 28- fuse fitted. Both were impact-fuses. DeVoil knew the immunization drill and unless he asked for advice I did not intend to be around when the thing was uncovered. It is much better for a young officer to sort things out for himself, and I was pleased at the idea that he would get a fine big bomb with a fairly simple fuse for his first.

Shuttering in place

About eleven o'clock one morning I had a telephone call from DeVoil. "We've uncovered part of the nose, sir. It's a Hermann but it's ticking." I was sceptical. A clockwork fuse in a Hermann was very, very, unusual. Again a bomb stethoscope is very sensitive to sounds of all kinds and false alarms often occur because of water dripping in the shaft or some other extraneous reason. So I told him I thought he must be mistaken. He said "Corporal Thom has heard clockwork fuses before, and he says it's ticking." I told him to get everybody off site, keep a stethoscope watch at 400 yards, and wait for me to join them. The bomb had fallen on open ground sheltered by trees on three sides. On the fourth, about three hundred yards away, was a secondary road. When I arrived this road had been closed and Don DeVoil was at the road junction, about eight hundred yards from the bomb. "It's stopped now, sir,'" he said. "It ticked for forty-five minutes altogether."

1,000 kg Bursledon bomb

My scepticism returned. I thought - well, it's his first after all, and he's doing the right thing and sticking to safety precautions. He probably feels uncertain. There seemed no point in delaying matters. I said to him: "Come on, we'll go down and look at the fuse. That'll settle it." We climbed down the shaft. There was another stethoscope besides the one at the watch point and DeVoil carried it. The bomb was lying nose up, at about forty-five degrees to the vertical, and the fuse-pocket - which in this type comes about halfway along the length of the case - was still well underground. I picked up a spade and carefully started to dig along the side of the nose but I had only made three or four spade cuts when DeVoil remarked abruptly: "It's ticking!!" I reached for the earphones. It was. I have never climbed out of a thirty feet shaft so quickly, before or since. Across the open track we were neck and neck. At the watch position four hundred yards away we both listened to the stethoscope, expecting the bomb to go up any moment.

After about ten minutes the ticking stopped again. The only thing to be done was to blow the thing up where it lay. The nearest house was five hundred yards off and with so large a bomb some windows and tiles might be damaged, but the possibility would have to be accepted. There was nothing to justify risking anyone's life. I asked what explosives there were available at the site and found DeVoil had two pounds of guncotton. This is not really enough applied to the nose of such a bomb, where the metal is thick, but I decided to have a try. The police who were on the spot went round warning householders of the coming bang and closed some more roads for fear of falling debris. Then DeVoil and I went back and placed the charge in position.

It was a bad move. The guncotton was insufficient to detonate the bomb and since the microphone had been removed when the charge was laid we were considerably worse off than before. I decided the best thing now would be to wait until morning, as this would give the fuse-clock a chance to run out its spring and detonate the bomb. If it did not, then it would be reasonably safe to approach it again. To our knowledge the fuse had started and stopped twice. It was therefore in a very sensitive condition and the shock it had been given by the guncotton would almost certainly have started it off or else jolted it in to a safer state.

However, this inference also proved of doubtful value. The bomb did not go off during the night and the next morning DeVoil and I returned and laid an adequate charge. Then just as we were tamping the new charge into position the fuse, to our horror, started ticking. Since it was only a matter of a minute's work we finished the job before bolting.

I can hardly recall a moment of greater satisfaction than when we sent up that Hermann. It would never tick again! Steel piles shot hundreds of feet into the air, but because of the depth of the shaft the explosion was contained within a chimney and the debris not widely scattered. Don DeVoil certainly had a stirring first bomb.

After

Nurse Gardner by Ken Groves (son-in-law)

The community of Titchfield had never been short of proficient nurses but in 1930 the 27-year-old nurse Dorothy Lawson descended on the village, having qualified as a State Registered Nurse and State Certified Midwife in Bromley, Kent.

Nurse Dorothy subsequently married a local man, Richard Gardner and became the indomitable Nurse Gardner. Records indicate that, during her time in Titchfield she delivered over 4,000 babies and, it was her claim, she never lost a mother. To describe her as formidable is an understatement. She steadfastly refused to allow the father to be present at the birth but she was worshipped by most of the mothers, largely due to her competence, dedication and diligence.

She is particularly remembered by the adult 'lads of the village', as the person they feared most, if she appeared on the scene when they were up to no good.

Eccentricity was, also, one of her traits and she had a tendency to drive down the middle of the road in her rush to reach a patient. This was OK during the War when she had one of the few cars in the village - a pre-war Morris 8 but this caused consternation later in her life. She officially retired in 1963 and Wilfred Pickles brought his radio show *'Have A Go'* down to celebrate the event, during which the Carnival Queen of the day presented her with a cheque from the people of Titchfield for £146, equivalent to about £3,500 to-day. Also, Gardner Road was named in commemoration of her efforts on behalf of the Parish.
In typical fashion, despite being warned not to, she continued to practice her skills when asked and finally died, aged 79, in 1982 having been blind for the previous five years due to diabetes.

Ben Waterfall

I had a Saturday morning job when I was about nine or ten. We had an old pram, which I used to wheel down to the Square because there was a gas showroom (where the Co-op is now). You could buy a gas stove there, but if you wanted some coke you would pay for it and they would give you a ticket. Then you would go down South Street and into Frog Lane and into the old gasworks and wait in the queue.

Ernie Privet would take your ticket and fill up a hessian sack. He was from Titchfield and knew all the Titchfield people. He'd say to me, "Who's this one for son?" "Oh that's for Uncle Jack." So he'd put an extra shovelful in. When he asked who it was for, if it was someone he liked, they'd get a bit extra. I used to make a little bit of pocket money on a Saturday morning for that, but you couldn't spend it on sweets because they were rationed.

Colin Wilton-Smith

"I remember the honesty and trust displayed by the occupiers - good old days!"

In January 1963 I started work as an articled pupil with Hall, Pain & Foster, Chartered Surveyors and Estate Agents, at 48 West Street, Fareham (now Beals Estate Agents). I was one of three articled pupils and we were required to collect rents on a Monday of each week. One week covered the Gosport area; the alternate week was Titchfield and the Western wards of Fareham.

The Titchfield rent round involved, amongst others, the collection of rents in Catisfield Lane, the centre of Titchfield village and areas close by - some 50 or 60 properties with weekly rents of anything between 10 shillings (50p) and 15 shillings (75p). I rode a BSA 250cc scooter, a lethal machine - lots of power and little stability. On one occasion, before the village was by-passed and when Catisfield Lane led to the village, I skidded into a ditch scattering the rent money amongst the leaves and with the scooter ending up somewhere down the road.

Rents in the village were collected mainly from East Street, the cottages in Church Path and West Street. In those days if the tenants were not in, the door was left unlocked and the rent and rent book would be on the table inside. Most of the tenants were employed in the market gardening/ strawberry industries and during the strawberry season, bags or punnets of strawberries would be left for me, testing my aptitude of riding the scooter fully laden.

At the time of the carnival the whole village was virtually closed down and we moved the rent day accordingly.

The rent round included the semi-detached villas on the north side of Hunts Pond Road. One of the tenants, a lady in her sixties provided a service to nearby residents of laying out the deceased on her parlour table. This was rather unnerving when trying to collect rents!

Apart from the main road, almost all the side roads in the area were unmade with the council just starting to adopt and surface these. Most of the fields were cultivated with strawberries but the developers were beginning to acquire this land. Hall, Pain & Foster acted as agents for many of the farmers and smallholders and I was involved in measuring up and preparing plans of land to be sold. We were still using steel chains as a measuring tool at this time with the units measured in links.

My abiding memory of these times was the simplicity of the homes from which I collected rents; most just had a front parlour and a very simple scullery or kitchen, very rarely was upholstered furniture present - just hard chairs and a kitchen table. I remember the honesty and trust displayed by the occupiers - good old days!

Leslie Ellis

On returning to England Leslie went back to Harrogate and worked in the casualty department of Harrogate hospital. It was there he met his wife Denise who was a nurse. Denise's family came from Switzerland but lived in Harrogate. Leslie and Denise were married in 1947.

In 1947 Dr Ellis heard from the chemist in Harrogate of a general practice for sale in Titchfield, Hampshire. The chemist's brother was Dr Windermer and he wanted to retire. Leslie and Denise bought the house and the practice at No. 1 Coach Hill and travelled down from Harrogate in an Austin 7. Dr Ellis practised in Titchfield until his retirement in 1985 aged 70. However, he still lives in the same house, and is now aged 101 years.

John Ekins

Soon after moving to Catisfield, I can remember being taken to Dr Windermer's surgery and a little later, with the advent of the NHS, meeting Dr Ellis for the first time. The consulting rooms were in what is now 'The Old Surgery'. The door from the street opened into the waiting room and you had to keep track of who was in front of you in the queue, there were no appointments then. My mother's rule of thumb was if there was a bicycle outside the wait would be longer. In fact we seldom waited as long as an hour - so it was much the same as today! Between the waiting room and the consulting room there was an anteroom where, I recall, Dr Ellis had a Bunsen burner for testing specimens. In those days there was much more touching and feeling of the patient, "Stick out your tongue, say Aah"; feel the glands in the neck, take your temperature and out with the stethoscope. There was much more interaction with the patient.

If you were really ill 'out of hours' then Dr Ellis or one of the partners would come to attend to you. Dr Ellis was in partnership with Dr Edwards who soon moved to concentrate on Locks Heath. Both had a good reputation but to a child Dr Edwards was a less forbidding presence than Dr Ellis. Dr Walsh joined a little later and seemed to split his time between Titchfield and Locks Heath.

Most ailments, especially coughs, would result in a prescription for some kind of jollop. Prescriptions would be made up at the chemist, still in the same shop today. I recall it being run by Mr. Dunne who lived over the shop but later moved to Catisfield. 'Be Done by Dunnes' was the banner he displayed at one carnival.

Although we lived next door to the Catisfield Post Office stores, for some reason my mother did not choose to shop there. We would have groceries delivered from Lusby's in Fareham. A Mr Goddard would come out on a bicycle to take a weekly order, which would be delivered a day or two later in cardboard boxes.

John Maginnis, *Folland Aircraft News-sheet, FANFARE, February 1952:*

"Have you heard the one about the Englishman, Irishman and Scotsman?"

George Templeman, Alex Wilson and John Maginnis

Well at Follands we have one of those stories which, although not so lewd as the usual type, has the greater merit of being true.
In our Process Department we have Mr George Templeman, who started with us as a Salt Bath operator in July of last year. During the following September, Mr Alex Wilson, was engaged in the same department for the same kind of work. In December, Mr John Maginnis joined us, same department, same job. These three men, now engaged upon this process work of annealing light alloys, met for the first time in Titchfield way back in 1940 when billeted with the 12th Commandos.

Operation Archery in Norway

They had terrific times together, having taken part in Operation Archery, the Lofoten Islands raids on Norway, when they went communication busting. They also went over to Normandy on D-Day,. The one point of that great event which, they seem to resent more than anything else, is the fact that they had to start out at the unearthly hour of 7 a.m. that morning. They set out 65 strong, but five hours later there were only 27 of them.

However these three came through safely and unlike most instances of this kind their forces friendship became cemented by coincidence. Each was a single man at that time and believe it or not each of them married his landlady of those early Titchfield days and they are settled in these parts, for good we hope!'

Mike Ferris

"Telephones were very rare among ordinary working people"

We used to supplement our coal ration by buying coke from the gasworks. Coke was not rationed. The major problem with coke however was transporting it home and many people used to line up on a Saturday morning to buy a bag, which they either took home in an old pram or perched on the frame of their bike. A woman's bike was best for this because the bag fitted in the 'V' without being obstructed by a crossbar.

The other supplement for the fire was timber of course and there was a plentiful supply of this available if you had the means to pay for a full load, and either a small truck, or horse and cart to collect it. A horse and cart was certainly the case with my family. This timber was obtained from a large storage area in Locks Heath, where timber recovered from the bombed-out houses in Southampton and Portsmouth was purchased and stored by a dealer. There was little that wasn't available from this depot and many sheds and pigsties were constructed from material purchased there. The timber for burning invariably consisted of nail-ridden floor joists and similar that all had to be sawn by hand to length and many saws were ruined by the nails.

Unloading hides into the tannery

The main industry in the village was the tannery, which processed several types of hides but principally cow hides. Most children from the school were shown around the tannery and other local places at some stage. Titchfield Mill was a working mill but I seem to recall that the miller told us, when we were shown around, that he did not produce flour, but largely ground oats and barley.

Telephones were very rare among ordinary working people. I knew of no one at all who possessed one. There was only one public telephone box in the village - situated at the bottom of Southampton Hill outside the public toilet. The Coach and Horses pub had a private telephone in their living quarters, which the landlady allowed people to use in an emergency. There was a telephone exchange in the village and this was situated in a cottage in Church Street. This was the old plug type operated manually. It eventually closed round about the early '50s when the automatic one was built at the top of Titchfield Hill on the corner of Highlands Road. When it was operating the old exchange was another building on the school's 'places to visit' list.

Victor Chase

I wasn't called up during the War because I was a mechanic at Boniface and Cousins garage and they did all the ARP stuff, ambulances and all that. They had several ambulances made up out of cars - cars were sometimes converted for the medical services during the War - and we used to do all that, plus the Fareham ambulances, so we worked on all those things.

Because I was in a reserved occupation I wasn't called up until 1946. I was lucky really because I should have been sent to Egypt by the army but I had a mate in the assignment office and he said to me, "When you go on parade tomorrow, they'll be asking for drivers and whatever you do don't tell them you can drive." I said "Why not?" and he said that all drivers were going to Egypt. As I only had a few weeks to go before being demobbed I didn't want to get posted abroad because that was for more time than I had left to serve. I would have liked to have gone abroad but not when I was coming out of the forces in a couple of weeks time. So I was lucky I had a mate in the office. I suppose I enjoyed my army career.

I was called up again after I'd been out of the army for a couple of years. I went to Bovington where I had a medical. I was sent home again because I was deaf. They were going to send me up to Scotland to get it checked, but the officer said it wasn't worth it and he told me to go home and see the doctor.

Peter Twiss OBE, DSC 1921 - 2011

Peter was the first person to fly above 1000 miles an hour in level flight. On 10 March 1956, he took his Fairey Delta 2 jet plane on two runs along the south coast and averaged 1132 mph between them. Lieutenant Commander Twiss already had two gallantry medals from his service during the War.

Peter was a larger than life character who was married five times and even had a role in the James Bond film 'From Russia with love' where he shot at Mr Bond from a Fairey Marine speedboat. He had previously flown a Fairey Swordfish torpedo plane in 'Sink the Bismark'.

He lived in South Street for more than 40 years and told his story in his autobiography 'Faster than the Sun'.

Church Chapel and Religion

Sheila Hignell

Dad and mum were married in 1936 at St Peter's Church here in Titchfield. The whole family were all married there, apart from my brother, and all have been christened there.

We remember when the Rev. Norman Miller came to Titchfield in 1946. He was a wonderful man. He transformed the church. When he arrived, water was dripping everywhere and he set up this restoration fund.

After the War, in 1947, rationing was still in place and life was still very difficult for people. St Peter's Church looked dark and dull and so, for Christmas that year, Steve Harris decided to provide the church with a Christmas tree. He and his family have continued this tradition to this day.

Queen's coronation lunch 1953

I remember Coronation day. The service was most amazing and the church was more crowded than ever before.

Mum was always helping others. She used to run old people to hospital when she could drive. Dad and her children were her main focus in life. She has just died, aged 101. She loved the village and the church. She used to collect people and take them to the community lunches even when she was older than the people she was picking up. She did this in her little old car for about 15 years.

The Rev. Norman Miller was very artistic. High above the door there is 'Jesus with the fishers of men'. In the '50s he got students from Portsmouth Art College to remodel it. They transformed it into a modern piece. Of course some people didn't like it.

The church fete was originally held in Hollam House. The first church fete was in vicarage gardens in 1947 or 48. The format has never changed and is basically the same to this day.

Churching of women – I was probably one of the last women to be churched in Titchfield in 1981 when I had my son. My mother had been churched with all of us. Just a very simple prayer saying thank God for the safe delivery of a baby.

John Ekins

The story is that on arriving in Catisfield, my grandfather attended St Columba Church, then in the 'Tin Tabernacle', which was situated near the new Limes housing development. He took his seat but evidently sat in the wrong place and was admonished. So he took himself down to St Peter's Church and joined the congregation there. Thus started our relationship with Titchfield and
St Peter's.

Norman Miller was the vicar through the late '40s and retired only in 1973. When he arrived the fabric of the church was in a poor state and Norman Miller worked tirelessly to restore the church and put it in good order. We still today benefit from his commitment and hard work.

In those days it seemed that the entire Church of England was celebrating matins at 11.15 am on a Sunday morning. As a child I found, and still do, matins a bit of a drudge with seemingly interminable canticles so I prefer evensong, which has fewer and shorter canticles. There was a proper choir at the evening services as well as for matins.

In 1956 my parents decided to be confirmed and I, a little reluctantly, joined them. Norman Miller prepared us for confirmation and in due course we were confirmed by Lancelot Fleming, then Bishop of Portsmouth and later of Norwich. Communion seemed only to be celebrated at 8 a.m. on Sundays. The protocol was then for communicants to return to their pews via the Southampton chapel which is what I still like to do today.

In the 1950s the garden fete was an even more significant event in the calendar than it is now. Its role then was to raise funds for the church restoration fund. Then it seemed quite an honour to be asked to help in the tea tent!

Titchfield Evangelical Church

There has been a church on the current site on the High Street for over 200 years. Originally the church was affiliated to the Congregational movement and remained with this denomination for many years. In the early 1900s they left the Congregational movement but later came back only to leave again.

In 1964 the church, which by this time was fully independent joined the Fellowship of Independent Evangelical Churches (FIEC) and has remained part of that movement ever since. The church has had its fair share of ups and downs but has maintained a presence on the High Street consistently over the years. Much modernisation has taken place inside to provide a comfortable, welcoming atmosphere, but the exterior has remained largely unchanged over the years.

Groups, Clubs and Societies

Over the years, Titchfield has been a thriving village, in part, because of the activities available and/or organised by and for residents. The following are details of just a few.

Unfortunately, many of the people who ran the groups did not keep a record of the brilliant work being done so we are unable to provide details of many of them. We know there has been a Red Cross group (see page 104), a football club, often known as Titchfield Wanderers, and the angling club to name three.

The Community Centre and the Boxing club gave us accounts of their organisations up to the present day. We have, therefore, included these so the information will be available for further generations.

We have also included something from Tessa Short so that people in future will know about the stones, the Christmas trees and the flags in the village.

Mary Burner

I personally did not go to any uniform clubs, but had friends who belonged to the Brownies and Guides, which met at the Parish Room.

The Scouts met in the Territorial Army (TA) centre and they used to have a musical section, which trained around the old TA car park. We used to hear them from our house, practising, playing and marching. They played at church events marching through the village. I am not sure when they disbanded and the Sea Scouts, that we have now at the Community Centre, began.

As a teenager in the '60s there was a club called the Stable d'Or at the Coach and Horses I remember. It was a live music club and was held in the old stables/barn behind the pub. Local bands played there and it was very popular. They held disco evenings too.

The Coach and Horses also held a monthly Folk Club up in the room at the back where the skittle alley was. It was very popular and had well-known local singers.

At one time a Young Rotoract club was started but I don't think that lasted too long - you had to leave when you were 21 I think!

Titchfield Bonfire Boys

Titchfield Bonfire Boys is the backbone of celebration in the village and has been organising the carnival since the 1880s. The organisation started with the burning of tar barrels as a form of protest but the target of this direct action has now been lost in obscurity. The following are some significant dates:

Carnival 2013

1919 Complaints from some residents that their paintwork was damaged following the burning of a tar barrel in the Square!

1945 Carnival stops during the War years but women and children walk the route to keep the spirit of the carnival alive.

1946 The carnival returns with all its pre-war vigour.

1964 Titchfield Carnival makes the British Pathé News film, which records the fun and games of Titchfield Carnival. It showed various decorated houses, people in fancy dress, decorated floats as well as various funny costumes. The narrator says the "Carnival is an open air fancy dress party ... and a must if visiting Britain."

Titchfield History Society - Peter Mills

The origin of the society is found in a short course on local history given by George Watts (the current President of the Society) early in the 1970s at the Titchfield Community Centre. Such was the enthusiasm generated by his course that a small group of like-minded members decided to set up a society to carry forward the study of the history of the village. Thus the society came into being, its original constitution declaring its aim to be, 'the study and research into publication of material concerning the history of the original and existing Parish of Titchfield.'

Publications have followed in extraordinary diversity and profusion. Three principal books span the history of the village. *Titchfield: a History* came first in 1982, then *Titchfield: a Place in History* in 1989, and finally *Titchfield: an Ancient Parish* in 2011, with reprints required for the first two. The society also published transcribed forms of the Titchfield Parish Registers for 1589 to 1634 and 1634 to 1678. Rendering the texts into modern English and indexing the results was a remarkable labour of love. Another important publication was *Titchfield at the Start of the Third Millennium*, an instant but comprehensive rendering of the village in the modern world.

Today the society continues on its vigorous way. A new website provides a helpful introduction. Seventy or more members regularly attend its monthly lectures. Its aims have expanded, with its amended constitution allowing, 'at the discretion of the committee, the study of matters of wider historical interest.' Nevertheless, the society always seeks to maintain a sharp focus upon the rich and diverse history of the remarkable village to which it belongs.

Earl of Southampton Trust

The first recorded charity in the Titchfield area was Robert Godfry's. He bought a farm near Funtley 'for the relief of the poor people of the town of Titchfield.' In 1620 an economic depression hit poor people. In response, Henry Wriothesley, the third Earl of Southampton, set up almshouses, small parcels of land and a charity 'for the setting the poor of the said Towne to work in clothing or some other good and profitable trade.'

Trustees have administered these and three other charities. They have provided payments for apprentices to learn a trade, provision of clothing and coal as well as providing pensions. These beneficiaries should 'be of a good character ... unable to maintain themselves by their own exertions.' They were given one shilling and six pennies a week, about seven and a half new pence.

In 1989 the charity was renamed The Earl of Southampton Trust and is a Relief in Need and an Almshouse charity. Look out for houses in the village with a plaque on them saying Earl of Southampton Trust.

Titchfield Remembers Project - Amanda Laws

In September 2013 I decided, with the help of a team of volunteers, to find out about the 41 First World War servicemen on the Church Memorial. The initial objective was to add their details onto various British Roll of Honour websites, but as our enthusiasm grew, so did the project. The final team of five: Phil Burner, Louise Bullivant, Dawne Dunton, Richard Boden, and myself, made local requests for information and posted on websites in order to make contact with relatives of those who died.

By using a range of online genealogy sites we established the basic facts about each serviceman and then went on to more specific military sites and visited museums. This was a steep learning curve for us, with little or no background in military history. Understanding the makeup of brigades and platoons and the roles of engineers and service battalions was all new. Soldiers moved regiment, even during the War itself, so the task to decipher which division or brigade was in which battle and to determine where each soldier had died was time consuming.

The Naval casualties were easier to follow, as when a ship was lost, details of the battle have, in most cases, been well documented. During research we found a further group of Titchfield born men who had a claim to be on the War Memorial. The criteria being - was the serviceman born in the Parish of Titchfield as it was in 1892, before Parish boundary changes? This led to a further nine being included in our research and in addition to this we started gathering stories and photographs about those who had survived the War.

We produced a body of work to exhibit in the Parish Rooms on 3rd August 2014 as springboard to collect further information. Locals and relatives came to add and amend what we had. We attempted to identify where each serviceman had been living prior to 1914 and the following month we gave our research to residents to produce a carnival commemoration window in their house.

The aim of the group for the final part of the project is to amend the Roll of Honour book in the church and to add the new names to the memorial by 2018.

Recent Titchfield history - Tessa Short

The illuminated Christmas trees outside houses were introduced in 1991 by Tessa Short. They were first put up in West Street, then Ron Knee took over South Street and also specified that the lights should be white in South Street. The trees now also appear at Christmas in the Square, High Street, East Street and Bridge Street. Tessa still organises the purchase and distribution of the Christmas trees.

Flags mounted on the walls of houses also began in West Street. They are all individual and many of the early ones were made by Grace Clark. She is also the person through whom bookings for the Parish Hall are currently made.

In the 1980s three sarsen stones were unearthed near Kites Croft when the new Warsash road was being built on the stream called the Brownwich Brook. Medieval people called them sarsen stones, meaning strangers. The three West Street stones weigh between half a ton and two tons and were brought to their present spot by members of the Titchfield Village Trust with the help of Raychem, the then owners of Kites Croft. This was achieved at a time when the West End pub was still open. The stones were placed during the time that the customers were imbibing, and when the customers emerged three large stones had appeared!

Every year the inhabitants of West Street have a sarsen stone celebration. The oak tree next to the stones was grown by Tessa Short's son and is now over 45 years old.

Titchfield Bowling Club - Gary Rathke

The Titchfield Bowling Club is situated in Bridge Street, Titchfield. Members have been playing Olde English Bowls there since 1923. It was resolved at the first meeting of interested parties to form the club and the offer of land at a nominal rent from Mr. J. H. H. Fielder was accepted. £20 towards the cost of laying the green was promised by a local gentleman. When the club was formed on 1st June 1923, there was a president and many vice presidents plus a club committee.

'The green of the Titchfield Bowling Club was opened by Colonel the Honourable C. Brabazon and afterwards a match was played between the members of the home club and Fareham Bowling Club, the result being a win for Titchfield by one point. After the match the visitors were entertained at the Queen's Head by the home bowlers when an enjoyable time was spent. A capital selection of music was provided by the Titchfield Brass Band under the direction of Mr. Westall. On the motion of Mr. W. Freemantle a hearty vote of thanks was accorded to the Fareham bowlers for the interesting game that they had been the means of providing. Mr. Leonard Trigg (Captain) in responding on behalf of the Fareham Club wished the Titchfield Club every success.'

'At the first annual meeting of the bowling club on 18th January 1924, the Hon. Sec. (M. Ernest C. Sutton) was able to present an eminently satisfactory report on the progress made by the Club during the first year of its existence. The membership of the club had now reached 40 players and several friends had indicated their intentions of becoming members as soon as the season reopened.'

After the above quotes, in *The Hampshire Telegraph & Post* in 1923 and 1924, there are no further records available until 1934. Minutes for the first ten years seem to have been lost. The club continued to survive though often had to rely on fund raising, such as running whist drives, to help supplement income. There were also no minutes for 1942 - 1944 when the club continued 'as best it could' during war time.

During the 90 years of the club's existence almost all the work on the green, the gardens and clubhouse has been carried out by volunteer members. Occasionally the club obtained a grant for equipment but usually fund raising was used to pay for a new mower. Cups for competitions were donated, rules were changed and reverted to previous rules and sometimes changed back yet again. Many social events were also organised including an annual dinner and dance.

There are no records as to when the clubhouse was built but in 1934 it is noted that water was connected and 'toilet basins' were provided by a member. Records show that members assisted with maintenance and cleaning of the clubhouse. The building had a new roof on several occasions. Once water was installed a committee meeting agreed that cups of tea could be provided for the members.

In 1959 ladies were allowed to join the club and in 1964 'It was proposed that the bucket in the ladies toilet be emptied fortnightly for the sum of £3. 3s. 0d.' It took until 2013, when a new clubhouse was built, for modern toilets to be installed! Electricity was also supplied to the new clubhouse, which replaced the generator that was purchased in 1999.

When the club was formed there were many officers and not many playing members. This was possibly because all the vice presidents had contributed in some way to the financing and/or founding of the club. Of course this was needed in the beginning but today the club is self-supporting and run by the Executive Committee of Titchfield Bowling Club. After 90 years the Titchfield Bowling Club continues to thrive.

The Women's Institute (WI) – Rita Prior

The National Women's Institute was 100 years old in 2015. Titchfield WI is 94 years old. The ideals of the WI are truth, justice, tolerance and fellowship. People often think of the WI members as 'jam makers', but the organisation actually exists to educate women to enable them to provide an effective role in the community, to expand their horizons and to develop and pass on important skills. Each WI is run separately but there are autumn and spring regional councils where delegates from each WI attend and then there is the national council.

Titchfield WI members helped and supported families in need during the War as did WI members throughout the country. Each group has regular meetings as well as such things as book clubs, walking groups, craft groups. They also have an interesting speaker every month.

There were so many members in the Titchfield WI that it split into two in about 1988, the Titchfield group and the Abbey group.

Titchfield Amateur Boxing Club (TABC)- Ken Charman

In July 2014, TABC was highly honoured by being awarded The Queen's Award for Voluntary Service. This is the equivalent to an MBE but for voluntary groups, and was presented to the Club by the Lord Lieutenant of Hampshire, Dame Mary Fagan.

It is likely that the Club was in existence before WW1. Lou Stamp remembers training in a room over a pub in the '50s, when Dereck Hoile was boxing for TABC. There is also a quote - '1937 the old Boy's School was leased to the Titchfield Boxing Club at £10 per year... the lease was extended to allow the club to obtain increased grants to enable main drainage, shower baths etc to be installed.' During WW2 the building became empty and deteriorated. 'Only temporary repairs could be carried out to the school roof in 1941, in view of the recent heavy air raids.'

In 1966 Dereck Hoile, one of a family of boxers, returned to the Club as a trainer and a pattern of shows developed, open to the general public, held twice each year at the Community Centre plus a dinner show each year. The dinner shows started at Clarence Pier in Southsea, progressed to South Parade Pier, then to the Pyramids Centre, and eventually to the Guildhall Portsmouth, which is still the venue for an annual dinner show. The Club joined forces with Eastleigh Lions Club and provided the boxing programme at various venues. For 20 years the Club hosted the annual three-way tournament between the Royal Navy, The Police and TABC held at South Parade Pier. In this period the first national title for the Club was won by

The Hoile boys

Bobby Elliott, who won the Junior ABA title. Sadly Bobby died at the early age of 26.

Local schoolboy boxers include Michael Goddard, Alex Burdon, Colin Matthews, Dennis Bennett, Patrick Levy, Leigh Medway, Terry Butler, Barry Todd and seniors Roger Johns, Les Skinner and Peter Blower were regularly boxing under trainers Dereck Hoile, Johnny Fuller and Jack Bennett.

From November 1971 the Club was run by Cmd. Matthew Todd, president, Mr. Charlie Bailey, chairman, Mr. Cyril Levy, vice chairman, Mr. H. Ord, secretary, Mr. P. Popely, treasurer, Messrs Jack Bennett, Dereck Hoile, and John Fuller, trainers, and committee members Messrs L. Clements, M. Jeffery, W, Eager, and J. Harrison. The Club met at the Titchfield Community Centre, where a gymnasium and facilities were newly set up. In 1971, several boxing tournaments were held and in 1972 a show was presented at Plesseys Ltd between TABC and Waterlooville ABC under the sponsorship of Fareham Lions Club.

From the earliest days, Doctor Ken Dunton gave his services freely to the Club by way of medical examinations, and acting as medical officer at all of the home shows. This was of immense assistance to the Club, as professional medical services are vital. Later in 1972, Ken Charman, joined the Club and took over as competition secretary. He is still active in the Club.

In 1975, Dereck Hoile left Titchfield ABC to start another club. The new head coach was Joey Peters. Joey's son, Jimmy Peters, was already boxing for the Club and was later joined by brother Jo Jo. Also at the club were Anthony Withey, Garry Skerrett, Matthew Castleton, Steve Michael, Paul Woodford, Timmy Henderson, Brindley Edwards, Mike Sharpe, Dave Grandon. Matt and Zac Broad, Mark and Gary Williams and Frank and Jamie Cooper. Joe's wife Ellen Peters took a keen interest in the Club and was the club consultant where weight and diet were concerned. Ellen Peters was a wonderful controlling and influential friend of the club.

The period in which Joe Peters, who in 1978, was joined by Lou Stamp, was the most successful in the history of the Club. Joe and Lou, helped by Tony Williams, formed the training team and national and international honours were won. TABC was in demand all over the country and attracted clubs and boxers from far and wide to its shows. Joe eventually became a professional trainer and Jimmy also turned professional, but the solid base remained. It was a hugely sad time when in September 2003 Joey Peters died, and before recovering from the grief, dear Ellen died in October 2006. The Peters family will be always thought of when TABC is mentioned.

In 1988 when the Community Association made changes to the buildings the club had to move elsewhere. As the millennium approached, discussions with Fareham Borough Council began, which were the beginning of plans for a dedicated gymnasium on the Titchfield recreation ground. The fine building in which the Club is now housed was largely funded by the club's own resources. It was officially opened on 25th January 2002 by the then Mayor of Fareham, Councillor Arthur Mandry.

During the planning and construction TABC was given very considerable help by local businessman John Hopkins. He became club president and a very dear friend. Sadly he died in May 2009. Councillor Malcolm Harper also gave the Club tremendous assistance. TABC is hugely indebted to a number of others including Tony Scopes-Upton for his support and generosity, Steve Cripps of Construction Company PLC, and David Ellis of D. Ellis, Electrical Contractors, and for many years C. D. Jordan and Son Ltd. There are many others who contribute to the fund of goodwill that TABC enjoys.

It is very doubtful if the Club could have succeeded in constructing its own premises without the dedication and skills of Lou Stamp, who after a period of 34 plus years is still the club's head trainer. Lou's loyalty and love of the Club is without parallel.

The past decade has seen the club go from strength to strength, now enjoying as strong a membership in numbers as ever before. Shows are regularly held at Sarisbury Green Social Club and one of the biggest dinner boxing tournaments outside of London is held each year at Portsmouth Guildhall. Arrangements for this important fund raising event are in the capable hands of Matt Castleton who had the first of his 57 bouts for TABC in March 1985. Tim Henderson has taken on the arduous job as competition secretary.

Assisting Lou Stamp the Club has eight ABA qualified coaches, Matt Castleton, Frank Cooper, Tim Henderson, James Norris, Gary Isles, Jason Moore, Wayne Matthews and Bradley Phillips. Most are ex TABC boxers. Wayne is one of three generations of a truly Titchfield family who have, or do, represent TABC. The Club also has numerous father/son combinations amongst its lengthy historic membership.

In 2014, the gymnasium was further extended, allowing for a larger floor area and facilities for disabled persons and female members. In 2015 planning permission was granted for further changing facilities and a larger gymnasium. We hope that boxing tournaments will be held in the gymnasium. TABC has always enjoyed its position in the community, and is still proudly affiliated to Titchfield Community Association. The Club has always looked for ways to help the less fortunate and its donations to charities run into tens of thousands of pounds.

The TABC has for many years proudly represented Titchfield and would like to think that it has earned a place in the folk history of the Village.

Titchfield Community Centre, D.J.L. Gibbs, Chairman

The early days: 1962 - 1985

It all started in January 1962 when the Territorial Army said that with the likely increased use of their Drill Hall, we would not be able to continue holding our various dances and functions there. In consequence, a meeting was called and it was decided to raise funds and obtain grants in order to build our own Community Centre. A steering committee was elected under the chairmanship of Wing Commander Denis Smith, which included the representatives of several local organisations. The main objective was to demonstrate that a need existed and that funds could be raised towards the cost of building and equipping our own Community Centre.

Classes were organised in people's houses and many fund raising events were held including a summer fete at West Hill Park School. Both Hampshire County Council and Fareham Borough Council (then Fareham B.D.C.) supported the idea in the form of grants, with the bulk of the money coming from the Government Education Fund. Some progress was made and land was purchased adjacent to the Queen's Head and the Parish Room; the latter being included in the architect's plans which were commissioned and prepared.

All this took many months to achieve and the financial position deteriorated. Grants were hard to obtain and it was feared that the size of the building we were attempting to finance was beyond our means. The prospect of building our own Community Centre for the Village seemed remote. However, just as all our plans appeared to be thwarted, a fortuitous change in central government policy presented us with a golden opportunity. The Territorial Army was to be completely reorganised and as a consequence the Titchfield Drill Hall would become surplus to requirements.

Immediate negotiations with the War Department Land Agents were initiated with a view to purchasing the Drill Hall for subsequent use as our community centre. Negotiations were frustratingly slow: 12 months after our initial approach little progress was apparent, and during this time the building was the subject of some vandalism. It was suggested that a quicker solution may be forthcoming if, instead of buying, we were to lease the building. This was finally achieved on the 1st October 1967 following a letter to the then Minister for War (Denis Healey).

At long last we had secured our base. Once in sole residence our principal objective was to develop and equip our community centre in order to provide a varied and expanding range of recreational pursuits for our members. A 'shoestring' budget necessitated our establishing working relationships with the Royal Navy, whose 'Surplus Stores' organisation along with the second hand equipment available from Hampshire County Council Education Department helped to furnish our 'home'.

As the finances of the Association improved, we were gradually able to replace the 'barrack-room' environment with a relaxed and friendly 'community' atmosphere. The close co-operation between the warden and the many committee and council members ensured an efficiently administered 'Centre'. Of course, there were differences of opinion, but these were always resolved in a spirit of co-operation and common purpose.

The pattern of recreation has, of course, altered as time has passed. In the 1970s there were regular dinners and dances every Friday and Saturday night - now it is mainly 'discos'. The type of classes run are different too - we started with millinery, tailoring and French: today it is bridge, yoga and keep-fit.

The Titchfield Community Association as it exists today has always been in the fortunate position of being able to pay its own way. In all, the Association has put many thousands of pounds into the building. As a result it has been able to obtain a number of grants from both the County and Borough Councils, which have supplemented the Association's finances for major development projects.

Up to date: 1985 - 2015

Both Hampshire County and Fareham Borough Councils supported the TCA through annual grants, which covered the majority of the staff wages.

As time progressed, however, government expenditure became tighter, and the money made available to support community centres such as Titchfield became more difficult to obtain until funding for running expenses stopped altogether, at which point the Community Association had to become self-funding. This was achieved through a lot of hard work by the warden, now the manager, the staff and the Association itself, developing and improving the facilities, which increased the revenue from hirings. Over the years, the usage of the Centre improved and the financial strength improved likewise.

Today the Centre is used by a large number of people and groups for a wide range of activities. Our regular groups become affiliated to the Association and contribute to the management and oversight of the Centre in return for discounted hire costs.

The Centre is still owned by Fareham Borough Council and the Community Association leases it and takes responsibility for the internal maintenance, whilst the Council remains responsible for the structure of the building. The Centre is run to professional standards and, although we no longer benefit from revenue support, we can and do apply for local authority funding for specific projects which has enabled significant enhancements to be made to the buildings, with extensions, upgrades and better furnishings.

We have a full-time manager, three part-time administration assistants and three part-time caretakers. Our facilities are in use seven days per week throughout the day and evening. We are now looking towards further improvements to the Centre with some exciting plans for internal decoration and external extensions. As well as our user groups pursuing their own activities, we have some groups who support those less able to care for themselves and are proud of our contribution to village and local community life.

Today we are one of the busiest, if not the busiest, community association and centre in Hampshire. We remain alive to the ever-present financial and operational challenges faced by community groups but are confident in our future. Whatever our history, the main objective has always been to provide the facilities which members in sufficient numbers require. The Titchfield Community Association has successfully fulfilled these aims.

The village would not be the same without it.

Shopping in Titchfield

For many years children have sung: "Rub a dub dub, three men in a tub. The butcher the baker the candlestick maker." Titchfield village did not have a candlestick maker but it had lots of shops that could provide local people with most of their every day essentials.

We have used *Kelly's Directory of Hampshire and the Isle of Wight* to provide a snapshot in 1939. It was the 20th edition and proudly boasted that it was "The oldest and largest Directory Publishers in the world". It was the yellow pages of its time. Unfortunately traders had to pay to have their names included so it does not give a full picture of all the shops and businesses in the area.

If you compare the village in 1939 and the present day you will notice that the shops and businesses are different. There were three banks in *Kelly's Directory*, but now we only have a cash machine. There were many independent traders providing bread, cycles, boot repairs etc. There were sweetshops and a toyshop which are now missing although the two supermarkets stock some of these items. In the twenty first century many people have cars and use supermarkets but in 1939 why did a small town like Titchfield have so many shops?

Kelly's Directory may have the answer. Lee-on-the-Solent has only three telephone numbers listed, one for the Rectory plus two farmers. Park Gate is not listed. Hook with Warsash has approximately half the numbers of entries as Titchfield, and the majority are fruit growers, market gardens and shellfish merchants. There are not as many entries for shops and the range is not as wide. It may be that the Titchfield shops served the whole area rather than just the village.

Here is a walk around Titchfield village with some of the contributors. They tell us how people shopped in the 1930s - '50s. They are Aimee St John (AS), Bessie Traves (BT), Donald Upshall (DU), John Ekins (JE), June Pellatt (JP), Mary Burner (MB), Sheila Hignell (SH), and Mike Ferris (MF). We have divided their stories into the four main streets of the village then included other businesses, deliveries, and sounds and smells.

East Street

These are the shops that I can remember in Titchfield around 1951. In East Street there was a Mr Rose, a grocer just up from the Wheatsheaf, I think it was about No. 5. We shopped here for some groceries. A bit further up at about No. 13 was Wally Bennett. He was a tobacconist so naturally he sold all of a smoker's requisites: he also sold quite a lot of stationery products

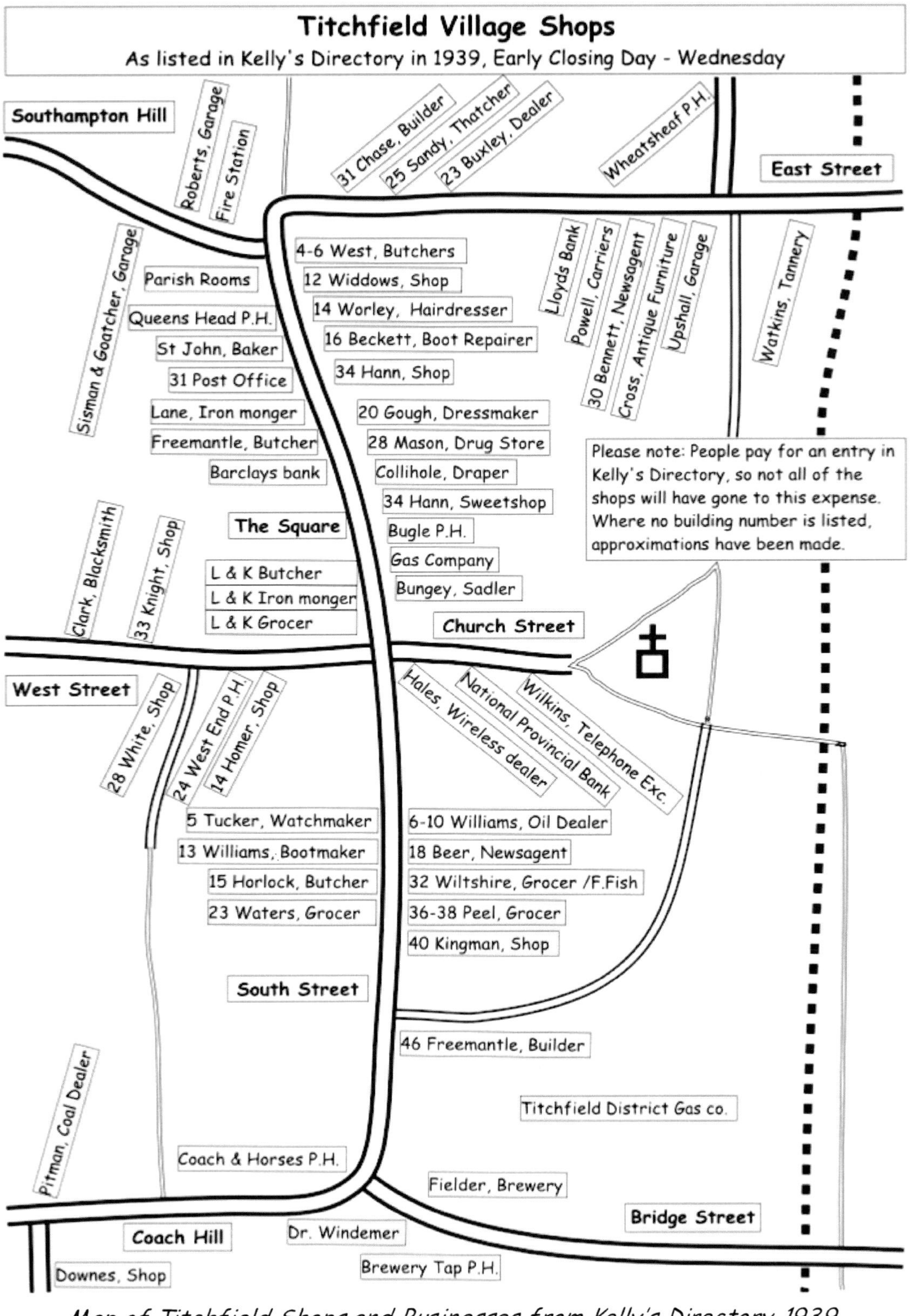

Map of Titchfield Shops and Businesses from Kelly's Directory 1939

including crepe paper which was much used in the carnival. In addition to the above he was a booking agent for Royal Blue coaches. He had lost an arm possibly in WW1. (BT)

At the top corner of East Street there was a bakery and this was also where I believe Lilly Judd, nee Gosling, who lived in East Street kept her pony and trap in which she delivered milk in the central village area. (MF)

Lilly Gosling (Judd) delivered the milk with her cart and the dairy was in her garden in East Street. (MB)

Around 1951 we also went for groceries at Roses which was a door or two along from the Wheatsheaf pub. I can remember walking back home with my sister in her pram. I could push it about half way up to where there was a manhole cover in the footway, somewhere just beyond what is now the start of the by-pass. A little further along East Street was a tobacconist cum newsagent cum stationer run by a Mr Bennett who had lost an arm, possibly in the first War. His shop was a bit of an Aladdin's cave with a memorable aroma of tobacco and paper. (JE)

High Street and the Square

In the High Street at No. 4, opposite the Parish Rooms, was a butchers, Mr Smith I think. A bit further along was the paper shop run by 'Fluff' Adams. (BT)

Opposite the Queen's Head was 'Fluff' Adams paper shop in what is now a house with bow fronted windows. Fluff was a popular village character who had an artificial arm under which he would tuck his papers. The only way you could detect the false arm was because he invariably wore a leather glove on it all the year round. (MF)

Some contributors have suggested that Fluff Adams lost his arm in WW1 but another suggested that it was the result of an accident at Bursledon brick works.

On the opposite side of the road was St John's Bakery and shop. (BT)

The St John's were there in the 1950s: hence the Old Bakehouse which is now the home of the physiotherapists. (JE)

The shop is the now hairdressers by the physiotherapists in the Old Bakehouse. Andrew St John's grandfather, Gordon, was a baker and ran the business. A fire was started in some rubbish bins and the corn store burnt down. The St John family did not want to make any

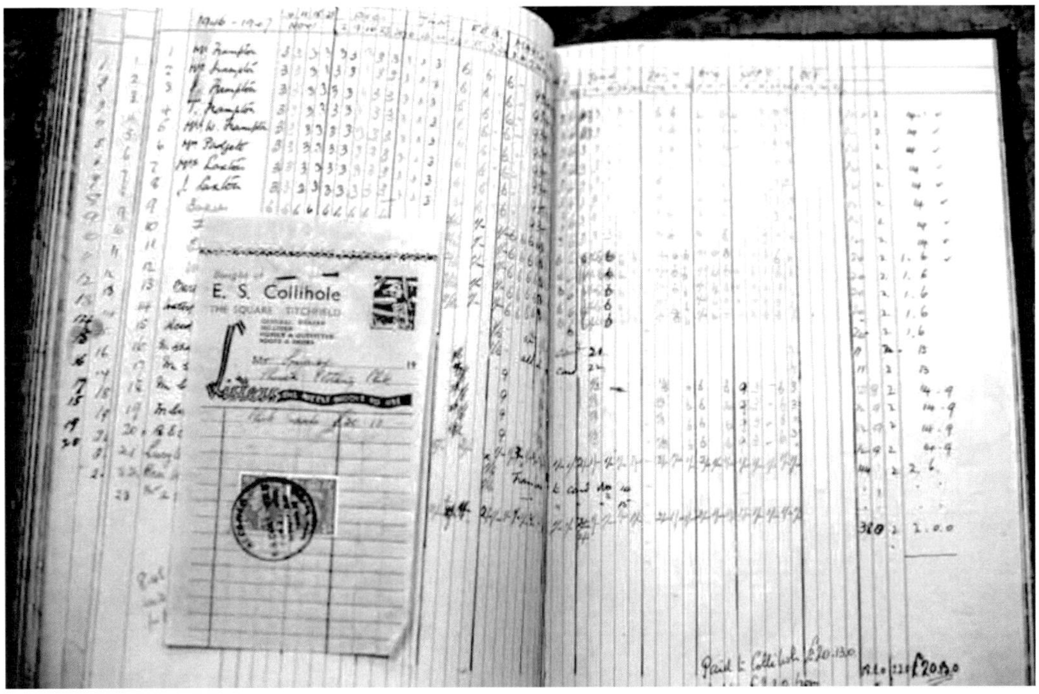

St Peter's Clothing Club ledger

Hampshire Records Office has the ledger from St Peter's Church. It shows that people would save small sums of money and then use it to buy cloth and clothes from Collihole. There were no credit cards then!

of the staff redundant but unfortunately the business had to close. (AS)

In the Square was the chemist, the pharmacist was a Mr Mason succeeded by Mr Dunn. It was in the same building, No. 28, as today and had large traditional coloured bottles in the window. Where One Stop is now was a shop called Collihole, this was a drapery shop, which sold a very wide range of men's, women's and children's clothes and sewing requisites. (BT)

Collihole also sold lino, shoes, wool, clothes for babies, children and adults, carpets, hats, cloths and brushes for all jobs. (MB)

Collihole was really a miniature department store. It was a very useful place for clothing and haberdashery and was sadly missed when it closed its doors and became One Stop. (JE)

There was a small sweet shop run by a Miss Hann and later, in the early '50s, by a Miss Bigwood. What is now the Co-op, I remember a wet-fish shop; it later became the gas showroom. On the corner of the Square and Church Street was Mr Bungey, Titchfield's saddler and harness maker. In the early '40s when I travelled a lot to be with Cyril, my husband, I asked Mr Bungay to make me a leather case for my gas mask. It was much more robust and durable for my travels. The original cases provided were made of cardboard and soon disintegrated. I still have this case now and it is still as good as new. (BT)

H. Bungey, Saddler and Harness Maker

On the west side forming the junction of West Street and the Square was Lankester & Crook. There was latterly three parts to this shop.
Part 1, now occupied by Penyards, was a large grocer and provisioner.
Part 2, now occupied by Dibbens, was an ironmonger.
Part 3, now occupied by Bath Travel, was as I first remember it, a tea room. It was later used as a butcher's shop by Lankester & Crook and they delivered meat. They were part of a local chain of shops in the Southampton area.

To the right of Lankester's in the late '40s was an antique shop, I think it was called Wimbush. Further to the right at about No. 31, in the late '40s or early '50s was another antique shop run by a Mr Collis. It then went onto be the paper shop and post office and later a betting shop; currently it is 'Memory Lane'.

The current Rowan's shop at the junction of South Street and Church Street was two businesses. The one on the left was a branch of the National Provincial Bank. On the right was a cycle shop run by Arthur Hales and no account of Titchfield shops in the 1950s would be complete without mention of Hales bicycle shop. (JE)

He fully refurbished and sold a wide range of bicycles, usually painted maroon and grey or bottle green and grey. He would sell you a new one if you could afford it as well as accessories. He also re-charged accumulators. These were small six-volt glass-cased acid batteries used to power the valve heaters for battery-powered radios. There were no transistors then. The high tension or higher voltage (HT) for the valves in these radios was from a 'dry' 90-volt battery. It must be remembered that the remoter areas of Titchfield and Brownwich did not have 'the electric' until the late '50s. Families usually had two accumulators; one being charged by Arthur and the other one in use. Changeover was normally part of the weekly trip into Titchfield on Saturday for the weekly shop. (BT)

The carpet shop was called Bettons and used to be on the other side of the Square before they moved to where the Rowan's Hospice shop is now.

There were no supermarkets or 'clicking' online for next day delivery! (MF)

My favourite shop was Mrs Bungey's toyshop on the corner of Church Street, next to where the Co-op is now. I was very keen on collecting Dinky toys and I can still remember the childhood delight at trying to decide which model to buy with my birthday money. The telephone exchange was in Church Street, two doors along from Arthur Hales and the bank. In the early '50s it was, of course, a manual exchange and one of the operators lived two doors away from us in Catisfield. (JE)

South Street

G.L. Williams' (Oily) shop

At Nos. 6, 8 and 10 South Street was Oily William's shop where, as you entered, a bell attached to the door would jingle and his wife would then come into the shop to serve you. It is now a private residence. Oily had another shop on the opposite side of the road: this sold hardware, ironmongery and household items and is now a planning consultancy, Brian Jezeph Consultancy Ltd. Oily also ran mobile shops, using vans, to all areas of the village, to Segensworth, in short to wherever there was a need for his services. All household requirements were sold from these mobile shops including paraffin from drums hung from the headlamps. The garage where he kept some of his stock and his vans is still there - the black corrugated tin building next to No. 8. (BT)

Oily Williams served paraffin into your own containers from a tank just inside the doors of his garage. He also travelled the village with a truck mounted with an oil tank and delivered to homes. The truck also had a can suspended and swinging about under the oil outlet spout. Although intended to catch drips, it rarely seemed to do so. Outside Oily's shop, the pavement had a permanent oil slick and a very strong smell. Oily also had a general ironmongery and store in a shop on the opposite side where the planning office is now. (MF)

Mum had paraffin cans lined up for him to deliver on a Saturday morning. We did not get the electricity until 1954 at Meon Bye, Triangle Lane. (SH)

Spencer and Penn's shoe shop in South Street was a handy place for shoe repairs or to buy shoes and its closure was another significant loss to the social fabric of the village. (JE)

In what is now Hallmark Jewellers, 13-15 East Street, was the village cobbler which became Spencer and Penn shoe shop. On the same side was Horace Walter's grocery store, the main food outlet in the village. On the other side, in part of the timbered cottages, was the fish and chip shop and next to it another small grocery shop run by Mrs Peel; a little further along was the post office. These are not all the shops, but were the principal ones. (MF)

There was another bakery behind the house at No. 17. This was used by the St. John's family. A few doors along at No. 25 was another grocer and provisioner, Mr Walters. The yard at the rear of this shop is now known as Wriothesley Court. I remember the fish and chip shop at No. 32. During the '40s there was a small grocery shop run by Mrs Peel at No. 38. Titchfield Post Office was then run by a Mr Jones from what is now the Red House. It was there until the mid-'60s.

Further along at No. 20, where the beauty parlour is now, was Dan Greenland's gents barber and tobacconist in the late '40s. On the opposite side of the street at No. 13 was Spencer and Penn, a shoe shop run by Jim Smith. Next door to him at No. 15 was Mr Horlock, the butcher. He was succeeded there by another butcher, Charlie Broomfield. It was he that moved the butchery business across the road to where Hadlow's is now. (BT)

No shop was open on Good Friday, Christmas and Easter. All the shops closed half day Wednesday and were 9-5 Monday to Friday, earlier closing on Saturday and closed all day Sunday. (MB)

On the day rationing stopped, the general store/sweet-shop near Bellfield, run by Mr Page, had Mars bars for sale, which we bought. We had 6d (2.5p) to spend which was a lot of money. (SH)

Other businesses

Titchfield Mill was the most amazing place and everyone who farmed went there to buy seeds plus hay and straw. It was owned by the Russsell Family and run as a sort of co-operative. (SH)

Deliveries

The Co-op served other areas with milk deliveries. Tom Parker's four-wheeled milk floats were drawn by wonderful animals. The driver would park at the end of a street and alight carrying his container of six pints of milk and then to progress from door to door along the street. The horse, without command, would keep pace with him and when the container required re-filling the float would be alongside him. Getting a Saturday morning job with a milkman was very popular amongst boys. It was the day that money was collected therefore the milkman appreciated help with the milk delivery whilst he was chasing the money. (MF)

People were still using horses and carts in the '50s for deliveries and general farm work. Tom Kill had a horse and cart, and his horse always had blinkers. I asked him why and he showed me - the horse didn't have an eye!

Heavy haulage in South Street

Mr Pitman delivered coal. He looked black and sooty and used to wear a leather coat to carry the bags of coal on his shoulders into the coal store.

The dustbin men came into your garden to collect the bins, which were heavy metal bins with lids. A very noisy job!

A rag and bone man used to call and a man used to come round asking if there was anything to sharpen - knives, scissors, garden shears, etc. The gypsies came round with things to sell - pegs, heather, flowers, etc. Onion Johnnies (real French men) called at the door selling the strings of onions.

My family were builders and a lot of reps used to call with huge cases of building trade items. These could be displays of tiles or flooring, using delicate bits of the actual tiles and wood, beautifully displayed, or drawings of bathroom and kitchen furniture. We still have these books today in the study.

The main Portsmouth to Southampton road came through the village, along East Street, until the new bypass was built by 1934. At one time two petrol stations faced each other at the bottom of Southampton Hill, when Southampton Hill was the A27. (MB)

There were three garages in Titchfield all selling petrol. Upshall, now branded as Titchfield Motor Works continues to flourish, Roberts, which was redeveloped as Village Gate housing and the Priory Garage which still exists but now mainly for car sales. Early in my recollection, a Mr Maltby ran Priory Garage on the new bypass. He lived in the bungalow next door. Early in the 1950s it was taken over by Mobil and run by Charlie Braid who had moved down from the West Midlands. (JE) *See Donald Upshall's account of Spitfire parts being made here in WW2 on page 70*

Edward 'Eddy' Upshall and Arthur Hales used to be partners in a combined cycle shop and accumulator battery business. But they separated and Arthur left to open the cycle shop in the Square. Eddy carried on repairing cars at the same site where his grandson Philip still runs the garage. (DU)

Sounds and Smells of Titchfield

The post office was always cool in summer and we could buy a red fizzy drink. Then in December it was warm and smelled of Christmas and paper chains. (JP)

At St John's bakers there was the smell of freshly baked bread from the bakery. There was a queue for hot cross buns on Good Friday when it opened, just to sell these, then it closed. (MB)

I remember the wonderful smell of St John's bakery, especially on a Good Friday when we ran to the village from Meon Bye to get our hot cross buns. (SH)

Wally Bennett's shop was a bit of an Aladdin's cave with a memorable aroma of tobacco and paper. (JE)

When Fielder's Brewery and the tannery were both working on the same day there was a horrible smell.

When the fire station siren went off it invited the fun of running up the road to watch the engine speed out of the station with the bells ringing. I remember steam engines as they rumbled through the village from Fareham Urban District Council (FDUC) making the houses shake (now they can be seen in Bursledon Brickworks Museum).

I also remember walking up to the railway bridge at Segensworth to watch the steam trains go over.

I could hear from East Street the cows and animals at Farmer Wolf's farm up at the barn. The cows made what seemed to me to be a horrible noise in the middle of the night. Also there were screech owls in the Holm Oak tree at the back of Maybury (MB)

South Street

Bus stop names

These are the names of the bus stops in the '50s as spoken in Titchfield. The names of the bus companies have changed. The buses that used to come through the village were the No. 77 Hants & Dorset, which was dark green with white mid-stripe, and the No. 45 Southdown Company - cream with light green panels. They were so reliable that people said that you could set your watch by them.

1. Wheatsheaf.
2. The Square.
3. The Coach. Coach and Horses pub (no longer there) on the corner of Coach Hill and South Street where the new houses are now.
4. Sam Page. Sam Page lived at the corner of Occupation Lane and Common Lane.
5. Brinnage. Where Brownwich Lane meets Common Lane.
6. The Sluish. The bottom of Hunts Pond Road, where the mini roundabout is now.
7. The Joe. The Sir Joseph Paxton pub on Hunts Pond Road.
8. Abshot Corner. Where Abshot Road meets Hunts Pond Road.
9. Dimmicks Corner. Where Church Road meets Hunts Pond Road.
10. Park Gate Corner. Where Hunts Pond Road meets Bridge Road.

Single decker in the High Street

An ABC of Hampshire dialect

Avoarhaand	before it happens
Baint	is it not?
Chewbacon	a yokel
Dimmet/dimpsey	dusk
Emmet	ant
Figgy pudden	a type of Christmas pudding
Gurt	very big
'appen	happen
Idhout	outside
Joaay	3d coin (1.25p)
Kiddil	kettle
Leerey	grumpy person
Maaeed	young girl, maid
Nammat	meal eaten by farm workers in the fields
Oi!	When shouted, to attract attention.
Pinchfart	a miser
Quag	boggy place
Randy	a party for a harvest etc.
Shrammed	frozen to the bone
Tafferty	not down to earth
Vaardin	farthing (0.1p)
Wedher	castrated ram
Yoa	ewe, female sheep
Yan tan tethera	shepherds' way of counting; one, two, three.
Zoa	sow, female pig
Zoider	cider

Snowy East Street

Part Four Bonus Pictures

Horse ploughing

Aunt Vi cockling

The Steve Harris lorry

Titchfield Abbey - fruit production

South Street Post Office

Mr Smith and Jerry

South Street

The Coach and Horses

Mabel Downes welcomes Chelsea Pensioners at the Coach and Horses

Queen Elizabeth and Prince Phillip Coronation portrait

Chelsea Pensioners at Coach & Horses

West Street

Jimmy Harris' funeral

Bet Veck and Paula Rogers with Lorna and Pudge outside St Peters

Significant Dates

1945 - **Titchfield tannery chimney blows down**
1946 **- Titchfield carnival restarts**
1946 - American dance craze 'Jitterbug' hits Britain
1947 - Britain suffers the coldest winter on record
- There is an outbreak of poliomyelitis (polio) in Britain
- India along with other British colonies gain their independence
1948 - Birth of the National Health Service
- Marshall Plan, American money to boost the War-torn European economies
1949 - British build de Havilland Comet - first commercial jet airliner
1950 - The *Archers* first broadcast
1951 - Treaty of Paris, six countries start the process of European Union
- British firm Ferranti deliver the first commercial computer
1952 - George VI dies and his daughter, aged 25, becomes Queen Elizabeth II
1951 **- Titchfield Gasworks closes**
1953 - First James Bond novel published
1954 - All rationing of food in Britain now finished
- Queen Elizabeth and Prince Philip came through Titchfield on their way from HMS Daedulus to Broadlands
1955 - The film *The Dam Busters* released
1956 - Double yellow lines now restrict parking
1957 - First Premium Bond winner selected by computer 'ERNIE'
1958 - Manchester United football team die in Munich Air Disaster
1959 **- Titchfield Bowling Club admits women members**
- Morris Mini goes on sale from £497
1960 - Beatles play their first gigs in Hamburg
1961 - TV series the *Avengers* arrives
1962 **- Titchfield Drill Hall morphs into Titchfield Community Centre**
- The Great Train Robbery - £2.5 million stolen from the Mail train
1963 - President Kennedy of USA is assassinated
- **Titchfield cloudburst - village flooded**
1964 - Radio Caroline starts broadcasting followed by other pirate radio stations

Bibliography and Further Reading

Fernley, Linda, (2014) *Hampshire Dialect*, Bradwell Books ISBN 978-8-90991-432-2.

Gebauer George, (2014) *Hitler Youth to Church of England Priest, My Biography*, self published.

Hartley, Major A B MBE RE (1958) *Unexploded Bomb, The story of bomb disposal.*

Scott, Kenneth, *HMS Tormentor*, Available by request from HCC libraries. A collection of documents and memories from people who served at HMS Tormentor.

Sturviant, Ray, (2011) *RAF Flying and Training and Support Units Since 1915* , Hamblin, ISBN 9780851303659.

Smith, David, (1997) *Four Centuries of the Earl of Southampton Trust* ISBN 09531904 0 4.

Titchfield History Society (1999) *Titchfield at the Start of the Third Millennium,* Titchfield History Society.

Titchfield History Society (4th Impression 2008) *Titchfield: A History,* Titchfield History Society.

Titchfield History Society (2011) *Titchfield: An Ancient Parish,* Titchfield History Society.

Twiss, Peter. 2000 *Faster than the Sun.* London: Grub Street Publishing. ISBN 1-902304-43-8.

Watkins, Peter R. (2010) *Villages of the Meon Valley, Aspects of their History.* Swanmore Books, ISBN 978-0-9541566-3-3.

Wheal, Ann, (2011) *A Scrapbook of WW2. A Collection of Personal Stories of Life During WW2*, Brinton Cottage Publishing, ISBN 978-0-9555988-2-1.

Woodford, Bryan, (2009) *Warsash and the River Hamble*, Warsash Publishing, ISBN 97809 48646843.

Woodford, Bryan, (2007) *Images of Warsash and the Hamble River*, Warsash Publishing, ISBN 978-0-948-64686-7.

WordWrights, (2007) *Eyewitness Account, True Stories From Those Who Were There*, Titchfield History Society, ISBN 978-09508131-5-8.

Other Resources

Fareham Museum, Westbury Manor. The resource room has many files of photo and documents.
hampshireculturaltrust.org.uk/**westbury-manor-museum**

Hampshire County Records Office. We researched Corporal Hill's diary, Titchfield Clothing club ledger, *Kelly's Directory* and photos including Titchfield National School.

www3.hants.gov.uk/archives

www.southdowns.gov.uk

www.facebook.com/pages/Titchfield-Nostalgia

www.wikipedia.org

www.google.co.uk

LIPSTICK CLAIR-OBSCUR

CLAIRE DAMON (DES GÂTEAUX ET DU PAIN)

PRÉPARATION

La crème pâtissière au café

Mettre le lait à bouillir. Battre les jaunes d'œufs avec le sucre et l'amidon de maïs afin de blanchir l'appareil. Une fois que le lait bout, verser sur le mélange. Mélanger. Remettre dans la casserole sur feu moyen. Mélanger constamment à l'aide d'une spatule. Dès que le mélange bout, mettre dans un saladier. Ajouter le beurre pommade. Réserver au frais 20 g de cette préparation pour la crème au beurre. Ajouter le café dans l'autre partie. Mixer à l'aide d'un mixeur plongeant. Réserver au frais.

La crème au beurre au café

Faire une crème anglaise. Pour cela, mettre le lait à bouillir dans une casserole avec le café. Battre les jaunes avec le sucre n° 1 pour que le mélange blanchisse. Une fois que le lait bout, le verser sur les jaunes et le sucre. Mélanger. Remettre à chauffer dans la casserole sans cesser de remuer. Dès que la crème anglaise atteint 85° C, transvaser dans un bol pour stopper la cuisson. Mixer la crème à l'aide d'un mixeur plongeant. Débarrasser dans un plat à gratin pour que le mélange refroidisse. Réserver au frais. Faire une meringue italienne. Mettre l'eau et le sucre n° 2 dans une casserole. Mettre les blancs dans la cuve du batteur dès que le mélange atteint 110° C. Lancer votre robot pour battre les blancs. Dès que le sirop de sucre atteint 121° C, le verser en filet dans la cuve du robot. Arrêter le robot une fois que le mélange est tiède. Réserver. Placer le beurre pommade dans la cuve du robot munie de la feuille. Incorporer la crème anglaise refroidie puis la meringue italienne. Une fois le mélange homogène, ajouter la crème pâtissière au café. Débarrasser dans un plat à gratin. Filmer au contact. Réserver au frais.

La mousseline au café d'Éthiopie

Dans la cuve du batteur munie du fouet, mélanger la crème au beurre au café avec la crème pâtissière au café. Une fois que le mélange est lisse et homogène, débarrasser dans un saladier.

Le croustillant à la vergeoise

Dans la cuve du batteur munie de la feuille, crémer le beurre et le sucre. Ajouter les ingrédients restants. Le mélange doit être souple. Étaler entre deux feuilles de papier sulfurisé à l'aide d'un rouleau à pâtisserie. Placer la préparation sur une plaque. Mettre un cadre au-dessus. Enfourner à 160° C pendant 17 min. À la sortie du four, détailler la préparation avec un cercle de 14 cm de diamètre afin d'avoir deux cercles de croustillant.

La crème d'amandes

Dans la cuve du batteur munie de la feuille, travailler le beurre jusqu'à ce qu'il devienne pommade. Ajouter d'abord les poudres, puis les œufs au fur et à mesure en prenant soin de corner les bords de la cuve, le fouet et le fond de la cuve. Ajouter la crème pâtissière mélangée avec le lait. Mettre la crème sur le croustillant à la vergeoise dans chacun des cercles. Poursuivre la cuisson : enfourner à 180° C pour 10 min.

Le biscuit à la cuillère

Monter les blancs tempérés. Ajouter progressivement le sucre. Arrêter le batteur, ajouter les jaunes. Faire tourner 1 seconde en 3e vitesse. Incorporer à la main la fécule et la farine tamisée. Mettre la préparation sur une plaque à trous recouverte de papier sulfurisé. Enfourner à 190° C de 4 à 5 min.

La crème brulée à l'eau de fleur d'oranger

Mettre la gélatine à tremper dans de l'eau froide. Faire une crème anglaise. Pour cela, chauffer le lait et la crème dans une casserole. En fouettant, blanchir les jaunes d'œufs et le sucre. Verser le lait et la crème chaude. Remuer. Remettre à cuire dans la casserole sur feu doux sans cesser de remuer jusqu'à ce que la préparation atteigne la température de 82° C. Ajouter la gélatine essorée, puis l'extrait d'eau de fleur d'oranger. Couler 120 g de préparation dans deux moules Flexipan de 14 cm de diamètre. Mettre la préparation dans le congélateur pour 6 h minimum afin de surgeler la préparation.

La chantilly au café d'Éthiopie

Mettre la gélatine à tremper dans de l'eau froide. Chauffer la crème fluide n° 1. Infuser le café moulu 2 min dans la crème. Chinoiser. Rectifier le poids de crème. Ajouter la gélatine, la crème froide liquide n° 2. Réserver au frais. Environ 12 h plus tard monter la crème en chantilly avec le sucre. Réserver au frais.

Le glaçage café

Hydrater la feuille de gélatine dans un bol d'eau froide. Faire bouillir la crème. Hors du feu ajouter la gélatine essorée. Verser la crème sur le chocolat. Ajouter le café. Mélanger à l'aide d'une Maryse. Verser le nappage à une température entre 70° C et 80° C sur l'appareil précédent. Mélanger. Chinoiser. Mixer. Utiliser le glaçage café à une température de 35° C.

Le glaçage ivoire

Utiliser le même procédé que pour le glaçage au café sans ajouter le café.

Montage et finition

Sortir la crème mousseline du réfrigérateur. Dans la cuve du batteur, battre la mousseline pour la rendre plus souple. La placer dans une poche à douille. Dans deux cercles de 2 cm de haut et 16 cm de diamètre, faire un cordon de crème mousseline café, poser le biscuit croustillant. Puis recouvrir de mousseline des bords jusqu'au centre, poser l'insert de crème brûlée à l'eau de fleur d'oranger en prenant soin de bien appuyer. Lisser avec la crème mousseline café. Surgeler la préparation pour environ 6 h. Pour l'autre partie du montage : sortir la crème chantilly au café du réfrigérateur. À l'aide d'un fouet monter la crème. Placer jusqu'à mi-hauteur des deux cercles de 16 cm la crème chantilly. Imbiber les biscuits à la cuillère avec l'expresso, les insérer en milieu de montage sur la chantilly. Ajouter la chantilly jusqu'en haut du cercle. Lisser à l'aide d'une spatule coudée. Surgeler la préparation pour 2 h au minimum. Décercler les cercles de mousseline au café. Floquer ces deux cercles avec le glaçage couleur café. Réserver au frais sur votre plat de service. Décercler les cercles de chantilly. Glacer avec le glaçage Ivoire. Poser les disques sur chaque cercle de mousseline. Attendre 6 h avant de déguster que l'entremets soit décongelé.

PARIS-TENU !

FRANÇOIS DAUBINET

Un électron libre au service de l'époustouflant

Pour tous ses desserts, il s'inspire d'un art, au sens très large du terme (peintures, sculptures, graffs). Son Paris-Tenu naît d'une sculpture, et de cette sculpture est venue l'idée du Paris-Brest, en une création jamais vue et complètement intime à François. Noisettes et sésame noir, point de départ épatant, prennent le palais, les glandes salivaires et la gorge à la première moitié de cuillère. Orbitent autour une infinité de micro-choux, crunchy et biscuités, un cake noisette et sésame noir, un croustillant noisette, une ganache noisette, un praliné sésame noir et une bavaroise noisette. Un travail titanesque (et téméraire). François pousse les limites de la création, tout en taillant à la perfection l'équilibre des goûts. Scotchant dans les deux. Un gâteau itinérant, proposé aux tea time *éphémères du chef, bientôt à Paris. Avant d'être chez lui, l'année prochaine…*

POUR 8 PERSONNES

Temps de préparation : 4 h • Temps de cuisson : 44 min environ • Temps de réfrigération : 4 h 20

INGRÉDIENTS

L'appareil du cake à la noisette

22,5 g de poudre de noisettes brute
11,2 g de cassonade
7,5 g de sucre muscovado
8 g de sucre glace
6,5 g de blancs d'œufs n° 1
1 g de sésame noir
7,5 g de jaunes d'œufs
10 g de farine type 55
1 g de levure chimique
0,1 g de sel fin
21,5 g de beurre noisette
25 g de blancs d'œufs n° 2
3,5 g de sucre semoule

Le sirop d'imbibage citron

60 g d'eau
60 g de sucre semoule
1 citron jaune

Le praliné au sésame noir

120 g de sésame noir Umami
80 g de sucre semoule
0,2 g de fleur de sel

Le croustillant praliné

20 g de beurre doux
20 g de sucre glace tamisé
24 g de Maïzena®
11 g de poudre d'amandes brute
0,4 g de sel fin
20 g de riz soufflé
5 g d'amandes hachées torréfiées
20 g de chocolat de couverture Opalys de Valrhona
25 g de pâte de noisettes

La ganache noisette

112,5 g de lait entier
12,5 g de crème liquide à 35 % de MG
0,5 g de sel fin
½ gousse de vanille
75 g de gianduja lait et noisette
75 g de pâte de noisettes

L'enrobage lacté et noisette

60 g de beurre de cacao
60 g de chocolat de couverture Jivara à 40 % de cacao de Valrhona
15 g de noisettes hachées et torréfiées

La bavaroise pralinée et noisette

2 g de gélatine de poisson en poudre
100 g de crème liquide à 35 % de MG
120 g de praliné noisette maison
150 g de crème montée souple

La pâte à choux

125 g de lait entier
125 g d'eau
115 g de beurre
5 g de sel fin
5 g de sucre semoule
140 g de farine type 55
250 g d'œufs entiers

Le glaçage au chocolat

9 g de gélatine de poisson en poudre
110 g d'eau
150 g de glucose
150 g de sucre semoule
100 g de lait concentré sucré
180 g de chocolat de couverture Andoa noir à 75 % de cacao de Valrhona
25 g d'huile de pépins de raisin

PARIS-TENU !

FRANÇOIS DAUBINET

RÉALISATION

L'appareil du cake à la noisette

Dans un robot coupe, mixer ensemble la poudre de noisettes, les sucres, les blancs d'œufs n° 1, le sésame noir, les jaunes d'œufs, la farine, la levure chimique et le sel. Ajouter le beurre noisette, homogénéiser. Monter les blancs d'œufs n° 2, en serrant progressivement avec le sucre semoule. Mélanger les deux masses délicatement à l'aide d'une Maryse. Mouler en demi-sphères de 3 cm. Enfourner à 165° C pour 13 min. À la sortie du four, démouler puis laisser tiédir sur une grille.

Le sirop d'imbibage citron

Porter l'eau et le sucre semoule à ébullition. Ajouter les zestes et le jus du citron. Imbiber les cakes tièdes dans le sirop tiède à une température d'environ 45° C.

Le praliné au sésame noir

Torréfier le sésame noir sur une plaque avec une toile en silicone de 8 mn à 160° C. Réaliser un caramel à sec. Pour cela, mettre le sucre dans une casserole sur feu doux et laisser caraméliser. Une fois que vous obtenez une couleur brun clair, ajouter la fleur de sel et verser sur le sésame. Refroidir à température ambiante. Mixer dans un robot coupe afin d'obtenir une pâte de praliné homogène. Attention : si votre appareil mixeur n'a pas assez de puissance, il risque de surchauffer.

Le croustillant praliné

Réaliser une pâte sucrée. Pour cela, placer dans la cuve d'un robot munie de la feuille ou dans un saladier le beurre mou le sucre glace. Crémer le mélange. Ajouter la Maïzena®, la poudre d'amandes et le sel. Une fois que le mélange est homogène, l'étaler à l'aide d'un rouleau à pâtisserie. Placer sur une plaque de cuisson avec une feuille de papier sulfurisé. Enfourner à 165° C pour 16 min. Laisser refroidir sur une grille. Hacher finement la pâte sucrée refroidie, ajouter le riz soufflé puis les amandes hachées. Mélanger. Faire fondre le chocolat de couverture Opalys, ajouter la pâte de noisettes et homogénéiser. Mélanger les deux masses et éparpiller sur une plaque, passer au froid pendant environ 20 min. Reprendre la masse une fois refroidie. La hacher grossièrement au couteau.

La ganache noisette

Porter le lait, la crème, le sel et la vanille à 85° C. Verser en plusieurs fois sur le gianduja haché finement et la pâte de noisettes afin de réaliser une belle émulsion, mixer pour parfaire celle-ci. Couler en demi-sphères de 3 cm et recouvrir de croustillant praliné haché. Placer au congélateur pour 4 h au minimum. Réserver au frais le restant de ganache pour la finition.

L'enrobage lacté et noisette

Fondre le beurre de cacao, ajouter le chocolat de couverture. Faire fondre l'ensemble à 45° C. Ajouter les noisettes hachées. Enrober l'insert de ganache noisette. Réserver.

La bavaroise pralinée et noisette

Mettre la poudre de gélatine dans l'eau. Porter la crème à 80° C, ajouter la gélatine réhydratée. Verser en plusieurs fois sur le praliné et réaliser une belle émulsion, mixer pour parfaire celle-ci. À 30° C, ajouter la crème montée. Mouler en moule sphérique. Réserver au réfrigérateur.

La pâte à choux

Porter le lait, l'eau, le beurre, le sel et le sucre semoule à ébullition. Hors du feu, ajouter la farine tamisée. Dessécher la panade sur le feu pendant 1 min. Verser la masse dans la cuve du batteur, ajouter très progressivement les œufs jusqu'à incorporation complète. Dresser de tout petits choux de 3 tailles différentes à l'aide d'une douille unie n° 3. Enfourner à 185° C de 10 à 15 min selon le four.

Le glaçage au chocolat

Réhydrater la poudre de gélatine dans de l'eau froide. Cuire l'eau, le glucose et le sucre semoule à 102° C. Ajouter la gélatine réhydratée, puis le lait concentré sucré. Verser sur le chocolat de couverture hachée et l'huile. Réaliser une émulsion, en mélangeant à l'aide d'une spatule. Mixer à l'aide d'un mixeur plongeant pour parfaire celle-ci. Attention de ne pas incorporer trop d'air. Réserver au frais. Utiliser le glaçage à une température de 40° C.

Montage et finition

Créer un insert de forme sphérique de 3,5 cm avec les éléments cités ci-dessus.

Partie inférieure, le cake imbibé, le praliné sésame noir. Partie supérieure, la ganache noisette, le croustillant praliné noisette. Déposer cet insert congelé dans la bavaroise pralinée et noisette, refermer avec la bavaroise pour former une sphère de 5 cm. Isoler les choux à l'aide de beurre de cacao. Déposer harmonieusement et un à un les petits choux de tailles différentes sur toute la sphère en les collant grâce au restant de ganache noisette. Enfin, glacer votre dessert avec le glaçage au chocolat.

ALI BABA

SÉBASTIEN DÉGARDIN

« On a rien inventé, juste un peu évolué »

Sébastien Dégardin aime la pâtisserie pour ce qu'elle est, pas pour ce qu'il en a fait. En immense modeste qu'il est, il considère que les dernières réelles créations remontent à la pâte à choux et au feuilletage, et que depuis, les pâtissiers travaillent autour de cela. Dans son cas, l'exercice vaut le détour, Sébastien signant des gâteaux d'une justesse et d'une gourmandise inouïes. Au sein même de son métier, il hiérarchise les envies. Pour une petite pulsion, une tarte aux pommes ou un éclair au chocolat. Pour un dîner entre amis, un panel de différents gâteaux, pour un dimanche en famille, un gros Paris-Brest ou un saint-honoré à partager. Le baba est à part. Celui de Sébastien, totalement dodu, est très malin. Au fond du contenant, un sabayon à la vanille, qui petit à petit récupère les effluves d'agrumes, vanille du gâteau très imbibé, au-dessus, un océan de moelleux et en ultime accessoire, une petite pipette de rhum, à doser. Et re-doser.

POUR : ENVIRON 10 BABAS

Temps de préparation : 1 h 30 • Temps de cuisson : 26 min • Temps de réfrigération/repos : 31 h

INGRÉDIENTS

La pâte à baba

20 g de raisins secs noirs de Smyrne
20 g de levure de boulanger
250 g de farine de gruau
62 g de beurre sec
10 g de sucre semoule
5 g de fleur de sel
175 g d'œufs
100 g d'eau
Quantité suffisante de beurre pommade

Le sirop d'imbibage

2 citrons jaunes
½ orange
750 g de sucre semoule
½ gousse de vanille
1500 g d'eau
Quantité suffisante de rhum

La crème légère à la vanille

180 g d'eau
100 g de sucre semoule
¼ de gousse de vanille
200 g de crème liquide à 35 % de MG
3,5 g feuilles de gélatine
45 g de jaunes d'œufs
3,5 g d'extrait de vanille

Le nappage à l'abricot

125 g de nappage abricotine
25 g eau

Montage et finitions

Quantité suffisante d'abricotine
Quantité suffisante de rhum
Quantité suffisante de pipettes en plastique

RÉALISATION

La pâte du baba

Hacher grossièrement au couteau les raisins. Mettre la levure de boulanger dans l'eau. Mélanger dans la cuve d'un batteur munie de la feuille, la farine et le beurre. Une fois que le mélange est sableux, ajouter la levure. Mélanger. Ajouter le sucre, le sel et les œufs un à un. Mélanger jusqu'à ce que la pâte soit homogène et brillante. Ajouter les raisins et laisser encore pétrir 3 min. Laisser la pâte lever entre 25 °C et 29 °C pendant environ 30 min puis dégazer la pâte. Pour cela, la mélanger rapidement afin que le gaz carbonique produit par la levure s'échappe. Mettre ensuite la préparation dans une poche à douille et garnir vos moules à savarins, préalablement graissés avec du beurre, de la préparation. Laisser pousser 30 min dans un endroit entre 25 °C et 30 °C. Une fois que la pâte a bien levé, enfourner à 180 °C pour environ 20 min. Retirer les babas de chaque moule. Les placer sur une grille et finir la cuisson 6 min à 180 °C de manière à ce que la cuisson soit uniforme. Après cuisson, débarrasser sur une grille froide et laisser sécher 1 nuit dans un endroit sec.

Le sirop d'imbibage

Prélever les peaux des agrumes à l'aide d'un Économe. Mélanger le sucre avec la vanille et les peaux des agrumes. Porter à ébullition la totalité des ingrédients sauf le rhum. Filmer et laisser macérer le sirop 24 h. Le lendemain, chinoiser le sirop à l'aide d'un chinois étamine. Porter à ébullition le sirop, poser les babas sur le sirop et les laisser s'imbiber généreusement. Poser sur une grille afin qu'ils s'égouttent. Arroser les babas avec le rhum.

La crème légère à la vanille

Faire un sirop. Pour cela, porter à ébullition l'eau et le sucre. Réserver. Gratter la gousse de vanille et l'ajouter à la crème. Laisser infuser 6 h minimum. Une fois que la crème est bien froide, enlever la gousse de vanille. Monter la crème au batteur à l'aide d'un fouet. Lorsque la crème tient sur le fouet du batteur, elle est prête. Réserver au réfrigérateur. Mettre à tremper la gélatine dans de l'eau glacée, réserver au froid. Mélanger les jaunes avec le sirop et l'extrait de vanille. Réchauffer l'ensemble au four à micro-ondes à faible puissance. Chinoiser. Réaliser une pâte à bombe. Pour cela, monter le mélange au batteur. Il doit blanchir et doubler de volume. Faire fondre la gélatine au bain-marie. Ajouter la gélatine dans la pâte à bombe. Ajouter un peu de crème, la crème montée et mélanger délicatement. Réserver jusqu'au montage.

Le nappage à l'abricot

Fondre le nappage avec l'eau et porter à ébullition. Réserver.

Montage et finition

Retourner les savarins et les napper avec le nappage abricot. Pocher dans des caissettes la crème légère à la vanille et poser les savarins dessus. Enfin, piquer dans le baba une pipette remplie de rhum.

LA TROPÉZIENNE

LAURENT FAVRE-MOT

Un peu de Marseille à Paris

Originaire du Var, Laurent n'a jamais réussi à trouver un gâteau plus préféré que la tropézienne. Elle regroupe ses deux lubies, la crème et la brioche, légères quand bien faites. Sa version barbotte dans la tradition, avec quand même une fantaisie notable sur la crème, assemblage de crème anglaise, de mascarpone, de chantilly et de vanille, le tout à peine sucré, un rôle qu'il préfère laisser aux grains de sucre qui croquent et crissent sur le sommet de la brioche. L'ensemble est lacté, fluide et aérien, et se passe allègrement d'eau de fleur d'oranger. Se fait simplement zester la peau d'une orange pour « pepser » le sirop de sucre dans lequel la brioche est « punchée ». La tropézienne se prend à deux mains, comme un sandwich, et se croque. Débarque pour l'hiver la copine au chocolat au lait, crème pralinée et noisettes caramélisées. Vivement le grand froid.

POUR 6 À 8 PERSONNES

Temps de préparation : 1 h • Temps de repos : 12 h • Temps de cuisson : 20 à 30 min

INGRÉDIENTS

La brioche
350 g de farine type 45
8 g de sel
45 g de sucre semoule
12 g de levure fraîche
5 œufs
220 g de beurre (à température ambiante)
Quantité suffisante de perles en sucre

La crème pâtissière Madame
La crème pâtissière
1 feuille de gélatine
2 gousses de vanille
250 g de lait entier
80 g de jaunes d'œufs
40 g de sucre semoule
15 g de fécule
La crème montée
200 g de crème liquide à 35 % de MG

RÉALISATION

La brioche

Placer la farine, le sel, le sucre, la levure et 4 œufs dans la cuve d'un batteur avec le crochet. Laisser pétrir pendant 10 min. Ajouter le beurre coupé en dés. Laisser pétrir pendant 7 min. Débarrasser dans un saladier. Filmer et réserver cette préparation 1 nuit au frais. Le lendemain, façonner la brioche afin qu'elle prenne la forme d'une boule. Laisser pousser 2 h à température ambiante. Battre le dernier œuf en omelette. À la fin du temps de pousse, lorsque la pâte a pris un peu de volume, étaler délicatement l'œuf à l'aide d'un pinceau sur le dessus de la brioche. Ajouter des perles de sucre. Enfourner à 170 °C pour 20 à 30 min de cuisson. À la sortie du four, laisser la brioche refroidir sur une grille.

La crème pâtissière Madame

La crème pâtissière

Placer la feuille de gélatine dans un bol d'eau froide. Fendre les gousses de vanille en deux, récupérer les graines. Mettre le lait avec les graines de vanille dans une casserole. Porter le tout à ébullition. Pendant ce temps, mettre les jaunes d'œufs dans un saladier, ajouter le sucre et la fécule. Battre la préparation à l'aide d'un fouet jusqu'à ce que celle-ci blanchisse. Une fois que le lait bout, le verser sur la préparation précédente. Retirer les gousses de vanille. Mélanger. Replacer la crème dans la casserole. Remettre le tout sur feu doux. Faire cuire en remuant constamment jusqu'à ce que la préparation épaississe. Débarrasser la crème dans un plat à gratin. Filmer au contact. Placer au frais pour minimum 2 h.

La crème montée

Placer la crème dans la cuve d'un batteur munie d'un fouet. Fouetter la préparation jusqu'à ce que la crème fouettée soit ferme. Débarrasser la préparation dans un bol. Placer la crème pâtissière froide dans la cuve de votre robot. Fouetter la préparation afin que le mélange devienne lisse. Ajouter la crème montée. Mélanger.

Montage et finition

Découper la brioche dans le sens de la longueur à l'aide d'un couteau scie. Mettre la crème pâtissière Madame dans une poche munie d'une douille lisse et ronde de 10 mm. Pocher de jolies boules de crème sur toute la moitié de la brioche, recouvrir avec le chapeau. Servir.

100 % NORMANDE

JEAN-FRANÇOIS FOUCHER

« Quand tous les produits viennent de la même région, ça s'accorde forcément »

Lorsqu'il vivait à Paris, Jean-François Foucher avait une maison en Normandie, avec un verger. À ce verger, il a eu envie d'offrir une pâtisserie, qui respecterait les saisons, la nature et les marchés : « Les cuisiniers l'ont compris depuis bien longtemps, qu'il fallait laisser décider les saisons. » En Normandie, pas besoin de se déplacer beaucoup pour faire un gâteau : les œufs, le lait, la crème, les pommes, la farine sont tous dans le même coin. Dans ce gâteau tacheté, on retrouve tous les codes de la pâtisserie normande, celle que Jean-François incarne. En un tube moderne et connoté vache, il réalise une sorte d'hybride entre la Tatin et le tiramisu. Ce gâteau se mange à l'assiette, couteau-fourchette, et à la première bouchée, c'est la crème – la vraie de vraie – qui s'impose, au bon goût de vache, acide et grasse, complètement divine et irremplaçable. Viennent ensuite les pommes à cidre, âpres et corsées, puis le sablé normand, rond, beurré, câlinant. Un gâteau qui sent bon la Normandie.

POUR 15 100 % NORMANDE

Temps de cuisson : 7 min • Temps de préparation : 1 h 30 • Temps de réfrigération : 30 h

INGRÉDIENTS

La marmelade de pommes
1 kg de pommes à cidre
200 g de sucre semoule n° 1
1 gousse de vanille
200 g de cidre
12 g d'agar-agar
20 g de sucre semoule n° 2

La crème
350 g de crème liquide à 35 % de MG
105 g de jaunes d'œufs
195 g de sucre semoule
73 g d'eau
10 g de gélatine en feuille
350 g de crème épaisse d'Isigny

Le sablé
400 g de beurre
1 kg de farine
150 g de fécule de pommes de terre
150 g de poudre d'amandes
25 g de sel
5 jaunes d'œufs

Montage et finition
Chocolat blanc

RÉALISATION

La marmelade de pommes

Peler et épépiner les pommes. Les couper en brunoise. Faire un sucre à sec avec de la vanille. Pour cela, mettre le sucre n° 1 et la vanille à chauffer dans une poêle. Déglacer avec le cidre. Cuire les pommes dans une étuve pendant 14 min. Mélanger l'agar-agar et le sucre n° 2. Incorporer ce mélange à la marmelade de pommes. Porter la marmelade à une température de 80° C. Débarrasser dans un cercle de 1 cm de haut et de 30 cm de diamètre. Réserver au frais.

La crème

Mettre la crème liquide dans la cuve d'un batteur. Fouetter jusqu'à ce que la crème soit montée. Réserver au frais. Mettre les jaunes, le sucre et l'eau dans une casserole. Fouetter l'ensemble jusqu'à ce que le mélange soit blanchi. Cuire sur feu doux en remuant sans cesse jusqu'à ébullition. Ajouter la gélatine préalablement ramollie dans de l'eau froide. Ajouter la crème épaisse, puis la crème montée. Réserver au frais.

Le sablé

Sabler le beurre avec la farine, la fécule, la poudre d'amandes et le sel. Ajouter les jaunes d'œufs. Réserver au froid 24 h. Détailler des rectangles de 10 cm x 1 cm sur une épaisseur de 2 mm. Cuire à 180° C pendant 7 min.

Montage et finition

Dans un tube de 3 cm de diamètre sur 10 cm de haut, disposer la crème avec une poche à douille puis la marmelade de pommes et enfin le sablé. Réserver au grand froid pendant 6 h. Démouler le tube et l'enrouler à l'intérieur d'un Rhodoïd imprimé « vache » grâce à du chocolat blanc. Réserver au réfrigérateur pendant 20 min et enlever le Rhodoïd.

L'OPÉRETTE

MARJORIE FOURCADE ET SAORI ODOI (FOUCADE)

Une pâtisserie saine et gourmande à la fois, lunaire parfois

Foucade est né d'une irrépressible envie de concilier sain et gourmand. Marjorie Fourcade, intolérante au blé et au lactose, n'a pas prévu de se contenter de fruits et de barres de céréales, et crée ce qui n'existait pas, une pâtisserie healthy *et bonne. Tout est frais, jusqu'aux pralinés et purées de fruits. L'opérette, version Foucade de l'opéra, est faite avec un chocolat récolté en biodynamie. À la dégustation, il ne faut pas décortiquer, mais bien prendre toutes les couches dans chaque cuillère, sans jamais isoler, sinon ce serait trop poivré ou trop fade ou trop fort, et seul le tout est harmonieux. L'opérette est puissante et douce à la fois.*

POUR 4 PERSONNES

Temps de préparation : 2 h 30 • Temps de cuisson : 24 min • Temps de réfrigération : 5 h

INGRÉDIENTS

Le crumble au chocolat

44 g de poudre d'amandes brute
1 g de farine de riz complet
30 g de sel non raffiné
12 g de cacao cru
22 g de sucre rapadura
15 g d'huile de colza extra-vierge première pression à froid
15 g de boisson de riz complet

Le croustillant

71 g de crumble cacao cru
36 g de chocolat de couverture cru à 70 % de cacao

Le biscuit au chocolat

34 g de jaunes d'œufs
16 g de sucre rapadura
72 g de blancs d'œufs
7 g de poudre de cacao cru

La chantilly au chocolat

145 g de crème minus L (sans lactose) à chauffer
89 g de chocolat de couverture cru à 70 % de cacao
11 g de chocolat de couverture cru à 100 % de cacao
218 g de crème minus L (sans lactose) froide

Le décor

200 g de chocolat de couverture cru à 70 % de cacao

Le sirop au chocolat

41 g d'eau
6 g de poudre de cacao cru
4 g de sucre rapadura

RÉALISATION

Le crumble au chocolat

Mélanger la poudre d'amandes, la farine de riz, le sel, le cacao en poudre et le sucre rapadura dans un cul-de-poule. Ajouter l'huile de colza puis mélanger à la main. Ajouter la boisson de riz et mélanger rapidement à la main. Étaler sur une feuille guitare sur une épaisseur de 7 cm pour faire le décor. Avec le reste, faire des miettes avec la pâte obtenue sur un papier cuisson qui serviront à faire la base du croustillant chocolat. Cuire au four à 160° C de 12 à 15 min. Passer au congélateur le décor pour le refroidir et ainsi le couper facilement. Découper des pièces de 1 cm x 1 cm pour en mettre 4 par portion individuelle.

Le croustillant

Broyer le crumble chocolat. Faire fondre le chocolat de couverture. Mélanger les deux à l'aide d'une Maryse. À l'aide d'une spatule coudée, étaler le croustillant au chocolat dans un cadre.

Le biscuit au chocolat

Monter les jaunes d'œufs avec la moitié du sucre rapadura au batteur avec un fouet. Monter les blancs d'œufs avec le reste de sucre rapadura. Mettre un peu de blancs d'œufs dans l'appareil avec les jaunes d'œufs puis mélanger au fouet. Remettre le mélange précédent dans les blancs d'œufs montés et mélanger à l'aide d'une Maryse. Ajouter le cacao cru en poudre et mélanger. Étaler sur une plaque de cuisson recouverte de papier cuisson à l'aide d'une palette coudée. Cuire au four à 190° C de 10 à 12 min. Une fois cuit, mettre le biscuit sur une grille.

La chantilly au chocolat

Chauffer la crème minus L dans une casserole. Faire fondre les chocolats de couverture avec la crème chaude. Mixer, incorporer la crème froide puis mixer tout ensemble. Réserver 5 h au minimum au frais. Mettre 165 g de chaque couche dans un cadre de 14 cm x 14 cm.

Le décor

Faire fondre le chocolat à 45° C puis laisser froidir jusqu'à 29° C. Remonter la température du chocolat jusqu'à 31-32° C. Étaler sur une feuille guitare. Couper en carrés de 5 cm x 5 cm pour les individuelles, de 3 cm x 3 cm pour les petits fours. Mettre le papier cuisson et les plaques sur les chocolats coupés.

Le sirop au chocolat

Porter tous les ingrédients dans une casserole à ébullition.

Montage et finition

Étaler sur une feuille guitare dans un cadre, le croustillant chocolat à l'aide d'une palette coudée. Monter la chantilly chocolat mousseuse, puis peser deux fois 165 g de chantilly. Étaler un peu de chantilly chocolat sur le croustillant. Détailler les biscuits en carrés de 14 cm x 14 cm. Poser un premier biscuit chocolat dans le cadre et l'imbiber de 25 g de sirop chocolat. Couler 165 g de chantilly chocolat dans un cadre et étaler à l'aide d'une spatule coudée. Poser le deuxième biscuit chocolat et renouveler l'opération. Stocker au réfrigérateur jusqu'à ce qu'il soit dur. Couper des portions individuelles ou des petits fours à l'aide d'un couteau chaud. Vous aurez environ 4 pièces individuelles et quelques pièces cocktails. Pour finir poser 4 petits carrés de crumble chocolat sur le dessus et déposer le décor chocolat en le collant avec un peu de chantilly chocolat.

TARTE CITRON & BASILIC

JACQUES GÉNIN

Jacques est à la pâtisserie ce que la petite robe noire est à la mode

Une béarnaise. Voilà ce qu'elle est, cette tarte, une béarnaise, et c'est bien pour cette raison qu'elle restera à vie l'amour sans faille de Jacques Génin. Une infusion de basilic dans une crème anglaise, le tout lié au beurre. Un peu comme un gâteau qui n'en serait pas un, le comble pour un cuisinier qui a fait des gâteaux sa vie. En dehors de cette recette, il n'aime pas la tarte citron, qu'il trouve trop lourde, trop acidulée, « comme un bonbon Krema ». La sienne est simplement acide, d'où le citron absolument vert, frais et parfumé. Le basilic camphré en rajoute une couche, il fait respirer ta tarte. L'acidité du citron s'exprime en premier, puis le craquant de la pâte et en dernier viennent le basilic et le beurre, comme une caresse toute douce.

La tarte une fois montée ne tient pas sur ses pattes, elle est toujours à la limite de craquer, dégouline à la coupe et se brise sous la cuillère. La tarte citron de Jacques Génin est fragile, complètement parfaite.

POUR 10 À 12 PERSONNES

Temps de préparation : 1 h 30 • Temps de cuisson : 20 min • Temps de réfrigération : 4 h 30

INGRÉDIENTS

La pâte (quantité volontairement supérieure)

125 g de sucre glace
30 g de poudre d'amandes
175 g de beurre à température ambiante
½ gousse de vanille
60 g d'œufs
2 g de sel
310 g de farine de gruau type 45

La crème citron basilic (quantité volontairement supérieure)

20 g de basilic
3 œufs
170 g de sucre semoule
180 g de jus de citron vert (6 à 10 citrons)
200 g de beurre doux
Le zeste de 3 citrons verts

RÉALISATION

La pâte

Placer dans la cuve d'un robot : le sucre, la poudre d'amandes, le beurre en cubes et la vanille. Mélanger à l'aide de la feuille. Ajouter les œufs. Mélanger de nouveau. Ajouter le sel et la farine. Mélanger. Placer la pâte entre deux feuilles de papier sulfurisé. Aplatir à l'aide d'un rouleau à pâtisserie la pâte sur une épaisseur de 0,5 cm. Réserver ainsi au frais pour 1 h 30. Prendre un cercle de 26 cm de diamètre. Beurrer le cercle. Foncer la pâte. Piquer la pâte à l'aide d'une fourchette et placer des poids de cuisson sur la pâte pour éviter qu'elle ne gonfle. Enfourner à 160 °C de 16 à 20 min. Astuce : afin d'avoir une cuisson uniforme, retirer le cercle vers la 13e min de cuisson.

La crème citron basilic

Ciseler les feuilles de basilic dans une casserole. Ajouter les œufs et le sucre. Mélanger. Ajouter le jus de citron. Cuire sur feu doux sans cesser de remuer. La crème doit épaissir. Aux premiers frémissements, bien avant ébullition, la retirer du feu. Filtrer la préparation à l'aide d'un chinois et d'une Maryse. Laisser l'appareil reposer jusqu'à ce que la température soit entre 45 °C et 50 °C. Incorporer le beurre coupé en dés. Émulsionner à l'aide d'un mixeur plongeant. Réserver la crème 3 h au réfrigérateur. Une fois qu'elle a la consistance d'un beurre pommade, garnir le fond de tarte à l'aide d'une spatule afin de lisser le dessus. Enfin, avec un zesteur (astuce : celui de la marque Microplane vous apportera des zestes très fins en un temps record), râper des zestes de citrons verts sur toute la surface de la tarte. Réserver la tarte au frais avant dégustation.

CARACAJOU

GUILLAUME GIL (COLOROVA)

« J'ai pas envie de réfléchir, je fais les gâteaux comme je les sens »

Pâtissier de formation, Guillaume Gil a quand même fait de la cuisine son quotidien chez Colorova, en plus de jouer à un jeu qu'il n'adore pas... Celui de la pâtisserie boutique. Pour contrer sa hantise des pâtisseries pâtissières, Guillaume cuisine chaque jour des gâteaux construits sur les goûts, pas trop nombreux et reconnaissables. Si certains sont graphiques, c'est non intentionnel, et plus le temps passe, plus Guillaume se détache de l'intellect, de la forme, des fioritures. À la question : « Que se passe-t-il à la première bouchée ? », Guillaume répond « C'est bon ! Le reste on s'en fiche. » La caracajou, construction parfaitement équilibrée autour du caramel, de la nougatine aux noix de cajou, du crémeux au chocolat lacté et de la mousse chantilly caramel, est à déguster silencieusement...

POUR ENVIRON 15 TARTELETTES

Temps de préparation : 3 h • Temps de repos : 37 h • Temps de cuisson : 20 à 27 min

INGRÉDIENTS

La pâte sucrée
125 g de beurre
125 g de sucre semoule
90 g d'œufs entiers
315 g de farine
3,5 g de levure

Le caramel à la noix de cajou
100 g de sucre semoule
50 g de glucose
200 g de crème liquide
50 g de beurre demi-sel
150 g de noix de cajou salées

La nougatine à la noix de cajou
150 g de sucre roux
150 g de glucose
150 g de beurre
150 de g noix de cajou en poudre

Le crémeux à la noix de cajou
50 g de jaunes d'œufs
25 g de sucre semoule
125 g de crème liquide
125 g de lait
150 g de chocolat lacté caramel Cacao Barry
1 feuille de gélatine
50 g de noix de cajou en poudre

La mousse de caramel
40 g de glucose
95 g de sucre semoule
80 g de crème liquide à 35 % de MG n° 1
1,5 feuille de gélatine
175 g de crème liquide à 35 % de MG n° 2
25 g de beurre demi-sel
40 g de jaunes d'œufs

Le glaçage
50 g de glucose
50 g de sucre semoule
80 g de crème liquide
180 g d'eau
60 g de chocolat lacté caramel de Cacao Barry
60 g de chocolat blanc Ivoire de Valrhona
1,5 feuille de gélatine

La chantilly
50 g de sucre semoule
250 g de crème liquide chaude
1 gousse de vanille
250 g de chocolat blanc
250 g de crème liquide froide

Montage et finition
Caramel
Noix de cajou

RÉALISATION

La pate sucrée

Mettre le beurre pommade et le sucre dans la cuve du batteur avec la feuille. Une fois que le mélange devient crémeux et homogène, ajouter les œufs. Lorsque la masse est une nouvelle fois homogène, ajouter la farine et la levure chimique tamisées. Dès que la préparation forme une boule, filmer au contact et laisser au frais 12 h.

Le lendemain, abaisser puis foncer la pâte dans des cercles à tarte. Astuce : si la pâte est trop friable, l'abaisser entre deux feuilles de papier sulfurisé. La replacer au frais pour une vingtaine de minutes. Enlever délicatement les feuilles et procéder au fonçage. Piquer la pate à l'aide d'une fourchette et placer des poids de cuisson sur la pâte pour éviter qu'elle ne gonfle. Préchauffer le four à 180 °C. Enfourner pour environ 12 min.

Pour le caramel à la noix de cajou

Mettre le sucre et le glucose dans une casserole sur feu moyen jusqu'à ce que le caramel prenne une jolie couleur brune. Déglacer avec la crème chaude et le beurre, poursuivre la cuisson. Dès que la masse devient homogène, passer le caramel au chinois puis le verser sur les noix de cajou concassées. Réserver.

La nougatine à la noix de cajou

Mettre le sucre et le glucose dans une casserole sur feu doux. Lorsque le mélange commence à fondre, ajouter le beurre en trois fois. Une fois le mélange homogène, ajouter les noix de cajou. Étaler le mélange entre deux feuilles de papiers sulfurisé. Enfourner à 180 °C entre 10 et 12 min. Détailler des disques avec un emporte-pièce rond d'un diamètre de 60 mm.

CARACAJOU

GUILLAUME GIL (COLOROVA)

Le crémeux à la noix de cajou

Faire une crème anglaise avec les jaunes, le sucre, la crème et le lait. Une fois que le mélange atteint 80 °C, le verser sur le chocolat concassé. Ajouter la gélatine et les noix de cajou. Mixer à l'aide d'un mixeur plongeant. Débarrasser en barquette et réserver au frais.

La mousse de caramel

Mettre 55 g de sucre et le glucose dans une casserole sur feu moyen jusqu'à ce que le mélange prenne une jolie couleur brune. Déglacer avec la crème chaude n° 1. Attention : il est important que la crème soit chaude afin d'éviter un choc thermique et donc des projections bouillantes. Incorporer le beurre puis la gélatine entre 25 °C et 30 °C.

Monter la crème n° 2 au batteur. Attention, elle doit rester mousseuse.

Mettre le sucre restant dans une casserole. Ajouter de l'eau de façon à simplement humidifier tout le sucre. Cuire le sucre jusqu'à 120 °C. Verser sur les jaunes en fouettant. Une fois que la préparation a blanchi, mélanger les deux préparations. Mouler rapidement avant que la mousse ne fige dans un moule en forme de palet de 60 mm de diamètre. Placer au congélateur pour 12 h.

Le glaçage

Cuire le glucose et le sucre au caramel brun. Déglacer avec la crème chaude et l'eau chaude. Une fois que la masse est homogène ajouter les chocolats. Lorsque la masse a réduit de moitié, incorporer la gélatine.

La chantilly

Faire un caramel à sec avec le sucre. Déglacer avec la crème chaude. Ajouter la gousse de vanille grattée. Laisser reposer couvert d'un film plastique pendant 1 nuit au réfrigérateur. Le lendemain, réchauffer la préparation. Puis, ajouter la crème froide. Remettre une nuit au frais, le lendemain monter en chantilly.

Montage et finition

Garnir les fonds de tarte avec le caramel à la noix de cajou. Mettre le crémeux à la noix de cajou dans une poche munie d'une douille d'un diamètre de 4 mm. Pocher le crémeux en escargot sur la tartelette. Déposer délicatement sur chacune des tartelettes les disques de nougatine. Sortir un palet de mousse caramel puis le glacer avec le glaçage caramel préalablement fondu au bain-marie. Placer le palet sur la nougatine. Monter la chantilly caramel au batteur muni de la feuille ou à la main avec un fouet. Mettre dans une poche munie d'une douille ronde de 20 mm. Pocher une belle boule en montant la poche. Décorer avec quelques noix de cajoux et du caramel.

ÇHOUQUETTES À LA VANILLE

STÉPHANE GLACIER

Le chou « chouquette », un gâteau bon et dodu

Meilleur ouvrier de France, pâtissier ne rime pas toujours avec gâteaux frimeurs et brillants. Stéphane Glacier, issu d'un père coiffeur, est tombé dans les gâteaux par hasard, pour ne jamais les quitter : un ami grossiste l'emmène voir une démonstration de sucre tiré, il est complètement fasciné et se lance. Aux États-Unis, Pierre Hermé et Jacques Torres lui trouvent une place de chef pâtissier, il en rentre plein d'expérience et animé d'une envie d'ouvrir… seul. Amoureux de la pâtisserie traditionnelle, il fait du chou (pâte à son sens la plus difficile à réaliser) son gâteau signature, sans le décliner. Ce sera chou à la crème ou pas de chou du tout. Son secret ? Réaliser une pâte à choux ferme, cuite au four à chaleur tournante pour obtenir un beau chou très développé… et plein de crème (100 g par gâteau). Un gâteau qui se mange à l'assiette, couteau et fourchette en main. Ou alors avec les doigts pour la version plus traditionnelle de la chouquette vide.

POUR 12 CHOUX

Temps de préparation : 1 h • Temps de cuisson : 25 min • Temps de réfrigération : 6 h

INGRÉDIENTS

La pâte à choux
375 g d'eau
125 g de lait entier
5 g de sel
15 g de sucre semoule
200 g de beurre
300 g de farine type 55 ou 65
500 g d'œufs
Quantité suffisant de sucre en grains

La crème pâtissière
400 g de lait
½ gousse de vanille
100 g de sucre semoule
90 g de jaunes d'œufs
30 g de poudre à crème
30 g de beurre

La crème chantilly
375 g de crème liquide à 35% de MG
1 gousse de vanille
50 g de sucre semoule

La crème diplomate vanille
600 g de crème pâtissière
425 g de crème chantilly

Montage et finition
Quantité suffisante de sucre glace

PRÉPARATION

La pâte à choux

Porter à ébullition dans une casserole l'eau, le lait, le sel, le sucre et le beurre. Tamiser la farine. À ébullition, retirer du feu et incorporer la farine tout en remuant. Reporter sur feu doux pour dessécher le mélange jusqu'à ce que la pâte n'adhère plus aux parois de la casserole. Vider la casserole dans la cuve d'un batteur munie de la feuille. Ajouter les œufs graduellement. Dresser la pâte à choux à la douille lisse ou cannelée sur une plaque recouverte de papier cuisson. Parsemer de sucre en grains. Cuire à 160 °C pendant 25 min. À la sortie du four, débarrasser les chouquettes sur une grille.

La crème pâtissière

Faire bouillir le lait, la vanille et la moitié du sucre. Fouetter les jaunes d'œufs avec le reste de sucre jusqu'à ce que le mélange blanchisse. Mélanger au fouet la poudre à crème dans les jaunes et le sucre blanchis. Verser 1/3 du lait bouillant sur le mélange ci-dessus. Mélanger. Reverser le tout dans la casserole avec les 2/3 de lait restant. Porter à ébullition tout en remuant constamment. Après 2 min d'ébullition, ajouter le beurre. Mélanger. Verser dans un plat à gratin. Recouvrir d'un film plastique au contact. Réserver au frais.

La crème chantilly

Faire bouillir 1/3 de la crème avec la gousse de vanille fendue et grattée ainsi que le sucre. Ajouter le reste de crème. Réserver au réfrigérateur jusqu'au lendemain. Retirer la gousse. Placer la crème dans la cuve d'un batteur munie d'un fouet. Monter en chantilly.

La crème diplomate vanille

Lisser la crème pâtissière en la fouettant dans un saladier. Incorporer délicatement à l'aide d'une Maryse la crème chantilly.

Montage et finition

Lorsque les chouquettes sont refroidies, percer chaque chouquette. Mettre la crème diplomate à la vanille dans une poche munie d'une douille de 8 mm. Garnir chaque chou avec la crème. Saupoudrer de sucre glace.

TARTELETTE NOISETTE

CÉDRIC GROLET (LE MEURICE)

Roi de sa génération, plus qu'une vocation, une vibration

Cédric Grolet est de ceux que l'on aurait aimé inventer, eut-on été doté d'une imagination aussi débordante. Véritable tourbillon de talent, infatigable et habité, Cédric dessine son nom avec les fruits sculptés, et à l'arrivée de l'automne tombe la noisette de l'arbre puis de ses doigts. Il la voit comme sa plus belle réussite, personnelle et jamais vue, striée comme une pièce en chocolat, une vraie prouesse. À la dégustation, il faut la couper en quatre par le haut, pour bien avoir de tout à chaque bouchée. Craque en premier la pâte sucrée, puis coule le praliné noisette, débarque la fleur de sel et prolonge le torréfié de la noisette grâce à la pâte sucrée garnie de crème noisette avec peau. Un ensemble absolument magistral de puissance, décliné pour Noël en bûche noisette, et pour les rois en galette noisette, blindée de praliné...
Vivement demain, et tous les jours suivants.

POUR 10 TARTELETTES

Temps de préparation : 3 h • Temps de cuisson : 20 min • Temps de réfrigération : 16 h

INGRÉDIENTS

La pâte sucrée
75 g de beurre
50 g de sucre glace
15 g de poudre d'amandes
1 pincée de sel de Guérande
1 pincée de vanille en poudre
30 g d'œufs
125 g de farine type 55

La crème noisette (quantité volontairement supérieure)
75 g de beurre
75 g de sucre semoule
90 g de noisettes mixées
75 g d'œufs
10 g de noisettes concassées grossièrement

La ganache montée noisette (quantité volontairement supérieure)
17 g de masse de gélatine
125 g de lait
40 g de noisettes torréfiées
50 g de chocolat Ivoire
80 g de pâte de noisettes
215 g de crème

Le caramel onctueux (quantité volontairement supérieure)
20 g de crème
50 g de lait
50 g de glucose n°1
1 gousse de vanille
2 g de fleur de sel
95 g de sucre semoule
105 g de glucose n° 2
70 g de beurre

L'insert caramel (12 g par pièce)
115 g de caramel onctueux
15 g de lait

Le praliné noisette (quantité volontairement supérieure)
200 g de sucre semoule
60 g d'eau
300 g de noisettes
2 g de sel fin

L'enrobage lait (10 g par pièce)
100 g de beurre de cacao
100 g de couverture lait

Montage et finition
Quantité suffisante de poudre or

RÉALISATION

La pâte sucrée

Mélanger dans la cuve d'un batteur munie de la feuille le beurre, le sucre glace, la poudre d'amandes, le sel de Guérande et la vanille en poudre. Émulsionner avec les œufs, puis ajouter la farine. Laisser la pâte filmée pendant 1 h au frais. Étaler la pâte sur 2 mm d'épaisseur. Foncer des cercles légèrement beurrés de 2 cm de hauteur sur 5 cm de diamètre. Laisser « croûter » une journée en chambre froide.
Mettre des billes de cuisson dans les fonds de tarte pour éviter que la pâte ne gonfle pendant la cuisson. Enfourner à 160 °C entre 12 et 16 min.

La crème noisette

Monter au batteur avec la feuille le beurre avec le sucre et les noisettes mixées. Incorporer les œufs graduellement. Stocker en poche, garnir chaque fond de tartelette précuit de 8 g de crème. Parsemer de noisettes torréfiées concassées grossièrement. Enfourner à 170 °C entre 6 et 8 min.

TARTELETTE NOISETTE

CÉDRIC GROLET (LE MEURICE)

La ganache montée noisette

Gonfler la gélatine dans de l'eau froide. Chauffer le lait, ajouter les noisettes torréfiées, puis mixer et laisser infuser 20 min. Chinoiser et repeser le lait. Chauffer le lait infusé. Réaliser une émulsion sur le chocolat Ivoire fondu, puis ajouter la masse de gélatine fondue. Mixer. Ajouter la pâte de noisettes, et la crème. Mixer. Réserver 12 h minimum au frais.

Le caramel onctueux

Chauffer ensemble la crème, le lait, le glucose n° 1, la vanille et la fleur de sel. Cuire le sucre et le glucose n° 2 à 185 °C, puis déglacer avec la crème chauffée. Cuire à 105 °C, puis chinoiser. Ajouter le beurre lorsque le caramel atteint 70 °C. Mixer.

L'insert caramel

Mélanger ensemble les ingrédients. Mouler dans des moules demi-sphères de 4 cm de diamètre : couler 12 g par pièce. Congeler la préparation.

Le praliné noisette

Astuce : pas le temps de faire un praliné ? Valrhona vous propose un super praliné.

Cuire le sucre et l'eau à 110 °C. Ajouter les noisettes légèrement torréfiées. Remuer sans cesse à l'aide d'une spatule pour éviter que le fond ne brûle. Le mélange va devenir sableux, c'est le sucre qui cristallise suite au choc de température. Il faut poursuivre la cuisson et continuer de remuer jusqu'à obtention d'un caramel foncé. Ajouter le sel, puis débarrasser sur un Silpat. Laisser refroidir. Mixer au robot afin d'obtenir un praliné d'une texture craquante. Garnir des moules demi-sphères de 2,5 cm de diamètre avec environ 8 g de praliné. Congeler la préparation.

L'enrobage lait

Fondre les ingrédients ensemble, puis mixer.

Montage et finition

Monter la ganache noisette mousseuse, garnir des moules demi-sphères de 45 mm, ajouter l'insert au caramel puis lisser à hauteur. Mettre au surgélateur jusqu'à ce que la ganache soit prise. Réserver au frais le reste de ganache noisette. Démouler les demi-sphères puis les sculpter avec le reste de ganache noisette de façon à former une pointe. Chauffer l'enrobage lait à une température entre 45 °C et 50 °C. Tremper les demi-sphères sculptées dedans puis les rayer tout de suite après à l'aide d'une brosse métallique, finir en poudrant d'or la demi-sphère, déposer la demi-sphère sur un Rhodoïd graissé. Prendre les fonds de tartes cuites et garnies de crème d'amande. Lisser à hauteur avec le caramel onctueux. Déposer la demi-sphère sculptée, finir par des brisures de noisette tout autour.

PARIS-BREST

OLIVIER HAUSTRAETE (BOULANGERIE BO)

« Manger mon Paris-Brest, c'est s'en mettre partout, même sur le nez »

Plutôt réputé pour ses gâteaux hybrides franco-japonais, Olivier ne désemplit pas d'amour pour les grands emblèmes de la pâtisserie française, tout particulièrement le Paris-Brest. Drôle de forme que ce choux géant, envoyant valser la traditionnelle roue ou la couronne de mini-choux. Pourquoi ? Parce que la plus gourmande façon de manger un gâteau est de croquer dedans et de s'en mettre jusqu'au nez. 120 grammes de mousseline au praliné lisse et d'un gros cœur de praliné grain pour plus de texture et de gourmandise. Couverts interdits, le Paris-Brest se mange avec les doigts, dans la rue, dans un parc, à même la boutique… pour le plaisir de l'instant.

POUR 10 CHOUX INDIVIDUELS

Temps de préparation : 1 h 30 • Temps de repos : 1 h • Temps de cuisson : 30 min

INGRÉDIENTS

Le craquelin amande
75 g de farine type 55
75 g de sucre en grains cassonade
75 g de poudre d'amandes
75 g de beurre extra-fin
1 g de sel fin

La pâte à choux
99 g de farine type 45
181 g d'eau
4 g de sucre semoule
4 g de sel fin
81 g de beurre extra-fin
181 g d'œufs frais

La crème mousseline praliné

La crème pâtissière
184 g de lait entier
91 g de sucre cristal
45 g de jaunes d'œufs frais
16 g de poudre à crème

La crème au beurre
160 g de sucre cristal
Quantité suffisante d'eau
80 g de jaunes d'œufs frais
320 g de beurre extra-fin
150 g de praliné grain amandes et noisettes maison (ou celui de Valrhona)

Montage et finition
50 g de praliné grain amandes et noisettes

RÉALISATION

Le craquelin amande

Tamiser les poudres ensemble, mélanger le tout avec le beurre tempéré jusqu'à obtention d'une pâte homogène. Étaler celle-ci à l'aide d'un rouleau à pâtisserie entre deux feuilles de papier sulfurisé. Réserver 1 h au frais avant de détailler à l'aide d'un emporte-pièce rond des disques de 7 cm de diamètre. Réserver à nouveau au froid avant utilisation.

La pâte à choux

Tamiser la farine. Faites bouillir ensemble l'eau, le sucre, le sel et le beurre. Retirer du feu, ajouter la farine en mélangeant vivement à l'aide d'une spatule sur feu doux jusqu'à ce qu'elle se détache bien des parois de la casserole et n'adhère plus à la spatule. Faire dessécher la pâte de 2 à 3 min. Débarrasser la pâte dans la cuve du batteur munie d'une feuille, incorporer les œufs petit à petit dans la pâte.

Dresser la pâte à choux avec une douille unie n° 18, sur une plaque recouverte d'un tapis Silpat ou d'une feuille de papier sulfurisé. Faire des dômes de 6 cm de diamètre. Placer sur le dessus un disque de craquelin. Préchauffer le four à 230 °C. Enfourner et cuire 1 min, puis éteindre le four. Laisser gonfler la pâte à choux de 6 à 7 min. Rallumer le four à 180 °C. Dès que la pâte à choux à une jolie couleur dorée, entrouvrir le four 10 secondes pour laisser s'échapper l'humidité, puis refermer et laisser finir de cuire (compter environ 30 min).

La crème mousseline praliné

La crème pâtissière

Porter à ébullition le lait avec 1/3 du sucre, mélanger les jaunes d'œufs à la poudre à crème et le reste de sucre. Délayer ce mélange avec la moitié du lait avant de l'incorporer dans le restant du lait. Porter la crème pâtissière à ébullition et laisser cuire 5 min en mélangeant vivement à l'aide d'un fouet. Débarrasser et conditionner la crème pâtissière en boîte hermétique, filmée au contact.

La crème au beurre

Mettre le sucre dans une casserole en Inox. Recouvrir d'eau afin que tout le sucre soit humidifié. Cuire à 121 °C. Lorsque le mélange atteint 110 ° C, faire émulsionner les jaunes d'œufs au batteur à l'aide d'un fouet. Enclencher le batteur à vitesse moyenne et verser le sucre cuit en filet sur les jaunes. Laisser refroidir à grande vitesse. Incorporer le beurre pommade petit à petit jusqu'à homogénéisation.

Une fois la crème au beurre refroidie, incorporer la crème pâtissière préalablement lissée et le praliné, puis émulsionner avant utilisation.

Montage et finition

Découper les choux un peu au-dessus du milieu, les déposer sur une grille. Garnir le fond du chou de crème mousseline et en son centre, placer le praliné grain (environ 5 g par choux). Dresser une rosace de crème mousseline praliné à l'aide d'une douille cannelée. Déposer le couvercle de pâte à choux préalablement emporte-piècé et saupoudré de sucre glace neige décor. Mettre les Paris-Brest au réfrigérateur quelques minutes puis servir.

LA CERISE SUR LE GÂTEAU

PIERRE HERMÉ

Gourmand né, un pâtissier habité, un talent insensé

Il habitait au-dessus de la boutique de son père, et n'a jamais imaginé faire autre chose que de la pâtisserie. Il débarque chez Lenôtre à 14 ans, frôle l'évanouissement quand il loupe une crêpe devant le grand Gaston, mais reste, progresse, grandit. Jamais il n'a eu l'impression de travailler, et voit ça comme une vraie chance. Il signe en 1992 son premier gâteau « d'architecte », idée alors reçue comme saugrenue, élaboré par le designer irlandais Yan Pennor's. L'idée de La Cerise sur le Gâteau était de proposer une forme que n'aurait jamais pu imaginer un pâtissier. Pierre Hermé avait envie d'utiliser le tout nouveau chocolat au lait de Valrhona de l'époque, le Jivara, et la noisette, accord parfait, s'est imposée d'elle-même. La recette est la même depuis 23 ans !

POUR 6 PERSONNES

Temps de préparation : 5 h • Temps de cuisson : 45 min • Temps de réfrigération : environ 16 h

INGRÉDIENTS

Le biscuit dacquoise aux noisettes
40 g de noisettes décortiquées du Piémont
75 g de sucre glace
65 g de poudre de noisettes
75 g de blancs d'œufs
25 g de sucre semoule

Le praliné feuilleté
10 g de beurre doux
50 g de gavottes
25 g de chocolat au lait Jivara à 40 % de cacao de Valrhona
100 g de praliné noisette à 60 % de noisettes

La ganache au chocolat au lait
250 g de chocolat au lait Jivara de Valrhona
2,3 dl de crème liquide à 35 % de MG

Les disques de chocolat au lait
200 g de chocolat au lait Jivara de Valrhona

La chantilly au chocolat au lait
210 g de chocolat au lait Jivara de Valrhona
3 dl de crème liquide à 35 % de MG

Montage de la base de la Cerise sur le Gâteau
Chantilly au chocolat au lait très froide
Biscuit dacquoise aux noisettes
Praliné feuilleté noisette
Fines feuilles de chocolat au lait
Ganache au chocolat au lait

La coque de chocolat au lait
Moule Cerise sur le Gâteau (Yan Pennor's)
400 g de chocolat au lait Jivara de Valrhona

Montage
6 parts de la base de la Cerise sur le Gâteau
Chantilly au chocolat au lait très froide
Coque de chocolat au lait
Le fondant amande pour la cerise
10 g de pâte d'amandes à 22 % d'amandes
20 g de fondant blanc confiseur
Quelques gouttes de colorant jaune d'œuf

Le sucre cuit rouge
150 g de sucre semoule
50 ml d'eau
Quantité suffisante de colorant rouge

La cerise en sucre rouge
1 cerise à l'eau-de-vie avec queue
10 g de fécule de pommes de terre
10 g de fondant amande pour cerise
Sucre cuit rouge

Finition
Poudre d'or alimentaire
Cerise en sucre rouge

RÉALISATION

Le biscuit dacquoise aux noisettes

Faire torréfier les noisettes au four à chaleur tournante à 160° C pendant 15 min. Retirer la peau. Les concasser. Dessiner au crayon à papier un cercle de 19 cm de diamètre sur une feuille de papier siliconé. Retourner la feuille sur une plaque de cuisson. Mélanger et tamiser le sucre glace et la poudre de noisettes. Dans le bol du robot équipé du fouet, monter les blancs en neige jusqu'à ce qu'ils deviennent opaques. Ajouter progressivement le sucre semoule en continuant à battre jusqu'à ce que se forment des crêtes fermes et brillantes. Retirer le bol du robot. À l'aide d'une Maryse souple, incorporer le mélange de noisettes et de sucre dans les blancs en neige. Déposer 1 cuillerée du mélange à chaque coin de la plaque de cuisson pour faire tenir la feuille de papier siliconé. Verser le mélange dans une poche plastique munie d'une douille n° 12. Dresser en spirale dans le cercle que vous avez dessiné sur le papier siliconé. Parsemer régulièrement la surface de la dacquoise de petits morceaux de noisette. Préchauffer le four à 165° C. Enfourner la dacquoise de 30 à 35 min jusqu'à ce qu'elle soit d'une belle couleur brun doré et ferme au toucher. Sortir la plaque du four. Faire glisser la feuille avec la dacquoise sur une grille. Laisser refroidir à température ambiante.

LA CERISE SUR LE GÂTEAU

PIERRE HERMÉ

Le praliné feuilleté

Faire fondre le beurre sur feu doux, dans une casserole, sans le laisser se décomposer. Le laisser refroidir. Émietter finement les gavottes. Faire fondre le chocolat entre 35° et 40° C au bain-marie. Mettre le praliné dans une terrine. Y ajouter le chocolat fondu, lentement, en tournant le mélange à l'aide d'une spatule. Incorporer les brisures de gavotte délicatement, puis le beurre fondu, sans cesser de tourner. Utiliser aussitôt.

La ganache au chocolat au lait

Hacher le chocolat. Faire bouillir la crème dans une casserole. Hors du feu, ajouter le chocolat en quatre fois, en tournant à l'aide d'une spatule pour lisser le mélange. Verser la ganache dans un plat à gratin recouvert d'un film alimentaire au contact de la ganache. Réserver au réfrigérateur pour au moins 4 h.

Les disques de chocolat au lait

Faire fondre le chocolat au lait au bain-marie à 50° C. Le tempérer, puis à l'aide d'une spatule, l'étaler sur une feuille plastique placée sur une plaque. Dès que le chocolat commence à figer, détailler 1 disque de 18 cm de diamètre. Le recouvrir d'une feuille de papier siliconé. Réserver au réfrigérateur.

La chantilly au chocolat au lait

Hacher le chocolat. Faire bouillir la crème dans une casserole. Hors du feu, ajouter le chocolat en trois fois, en fouettant pour lisser la préparation. Verser la préparation dans un plat à gratin. Recouvrir de film alimentaire au contact de la crème. Réserver au réfrigérateur pendant 12 h. La maintenir entre 2° et 4° C pour éviter qu'elle ne se décompose au moment d'être foisonnée. Il suffit d'1 min pour obtenir une texture parfaite.

Montage de la base de la cerise sur le gâteau

Dans un cul-de-poule, foisonner la chantilly au chocolat au lait. Sur une plaque en Inox revêtue d'une feuille de papier siliconé, placer 1 cercle en Inox de 18 cm de diamètre et de 3 cm de hauteur. Poser successivement le biscuit dacquoise. Par-dessus, étaler finement 100 g de praliné feuilleté à l'aide d'une palette. Puis ajouter 1 disque de fines feuilles au chocolat au lait. Enfin, mettre 110 g de ganache et un second disque de fines feuilles de chocolat au lait. Laisser figer au réfrigérateur de 15 à 20 min. Garnir ensuite de chantilly, lisser le cercle à ras et surgeler. Une fois mi-congelé, décercler le gâteau et le couper en 8 parts égales. Stocker au congélateur, sous film plastique.

La coque de chocolat au lait

Préparer le moule. Pour cela, le nettoyer à l'aide d'un coton et l'utiliser à une température comprise entre 18° et 20° C.

Mettre le chocolat au point. Pour cela, mettre le chocolat haché à l'aide d'un couteau-scie à fondre dans une jatte posée dans une casserole au bain-marie. Remuer. Lorsque le chocolat atteint la température de 45°-50° C, retirer aussitôt la jatte du bain-marie. Le placer dans une seconde jatte remplie d'eau avec 5 glaçons. Remuer par intermittence le chocolat fondu pour éviter qu'il ne fige. Dès qu'il a atteint la température de 26°-27° C, remettre la jatte dans la casserole au bain-marie. Dès que la température a atteint 29°-30° C, prendre une louche et garnir le moule à ras de chocolat. Tapoter le moule pour faire remonter à la surface d'éventuelles bulles d'air. Retourner le moule dans la jatte de chocolat, puis sur une grille posée sur une plaque revêtue d'une feuille de papier siliconé pour permettre à l'excédent de chocolat de s'écouler. Lorsque le chocolat commence à figer, ébarber à ras à l'aide d'une palette non coupante. L'épaisseur idéale de la coque doit être d'environ 2 mm. Procéder au montage de la Cerise sur le Gâteau.

Montage

Étape 1

Laisser décongeler complètement les parts de la base de la Cerise sur le Gâteau avant de procéder au montage.

Dans un cul-de-poule, foisonner la chantilly au chocolat au lait à une température comprise entre 2° et 4° C. Remplir une poche jetable sans douille. Garnir la coque de chocolat au lait d'un peu de chantilly. Saisir une part de base, la retourner et planter la pointe d'un couteau dans la dacquoise. La déposer dans le fond de la coque. Garnir le pourtour de la première part d'un peu de chantilly. Empiler successivement les parts dans la coque de chocolat. Entre chaque part, mettre un peu de chantilly, à la fois pour les faire adhérer entre elles et pour obstruer d'éventuels espaces. Lisser à ras avec de la ganache. Appliquer un triangle de feuille de papier siliconé puis retourner l'édifice, côté droit face à vous. Le démoulage est délicat. Retirer les élastiques puis la partie du moule en plâtre. Faire passer vos doigts entre les deux parties du moule en silicone. Détacher la partie droite du moule en commençant par le bas mais sans toutefois décoller le sommet du gâteau. Poursuivre en détachant la seconde partie puis, en tout dernier, le sommet.

Étape 2 : le fondant amande pour la cerise

Malaxer séparément la pâte d'amandes et le fondant pour les assouplir. Les assembler et mélanger. Chauffer au four à micro-ondes à 50° C avant d'ajouter le colorant. Utiliser aussitôt.

Étape 3 : le sucre cuit rouge

Dans une casserole, faire cuire le sucre et l'eau jusqu'à 120° C environ. Ajouter le colorant et poursuivre la cuisson jusqu'à 160° C. Utiliser aussitôt.

Étape 4 : la cerise en sucre rouge

Égoutter la cerise puis la poser sur du papier absorbant. Saupoudrer la cerise légèrement de fécule de pommes de terre. Tremper ensuite la cerise dans le fondant amande. La suspendre par la queue afin de laisser s'écouler l'excédent. Une fois le fondant figé, couper l'excédent et laisser refroidir. Procéder de même avec le sucre cuit rouge. Laisser s'écouler l'excédent et le couper à l'aide de ciseaux. Conserver la cerise, une fois refroidie, dans une boîte hermétique avec des pastilles anti-humidité.

Finition

Mélanger la poudre or avec un peu d'eau ; puis au pinceau appliquer cinq traits d'or en suivant les rainures situées sur la partie frontale de la coque. Déposer la Cerise sur le Gâteau sur un plat de présentation. Posez la cerise en sucre rouge au sommet. Réserver au réfrigérateur.

TARTE CHOCOLAT « RENDEZ-VOUS »

JEAN-PAUL HÉVIN

Un chocolatier au service du bon

Avant d'être un chocolatier, Jean-Paul Hévin est un dégustateur, capable les yeux fermés de retrouver l'origine d'une fève. Ce travail de passion le propulse au sein de la poignée des meilleurs chocolatiers de la capitale, et les gâteaux suivent. Parfaitement structurés, chirurgicalement tempérés, divinement équilibrés, la gamme pâtissière de Jean-Paul Hévin est renversante de gourmandise. Sa tarte au chocolat, probablement le candidat idéal pour une première fois, est un modèle du genre. Tout y est. La pâte sucrée au chocolat, régulière, impeccablement cuite et toute « crissante » sous la première dent, la ganache au chocolat et à la crème fleurette, et après croc, le mélange des deux. Le meilleur moment.

POUR 5 PERSONNES

Temps de préparation : 25 min • Temps de cuisson : 20 min • Temps de réfrigération/Repos : 4 h

INGRÉDIENTS

La pâte sucrée au chocolat

20 g de chocolat de couverture à 68 % de cacao
105 g de beurre mou
65 g de sucre glace
22 g de poudre d'amandes
0,25 g de vanille en poudre
1 pincée de sel
35 g d'œuf
175 g de farine

La ganache au chocolat

170 g de chocolat de couverture à 63 % de cacao origine Pérou
250 g de crème fleurette
10 g de sucre inverti

Montage et finition

2 aiguilles en chocolat
1 meringue
Quantité suffisante de poudre or

PRÉPARATION

La pâte sucrée au chocolat

Faire fondre le chocolat au bain-marie.Dans un récipient, mélanger délicatement le beurre, le sucre glace, la poudre d'amandes, la vanille et le sel. Incorporer l'œuf puis la farine et le chocolat fondu. Mélanger jusqu'à obtenir un mélange homogène. Protéger la préparation recouverte d'un film alimentaire au réfrigérateur pendant 2 h. Étaler la pâte à l'aide d'un rouleau à pâtisserie le plus finement possible en formant un disque. Foncer un cercle de 22 cm de diamètre. Piquer la pâte et y placer des billes de cuisson afin d'éviter que celle-ci ne gonfle à la cuisson. Enfourner à 180 °C pour environ 20 min. Laisser le fond de tarte refroidir une fois sorti du four. Dès qu'il est froid, chablonner l'intérieur avec le chocolat couverture 68 % fondu. C'est-à-dire, à l'aide d'un pinceau recouvrir l'intérieur du fond de tarte d'une fine couche de chocolat. Cela permet de l'isoler de l'humidité et donc de garder une pâte croquante. Réserver à température ambiante.

La ganache au chocolat

Hacher le chocolat et mettez-le dans un saladier. Faire bouillir la crème fleurette avec le sucre inverti. Verser la préparation en 3 fois sur le chocolat. Mélanger jusqu'à ce que la préparation soit homogène.

Montage et Finition

Couler la ganache au chocolat encore chaude dans le fond de tarte. Laisser la tarte 2 h à température ambiante (18-20 °C). Disposer 2 aiguilles en chocolat et 1 goutte de meringue française enrobée puis recouverte de poudre or.

COOKIES MULTIGRAIN

MOKO HIRAYAMA ET OMAR KOREITEM (MOKONUTS)

Le meilleur cookie de Paris. Le plus libre, aussi.

Ex-avocate à New York, Moko est un ouragan de folie, de joie et de bonhommie. Le cookie, c'est toute son enfance aux États-Unis, et n'étant pas pâtissière de formation, elle n'y voit aucune limite. Elle crée comme elle respire, d'un cookie chocolat blanc/olive noire à un cookie maïs/romarin. Si ça ne fonctionne pas, elle recommence. À la base de ce petit gâteau, elle voit un champ des possibles infinis, où tout logerait gaiement, sans jamais s'arrêter. Pas forcément à la recherche d'un goût, les cookies de Moko poursuivent une curiosité, un peu comme un biscuit libre et vivant, à la texture inouïe et aux associations prodigieuses. Son petit bijou, c'est le cookie graines/chocolat noir, qui « pop et crunch » sous la dent, à différents niveaux. Il croque d'abord au bord, puis les graines éclatent au cœur, et le chocolat fond partout.
Le Graal du cookie.

POUR ENVIRON 15 COOKIES
Temps de préparation : 30 min • Temps de cuisson : 12 min

INGRÉDIENTS
La pâte de cookies
80 g de flocons d'avoine
90 g de mélange de graines (graines de courge, tournesol, lin etc)
125 g de farine
8 g de levure chimique
2 g de sel
115 g de beurre doux
130 g de sucre semoule
1 œuf
150 g de chocolat noir en morceaux

RÉALISATION
Mélanger les flocons d'avoine, les graines, la farine, la levure et le sel. Réserver. Mélanger le beurre et le sucre jusqu'à obtention d'une texture homogène. Ajouter l'œuf et mélanger. Ajouter la mixture de farine et graines et incorporer le tout délicatement. Ajouter le chocolat noir. Diviser, à la main, la pâte en 15 petites boules et répartir sur une plaque recouverte de papier sulfurisé. Enfourner à 180 °C pour environ 12 min. Les cookies doivent avoir une jolie coloration blonde.

TARTE AUX POMMES

SHINYA INAGAKI (BOULANGERIE DU NIL - TERROIRS D'AVENIR)

Des gâteaux de la ferme, essentiels et tellement bons

Si toute la terre était aussi belle que Samuel Nahon et Alexandre Drouard la voient, le futur serait évanouissant de beauté. Leur terroir est beau, rare et vrai. Depuis récemment, leur boulangerie aussi. Shinya Inagaki en a fait sa cour, désireux d'y livrer une image de beau français : du bon pain et du bon vin. Passionné par les variétés anciennes de blé, leur culture et leur transformation à la ferme, Shinya rejoint l'aventure formidable de Samuel et Alexandre, celle de mettre en avant un savoir-faire ancré dans un terroir. Avec les saisons comme cœur de métier, il y signe des gâteaux de boulanger, ultra-bons puisque faits simplement, avec d'excellents produits. Grand fou de crème d'amandes, déjà phare dans la barre au chocolat et aux amandes, ou dans le croissant aux amandes, Shinya ne pouvait qu'en gaver sa tarte aux pommes, complètement divine, et complètement « si-je-ne-devais-en-choisir-qu'une-ce-serait-celle-là ». À la première bouchée, tout se mélange, rien ne prend le dessus sur rien, et on a une fonte idéale et merveilleuse de la pâte sucrée, la crème d'amandes et les pommes tout juste fondantes.

POUR 4 PERSONNES

Temps de préparation : 45 min • Temps de repos : 2 h • Temps de cuisson : 45 min

INGRÉDIENTS

La pâte sucrée

65 g de beurre mou
40 g de sucre glace
15 g de poudre d'amandes
110 g de farine type 65
1 pincée de sel
1 petit œuf

La crème d'amandes

50 g de beurre mou
50 g de sucre blond
1 petit œuf
50 g de poudre d'amandes

Le dressage

1 grosse pomme

RÉALISATION

La pâte sucrée

Dans la cuve d'un batteur munie de la feuille, mélanger le beurre mou et le sucre glace jusqu'à obtention d'un appareil homogène. Ajouter la poudre d'amandes, la farine et le sel. Mélanger. Incorporer l'œuf. Travailler jusqu'à obtention d'une boule compacte. Filmer au contact et réserver au frais pendant minimum 2 h.

La crème d'amandes

Préchauffer le four à 220 °C.

Mélanger le beurre mou avec le sucre blond. Ajouter l'œuf puis la poudre d'amandes. Mélanger.

Montage et finition

Étaler la pâte dans un moule à bord haut de 16 cm de diamètre. Piquer la pâte. Placer la crème d'amandes en couche épaisse. Disposer sur le dessus des rondelles de pomme très fines. Faire cuire 45 min à 220 °C.

SAINT-HONORÉ

LAURENT JEANNIN (LE BRISTOL)

Des gâteaux d'une élégance abyssale

En plus d'être le saint patron des boulangers, Saint-Honoré est la rue du Bristol, Laurent Jeannin n'avait pas tellement d'autre choix que d'en faire son dada. Un dada qui trotte bien, et différemment : deux sortes de pâtes (à choux et feuilletée), deux sortes de crème (pâtissière/fouettée et chiboust/fouettée), et deux sortes de caramel (crème au caramel demi-sel et caramel croquant). Dernière touche, sa forme élancée. Sous tant d'élégance, un feuilletage rempli d'une crème pâtissière allégée à la crème fouettée et vanille, un caramel craquant sur toute la surface, et des choux bien dorés garnis d'un caramel demi-sel et d'une crème chiboust, détendue à la crème chantilly. Tout ce que Laurent Jeannin recherche, c'est l'émotion, à la fois sur les textures et sur les goûts. La chantilly prend le palais tout de suite, puis la chiboust, puis le caramel des choux. Arrivent en fin de bouche le feuilletage bien poussé et le caramel craquant, comme un rappel de gourmandise.

POUR 4 PERSONNES

Temps de préparation : 1 h • Temps de cuisson : 30 à 40 min • Temps de réfrigération : 10 min

INGRÉDIENTS

65 g de pâte feuilletée du boulanger ou maison
Farine
Huile pour la plaque

La pâte à choux
80 g d'eau
80 g de lait
6 g de sucre semoule
5g de sel fin
65 g de beurre
150 g de farine
160 g d'œufs frais

Le caramel
40 g d'eau
160 g de sucre semoule
25 g de sirop de glucose

La crème chiboust
2/3 d'une feuille de gélatine
80 g de lait
½ gousse de vanille
40 g de jaunes d'œufs
35 g de sucre semoule
8 g de fécule de maïs ou de poudre à flan
50 g de blancs d'œufs

La chantilly
145 g de crème liquide
15 g de mascarpone
12 g de sucre semoule
½ gousse de vanille

RÉALISATION

La pâte à choux

Dans une casserole, porter à ébullition l'eau, le lait, le sucre, le sel et le beurre. Hors du feu, ajouter la farine tamisée. Mélanger jusqu'à ce que la pâte soit homogène. Remettre la casserole sur feu doux en remuant énergiquement 1 min pour dessécher la pâte. Mettre la préparation dans la cuve d'un batteur munie du fouet. Faire tourner à vitesse moyenne. Incorporer les œufs petit à petit de façon à obtenir une pâte lisse, homogène et brillante. À l'aide d'un rouleau à pâtisserie, étaler très finement (2 mm d'épaisseur) la pâte feuilletée, tout en la farinant légèrement. La déposer sur une plaque et la faire durcir environ 15 min au réfrigérateur. Sortir la pâte et la piquer à l'aide d'une fourchette. À l'aide d'une assiette retournée, découper un disque d'environ 18 cm de diamètre. Poser ce disque sur la plaque de pâtisserie légèrement graissée et essuyée. Dresser sur le pourtour du feuilletage une couronne de pâte à choux et, à côté sur la plaque, une vingtaine de petits choux de 2 cm de diamètre environ avec une douille ronde unie n° 7. Préchauffer le four à 230 °C. Enfourner et cuire 1 min, puis éteindre le four. Laisser gonfler la pâte à choux de 6 à 7 min. Rallumer le four à 180 °C. Dès que la pâte à choux a une jolie couleur dorée, entrouvrir le four 10 secondes pour laisser s'échapper l'humidité, puis refermer et laisser finir de cuire (compter environ 30 min). Dès la sortie du four, mettre les choux et le fond du Saint-Honoré sur une grille et laisser refroidir.

Le caramel

Dans une casserole, porter à ébullition l'eau et le sucre sur feu doux, ajouter le sirop de glucose et laisser cuire jusqu'à obtention d'un caramel clair. Tremper les choux et les laisser de côté. Décoller chaque chou une fois que le caramel a figé.

La crème chiboust

Mettre la gélatine à ramollir dans l'eau froide. Porter à ébullition le lait avec les graines de la ½ gousse de vanille. Laisser infuser 5 min. Filtrer dans une passoire. Dans un bol, mélanger les jaunes d'œufs et 8 g de sucre semoule. Ajouter la poudre à flan. Porter à nouveau le lait vanillé à ébullition. Hors du feu, le verser dans le mélange aux œufs. Faire bouillir 1 min. Hors du feu, incorporer la gélatine égouttée. Monter les blancs d'œufs en neige avec le sucre semoule restant. Incorporer à la préparation précédente chaude. À l'aide d'une poche munie d'une petite douille unie, garnir les petits choux de crème chiboust par le fond. Garnir également l'intérieur de la couronne. Réchauffer le caramel. Tremper légèrement le fond de chaque chou, coller sur la couronne. Réservez le Saint-Honoré 10 min au frais.

La chantilly

Fouetter ensemble la crème, le mascarpone, le sucre et les graines de la ½ gousse de vanille jusqu'à obtention d'une chantilly.

Montage et finition

Sortir le Saint-Honoré du réfrigérateur, décorer le centre de crème chantilly avec une douille à Saint-Honoré et servir.

PIE MATCHA

ANTOANETA JULEA ET SAYAKO TSUJI (AMAMI)

Ou la naissance d'un conte de fées

Antoaneta et Sayako se sont rencontrées au Cordon Bleu à Paris, il y a presque dix ans. L'une est canadienne d'origine roumaine, l'autre américaine d'origine japonaise, les idées fusent et les gâteaux naissent sans cesse, habités par cette envie de tester, sans idée reçue, des recettes. Formées respectivement chez Rochoux et au Crillon, elles décident de se lancer, « quitte à travailler dur pour les autres, autant le faire pour soi-même ». Elles commencent petit, avec des caramels préparés dans leur appartement, vendus sur Internet. Les commandes explosent, elles ouvrent Amami en décembre 2015. Naît très vite la pie matcha, hybride idéal entre l'Amérique et le Japon. L'appareil se rapproche de celui du flan, en beaucoup plus crémeux, une richesse contrebalancée par le côté iodé voire amer du matcha bio de la maison Jugetsudo. Le résultat est scotchant.

POUR 4 PERSONNES

Temps de préparation : 30 min • Temps de repos : 4 h • Temps de cuisson : 1 h 15

INGRÉDIENTS

La pâte

340 g de farine
15 g de sucre semoule
1 cuil. à café de sel
250 g de beurre
100 g d'eau froide

La crème au matcha

110 g de beurre
130 g de sucre semoule
½ cuil. à soupe de farine
¼ de cuil. à café de sel
½ cuil. à soupe de matcha en poudre
4 œufs
450 ml de crème liquide
½ cuil. à café d'extrait de vanille

RÉALISATION

La pâte

Dans un saladier, verser la farine, le sucre et le sel. Ajouter le beurre préalablement coupé en cubes. Sabler le mélange à la main. Verser l'eau bien froide. Mélanger. Une fois que la pâte forme une boule compacte et homogène, couper la pâte pour former deux pâtons. Laisser reposer au réfrigérateur pendant 2 h. Avec le premier pâton, former un disque assez grand pour déborder un peu du haut du moule de la tarte (22 cm de diamètre). Couper les bords à l'aide d'un couteau. Étaler le deuxième disque pour le décor. Couper la pâte en trois fines bandes et faire une tresse. À l'aide d'un pinceau imbibé d'eau, coller la tresse sur le rebord de la pâte foncée. Laisser reposer au réfrigérateur pendant au moins 1 h. Poser dans le fond un papier sulfurisé et recouvrir de billes de cuisson. Astuce : pas de billes de cuisson ? Du riz ou des lentilles feront très bien l'affaire. Préchauffer le four à 175 °C. Faire cuire à blanc pendant 15 min. Retirer la feuille et les billes puis poursuivre la cuisson 15 min. Sortir le fond de tarte du four lorsque la pâte est bien dorée.

La crème au matcha

Faire fondre le beurre. Mélanger au fouet le sucre, la farine, le sel et la poudre de matcha. Incorporer le beurre fondu dans le mélange sec, puis les œufs un par un. Ajouter la crème et l'extrait de vanille. Passer le mélange à la passoire fine puis le couler dans le fond de tarte. Enfourner à 175 °C pendant 10 min. Puis prolonger la cuisson à 150 °C pour 30 min. Le centre de la tarte reste légèrement tremblant. Une fois que la tarte est à température ambiante, la placer 1 h au frais.

FLAN GRAND-MÈRE

LOGAN ET BRADLEY LAFOND (ERNEST ET VALENTIN)

Les frangins passionnés et passionnants, au talent inouï

« Logan et Bradley, ça faisait quand même moyen comme nom de boulangerie, donc on a pris les prénoms de nos grands-pères, Ernest et Valentin. » Grands-pères qui n'étaient pas boulangers, on est bien loin du cliché de la transmission familiale, l'histoire, ils l'ont dessinée eux-mêmes. Ils avaient envie d'emporter une partie d'eux-mêmes dans l'aventure, même nuageuse, même lointaine, de ceux qui leur ont transmis les valeurs du bien manger. Le flan grand-mère n'a, encore une fois, de familial que le nom et ne vient pas de la leur, mais représente à leurs yeux le summum du gâteau de boulanger, si difficile à trouver bien fait. Bradley, le pâtissier, s'attèle à l'appareil et Logan, le boulanger, met la main à la pâte qu'il cuira derrière au four à pain. Le rendu est caramélisé sur le dessus, flageolant à cœur, à la texture de crème brûlée, crémeuse et lactée, pleine de vanille Bourbon longue et ronde. Une constante à épouser.

POUR 6 À 8 PERSONNES

Temps de préparation : 1 h • Temps de cuisson : 20 à 40 min

INGRÉDIENTS

La pâte brisée

200 g de farine type 45
100 g de margarine
4 g de sel
50 g d'eau

La crème pâtissière

750 g de lait
250 g de crème liquide à 35 % de MG
200 g de sucre semoule
1 gousse de vanille
85 g de Maïzena®
100 g d'œufs

RÉALISATION

La pâte brisée

Mettre tous les ingrédients dans la cuve d'un batteur. Mélanger avec le crochet jusqu'à ce que la pâte soit homogène. À l'aide d'un rouleau à pâtisserie, étaler la pâte sur 3 mm d'épaisseur. Foncer un cercle de 22 cm de diamètre. Réserver au frais le temps de préparer la crème pâtissière.

La crème pâtissière

Dans une casserole, faire chauffer le lait et la crème liquide avec les trois quarts du sucre. Fendre la gousse de vanille en deux et gratter pour récupérer les graines. Ajouter la gousse et les graines dans le lait. Mettre le sucre restant, la Maïzena® et les œufs dans la cuve d'un batteur. Fouetter la préparation jusqu'à ce que le mélange soit légèrement blanchi. Dès que le mélange de crème, de lait et de sucre est en ébullition, en verser une partie sur les œufs, le sucre et la Maïzena®. Mélanger. Remettre le tout dans la casserole. Fouetter énergiquement pour obtenir un mélange lisse et homogène. Verser à l'aide d'une louche la crème obtenue dans le cercle foncé avec la pâte brisée. Suivant votre four, enfourner à 260 °C pendant 20 min pour une cuisson à la sole, ou enfourner à 180 °C pendant 40 min pour une cuisson à chaleur tournante.

À la sortie du four, le flan doit être doré et gonflé. Le laisser refroidir à température ambiante. Une fois froid, le décercler. Mettre le flan dansun plat de service. À la dégustation, le flan doit être crémeux et fondant en bouche.

LE CITRON

ALEXIS LECOFFRE ET SYLVESTRE WAHID (GÂTEAUX THOUMIEUX)

Un pâtissier et un chef doublement étoilé : le duo idéal et percutant

Pour Sylvestre et Alexis, une tarte citron, « gustativement » en tout cas, doit être accessible à tout le monde. Leur version est sans pâte ni biscuit, texture remplacée par la coque au chocolat blanc, et dans une forme presque de goutte, dodue et rassurante. Au cœur, une ganache montée au citron, du jus de citron, des zestes de citron, tous jaunes, tous acidulés. Au cœur du cœur, un confit de citron vert, détendu au jus d'orange. Le sucre est apporté par la coque, tout le reste se concentre sur la fraîcheur et l'acidité. Une prouesse assez remarquable, d'arriver à un équilibre gras/sucre/acidité sans même avoir besoin de suprêmes d'agrumes, simplement quelques billes de citron caviar pour le panache. Une très jolie façon de raconter un citron.

POUR 10 PIÈCES

Temps de préparation : 1 h 45 • Temps de réfrigération : 36 h

INGRÉDIENTS

La ganache montée citron

3,5 feuilles de gélatine
600 g de crème liquide
10 g de zestes de citron
175 g de chocolat blanc Concerto de la Chocolaterie de l'Opéra®
200 g de jus de citron jaune

Le confit citron vert

30 g de citron vert
30 g de jus d'orange
40 g de sucre semoule n° 1
1 pincée de sucre semoule n° 2
La pointe d'un couteau de pectine NH (astuce : pas de pectine ? Un autre gélifiant fera l'affaire)

L'enrobage au chocolat blanc

250 g de beurre de cacao
250 g de chocolat blanc Concerto de la Chocolaterie de l'Opéra®

La meringue italienne au citron vert

315 g de sucre semoule
80 g de jus de citron vert
105 g de blancs d'œufs

Montage et finition

Quantité suffisante de poudre or
Quantité suffisante de feuille d'or

RÉALISATION

La ganache montée citron

Réhydrater la gélatine dans de l'eau bien froide. Faire bouillir 1/3 de la crème avec les zestes de citron puis ajouter la gélatine et verser en deux fois sur le chocolat blanc. Mélanger. Incorporer le reste de la crème puis chinoiser et une fois le mélange froid, ajouter le jus de citron puis mixer. Attendre 24 h avant utilisation.

Le confit citron vert

À l'aide d'un couteau, couper grossièrement le citron vert puis le passer au mixeur. Mettre dans une casserole le jus d'orange, le citron vert haché et le sucre semoule n° 1. Chauffer à 50 °C puis incorporer le sucre n° 2 préalablement mélangé à la pectine NH. Porter à ébullition puis baisser le feu et laisser cuire environ 15 min. Laisser refroidir. Réserver au frais.

L'enrobage au chocolat blanc

Faire fondre le beurre de cacao à 45 °C puis verser sur le chocolat blanc et mixer. Utiliser à 50 °C.

La meringue italienne au citron vert

Cuire le sucre et le jus de citron à 110 °C. Monter les blancs d'œufs. Poursuivre la cuisson du sirop jusqu'à 121 °C. Verser sur les blancs, serrer la meringue jusqu'à obtention d'un bec d'oiseau. Cette action de fouetter les blancs d'œufs déjà montés en neige en ajoutant du sucre va permettre de raffermir leur consistance.

Montage et finition

Dans la cuve d'un batteur munie d'un fouet, monter la ganache citron jusqu'à ce qu'elle tienne sur le fouet. Garnir une poche à douille de ganache citron et remplir au ¾ un moule en silicone de forme sphérique. À l'aide d'une palette, remonter la ganache citron sur les bords du moule. Garnir une poche à douille de confit citron vert et mettre 10 g au milieu du moule. Compléter le ¼ restant de ganache citron puis lisser à hauteur du moule et mettre au congélateur pour environ 12 h. Une fois la sphère congelée, démouler puis insérer une pique par la base de la sphère. Tremper les sphères dans le mélange beurre de cacao et chocolat blanc et remettre 10 min au congélateur. Puis tremper les sphères dans la meringue. Enlever la pique à l'aide d'une fourchette puis poser sur assiette. À l'aide d'un chalumeau, colorer légèrement la meringue, souffler de la poudre or puis déposer de la feuille d'or au sommet.

CAKE CUBE AU SÉSAME NOIR

YANN LE GALL (LES SOURIS DANSENT)

« Je suis un peu feignant, alors je fais dans l'ultra-simple »

De son amour pour le Japon, Yann tire le graphisme des gâteaux, qu'il exprime dans leurs formes. Côté goûts, il les aime simples, reconnaissables et rassurants. Au cours de l'un de ses voyages, il découvre le cake cube, sorte de gâteau japonais hyper aérien monté en cube, avec beaucoup de chantilly à l'intérieur et une fine plaque de chocolat sur le dessus. Il a adoré, et ne les a jamais retrouvés ailleurs. Sa version se passe de la feuille de chocolat, et envoie valser les codes classiques de la pâtisserie qui voudraient que toutes les textures soient représentées. « Ici, c'est mou sur mou, sans craquelin ni croustillant ! », une texture assez proche du soufflé. Celui au sésame noir, est le favori de la maison. À la première bouchée, le moelleux s'impose, suivi de près par la puissance du sésame noir et la chantilly légère qui tempère. Un gâteau doux et vif.

POUR 8 CHOUX

Temps de préparation : 2 h • Temps de cuisson : 36 min • Temps de réfrigération : 30 min

INGRÉDIENTS

La pâte à choux
95 g d'eau
35 g de beurre
½ pincée de sel
35 g de farine
5 g de poudre de charbon
4 œufs moyens

Les langues de chat
50 g de beurre pommade
50 g de sucre glace
50 g de blancs d'œufs
50 g de farine
½ cuil. à café de poudre de charbon

La crème pâtissière au sésame noir
250 g de lait
2 jaunes d'œufs
32,5 g de sucre semoule
22 g de Maïzena®
20 g de pâte de sésame noir

La chantilly au sésame noir
150 g de crème liquide à 35 % de MG
15 g de sucre glace
1 cuil. à café de pâte de sésame noir

Montage et finition
Quantité suffisante de graines de sésame noir
Quantité suffisante de chantilly au sésame noir
8 langues de chat en spirales

RÉALISATION

La pâte à choux

Mettre à chauffer l'eau, le beurre et le sel dans une casserole jusqu'à une légère ébullition. Ajouter, hors du feu, la farine et la poudre de charbon. Mélanger jusqu'à obtention d'une pâte homogène. Remettre la préparation sur feu doux et dessécher durant 1 min la pâte. Transvaser la pâte dans un saladier. Ajouter, en plusieurs fois, les œufs battus en omelette. Mélanger énergiquement entre chaque ajout d'œuf. Mettre la pâte à choux dans une poche à douille. Sur une plaque recouverte de papier sulfurisé, déposer 8 moules carrés de 5 cm x 5 cm. Pocher la pâte dans le fond des moules. Mettre une autre plaque de cuisson sur les moules. Enfourner à 180 °C pour 30 min. Démouler à la sortie du four le plus vite possible. Réserver sur une grille.

Les langues de chat

Fouetter le beurre et le sucre dans un saladier afin de rendre le mélange homogène. Ajouter les blancs, la farine tamisée avec la poudre de charbon. Mettre la préparation dans une poche sans douille. Couper le bout de la poche et faire des spirales sur une plaque de cuisson recouverte de papier sulfurisé. Enfourner à 170 °C pour 6 min.

La crème pâtissière au sésame noir

Dans une casserole, faire bouillir le lait. Dans un saladier, fouetter les jaunes avec le sucre, la Maïzena® et la pâte de sésame noir. Verser un peu de lait bouillant pour délayer le mélange. Reverser le tout dans la casserole. Cuire sur feu moyen jusqu'à l'obtention d'une légère ébullition. Débarrasser la crème pâtissière dans un plat à gratin. Filmer au contact. Réserver au frais pendant environ 30 min.

La chantilly au sésame noir

Placer la crème liquide froide et le sucre glace dans la cuve d'un batteur munie du fouet. Battre l'ensemble jusqu'à ce que la chantilly tienne au fouet. Ajouter la pâte de sésame noir au dernier moment. Mélanger délicatement. Réserver au frais.

Montage et finition

Sortir la crème pâtissière du réfrigérateur et la mettre dans un saladier. Ajouter quelques graines de sésame noir. Fouetter la crème afin de la détendre. Placer la crème pâtissière dans une poche munie d'une douille de 8 mm de diamètre. Percer chaque cube à l'aide d'une petite douille. Garnir chaque chou de crème pâtissière au sésame noir. Ajouter sur le dessus des pointes de chantilly et 1 langue de chat.

LE CROUSTI BREIZH

PIÈR-MARIE LE MOIGNO

Une nouvelle façon d'approcher le kouign-amann, ludique et addictive

En juin 2014, le projet rêvé de Pièr-Marie Le Moigno est tracé : apporter, en Bretagne, une manière de pâtisser façon hôtellerie, avec un renouvellement régulier des cartes, comme au restaurant, du sur-mesure, dans une gamme courte, fraîche, locale et journalière, en direct du marché. Fou de ses origines, Pièr-Marie cherche une autre façon de raconter le kouign-amann, en une interprétation plus contemporaine, plus mignonne, plus snack… la chips de kouign-amann, celle qu'on aurait aimé inventer nous-mêmes. Roulé, détaillé puis cuit dans des moules spéciaux, le dénouement se joue brillant : pâte feuilletée serrée, volontairement pas développée, croustillante et ultra-caramélisée, un scandale d'addiction. Les chips sont plus ou moins épaisses, toutes sont inégales, certaines sont moelleuses, d'autres totalement crunchy, un résultat que le chef adore. Une chips peut en cacher une autre, toute autre.

POUR UNE TRENTAINE DE CROUSTI BREIZH

Temps de préparation : 1 h • Temps de cuisson : 15 min • Temps de réfrigération : 2 h

INGRÉDIENTS

La pâte levée feuilletée

7 g de levure fraîche
270 g d'eau froide
5 g de sel de Guérande
450 g de farine type 45
3 g de vanille en poudre
20 g de beurre fondu doux
330 g de beurre sec
150 g de sucre semoule
150 g de sucre cassonade

RÉALISATION

La pâte levée feuilletée

Délayer la levure dans un peu d'eau. Verser dans la cuve d'un batteur l'eau avec le sel, la farine et la vanille. Commencer à mélanger doucement avec la feuille du batteur. Ajouter le beurre fondu. Travailler ensuite la pâte avec le crochet de votre batteur pour lui donner du corps et ainsi qu'elle se décolle des parois de la cuve. Mettre cette pâte en boule. Filmer au contact. La réserver au frais pendant 30 min minimum.

Après ce temps de repos, dégazer la pâte sur votre plan de travail. Pour cela, écraser la boule avec la paume de la main. Cela va permettre à la levure de trouver de nouveaux nutriments pour pousser.

Étaler la pâte en un grand carré. Astuce : ne pas hésiter à mettre régulièrement une fine pellicule de farine sur votre plan de travail afin d'éviter que la pâte ne colle. Poser le beurre au centre qui doit être dans un format carré plus petit que celui de la pâte. Replier chaque côté de la pâte sur le beurre. Souder les bords. Étaler le carré en longueur. Le pâton est à la bonne taille lorsqu'il est trois fois plus long que large. Faire un tour simple en repliant trois fois le rectangle sur lui-même comme un portefeuille. Tourner votre pâton à 90° afin d'avoir la pliure sur le côté. Laisser la pâte reposer 30 min au réfrigérateur. Réaliser la même opération pour faire le deuxième tour en faisant attention d'avoir toujours la pliure sur le côté. Avant de faire le pliage en portefeuille, saupoudrer par-dessus la totalité des deux sucres. Cela permettra au crousti breizh d'avoir un petit goût caramélisé. Faire le pliage en portefeuille, puis placer au frais pour 30 min environ. Après la réfrigération, étaler une nouvelle fois la pâte.

Puis rouler la pâte afin d'obtenir un rouleau de 5 cm de diamètre. Laisser au froid environ 30 min. Détailler des lamelles de 2 mm d'épaisseur. Laisser pousser les lamelles sur une plaque recouverte de papier sulfurisé à environ 24 °C. Enfourner à 180 °C pour 15 min environ. Contrôler la cuisson par la coloration du caramel. Laisser tiédir sur une grille et déguster.

GÂTEAU BASQUE

GÉRARD LHUILLIER (LE MOULIN DE BASSILOUR)

Le Moulin de Bassilour, nectar du gâteau basque

Boulangerie depuis plus de 80 ans, Le Moulin (toujours en activité) de Bassilour est au gâteau basque ce que la charentaise est à la pantoufle : sacré, transgénérationnel, indémodable. Crème pâtissière au lait et aux œufs de la ferme, pâte sablée pur beurre à la farine de maïs et de blé ultra-friable, touche de rhum, jamais la recette ne changera. Et jamais la recette ne fuira, aujourd'hui inconnue même des salariés du Moulin. Gâteau basque à la crème ou gâteau basque à la confiture de cerises, il ne sera pas non plus question d'élargir la gamme. Gérard Lhuillier, troisième génération de boulanger, propose ici une recette traditionnelle de gâteau basque, à reproduire à la maison. Pour goûter le vrai du Moulin, il faudra se rendre à Bidart…

POUR 4 PERSONNES

Temps de préparation : 20 min • Temps de repos : 2 h • Temps de cuisson : environ 40 min

INGRÉDIENTS

La pâte
120 g de beurre doux
200 g de sucre semoule
300 g de farine type 55
11 g de levure chimique
3 pincées de sel
2 œufs
2 cuil. à soupe de rhum brun

La crème
500 g de lait
3 œufs
125 g de sucre semoule
40 g de farine type 55
2 cuil. à soupe de rhum brun

Montage et finition
1 œuf

RÉALISATION

La pâte

Dans un batteur muni d'une feuille, crémer le beurre pommade et le sucre. Ajouter la farine, la levure, le sel, les œufs et le rhum. Dès que la pâte est homogène, former une boule. Filmer au contact. Réserver au frais pour 2 h minimum.

La crème

Dans une casserole, faire chauffer le lait. Dans un saladier, fouetter les œufs et le sucre jusqu'à ce que le mélange blanchisse légèrement. Ajouter la farine et mélanger. Dès que le mélange est homogène, le verser dans la casserole avec le lait. Remuer jusqu'à ce que le mélange soit à ébullition. Poursuivre la cuisson de 3 à 4 min en remuant énergiquement. Hors du feu, ajouter le rhum. Débarrasser dans un plat à gratin. Filmer au contact. Réserver au frais.

Montage et finition

Beurrer un moule à gâteau rond. Séparer la pâte en deux morceaux équivalents. Abaisser les deux bouts de pâte sur une épaisseur d'environ 5 mm. Placer un morceau de pâte dans le fond du moule. Ajouter la crème tiède (environ 25 °C). Refermer avec la pâte restante. Enlever les morceaux de pâte qui dépassent. Battre l'œuf dans un bol. À l'aide d'un pinceau, dorer le dessus du gâteau. Rayer le gâteau à l'aide d'une fourchette. Enfourner à 160 °C pour environ 40 min. Démouler une fois le gâteau refroidi.

SABLÉS

FIONA LELUC, VINCENT LELUC ET FATINA FAYE (BONTEMPS)

Le petit gâteau sur le bout des doigts

Que du bon temps à prendre chez Bontemps, toujours de bonne trempe et de très bon ton.
D'un péché mignon, Fiona et Vincent ont ouvert boutique, avec un principe limpide : proposer uniquement ce qu'ils aimaient le plus. La crème de la crème de la gourmandise ultime. Bontemps inonde d'irrésistible, du petit sablé Bontemps aux citrons de Sicile au sablé pétale à la framboise en passant par la tarte sablée au gianduja de noisettes du Piémont, avec une gamme de biscuits complètement renversante, complètement addictive, et complètement… inimitable. La recette Bontemps, secrète et intouchable, ne voyagera pas ! La légèreté du sablé, son craquant salin et la rondeur de sa crème ne répondront qu'à la porte de Bontemps. Sa version « à la maison » cependant, proposée ici-bas par ses créateurs, jouera les alternatives pour les plus aventuriers.

POUR UNE VINGTAINE DE PETITS SABLÉS

Temps de préparation : 20 min • Temps de cuisson : 15 à 20 min • Temps de réfrigération : 1 h

INGRÉDIENTS

170 g de beurre pommade
60 g de sucre glace
200 g de farine
1 pincée de fleur de sel

RÉALISATION

Mettre le beurre pommade et le sucre glace dans un cul-de-poule ou dans le bol d'un robot. Mélanger au fouet ou avec la feuille du robot pour obtenir une crème.
Ajouter la farine et la pincée de sel. Mélanger jusqu'à obtenir une pâte à peine homogène (attention, il ne faut pas trop travailler la pâte). Astuce : étaler la pâte entre deux feuilles de papier sulfurisé pour éviter qu'elle ne colle (environ 5 mm d'épaisseur) et réserver au frais pendant 1 h.
Utiliser un emporte-pièce rond pour détailler des ronds de pâte. Utiliser un emporte-pièce rond de plus petite taille pour trouer l'intérieur. Poser la pâte découpée sur une plaque de cuisson recouverte de papier sulfurisé. Cuire au four à 160 °C de 15 à 20 min.

LES NUSSCHNITTLIS

RAOUL MAEDER

Un amour latent pour l'Alsace, en plein cœur des épices

Père alsacien, Raoul s'intéressera à ses origines bien plus tard, en commençant à la Maison du Chocolat. Puis l'idée de vendre des gâteaux qui puissent voyager fait son chemin, et il revient à son Alsace adorée. Ce gâteau, une pâte sablée/cannelle volontairement bien poussée en cuisson et un crousti-moelleux à l'intérieur, donne une impression de chaud en bouche. La mastication, liée aux arômes, allonge le goût, la gorge monte en température. Les épices, l'un des plus beaux héritages de l'Alsace, jouent fort leur carte aussi. Les gens viennent pour ça. Jamais Raoul ne se lassera de cette pâtisserie de transmission, toutes les recettes viennent de son père. À chacun sa madeleine.

POUR 8 NUSSCHNITTLIS

Temps de préparation : 45 min • Temps de cuisson : 30 min • Temps de réfrigération/repos : 36 h

INGRÉDIENTS

La pâte linzer
40 g de sucre glace
40 g de sucre semoule
80 g de beurre blanc
1 œuf
1 pincée de sel
6 g de cannelle (1 cuil. à café)
20 g de poudre de noisettes
200 g de farine
1 cuil. à café de carbonate d'ammonium

La confiture framboises
120 g de confiture de framboises

L'appareil à nusschnittlis
100 g de sucre semoule
18 g de poudre de noisettes
18 g de noisettes effilées
18 g de poudre d'amandes
18 g d'amandes effilées
5 g de cannelle
50 g de blancs d'œufs

RÉALISATION

La pâte linzer

Mettre tous les ingrédients dans l'ordre dans la cuve d'un batteur. Pétrir la pâte à l'aide de la feuille. Une fois que la pâte est homogène et forme une boule, filmer au contact et conditionner pour 12 h au réfrigérateur. Abaisser la pâte sur 2 mm d'épaisseur, foncer plusieurs cercles.

La confiture framboises

Garnir chaque fond de tarte de 15 g de confiture de framboises.

L'appareil à nusschnittlis

Mettre tous les ingrédients dans une casserole et chauffer l'appareil en remuant constamment. Retirer avant ébullition et garnir les fonds de tarte. Laisser sécher 24 h à température ambiante. Enfourner à 150° C pendant 30 min position chaleur tournante. Décercler les nusschnittlis et servir.

TARTE CHOCOLAT NOIR & ORANGE

GILLES MARCHAL (MAISON CHAUDUN)

Et contre toute attente, il boucle la boucle chocolatée

Ce petit faible, il l'a toujours eu pour le style Chaudun, précurseur du genre avec ses moulages faits main. L'opportunité a d'abord été de reprendre l'atelier pour en faire la pâtisserie Gilles Marchal, et quelques mois plus tard, c'est finalement l'atelier… et la maison que Gilles reprendra. Un nom sur un autre nom, chacun passionné et fou d'amour pour le chocolat, ne peut qu'étinceler. Au-delà des fondants et des marbrés, la tarte chocolat est une référence emblématique du chocolat. Monsieur Chaudun avait arrêté les gâteaux, Gilles Marchal leur a redonné vie, dans un style de chocolatier pur. Tant que le goût suit, Gilles aime les gâteaux bijoux, qui attrapent l'œil pour ne plus le laisser s'échapper. Cette tarte coche les deux cases, et pas qu'un peu : pâte sucrée bien régulière et dorée, puissance du chocolat à la fois douce et cacaotée de la crème anglaise au chocolat noir, surprise acidulée des agrumes confits, puis régression complète avec le glaçage. Le gâteau qui reste.

POUR 6 PERSONNES

Temps de préparation : 1 h 30 • Temps de repos : 28 h • Temps de cuisson : 25 min

INGRÉDIENTS

La pâte sucrée

150 g de beurre doux AOC
120 g de sucre glace
30 g d'amandes en poudre fine
1 œuf entier
¼ de gousse de vanille Bourbon
2 belles pincées de sel fin
300 g de farine type 45 bio

Le crémeux au chocolat noir grand cru

125 g de lait entier
125 g de crème liquide
2 jaunes d'œufs
190 g de chocolat noir à 66 % pur Caraïbe de Valrhona

Le glaçage cacao

10 g de feuilles de gélatine
180 g d'eau minérale
200 g de sucre semoule
70 g de cacao en poudre
125 g de crème liquide à 35 % de MG

Montage et finition

Aiguillettes d'orange confite
Crème d'orange de Sovéria
Feuilles d'or

RÉALISATION

La pâte sucrée

Couper le beurre en petits morceaux. Ajouter le sucre glace et la poudre d'amandes. Malaxer légèrement, ajouter l'œuf, la vanille, le sel fin et la farine. Mélanger jusqu'à obtention d'une pâte bien homogène. Étaler directement entre deux feuilles de papier sulfurisé à 3 mm d'épaisseur. Laisser reposer au frais 2 h. Beurrer un cercle à tarte de 18 cm de diamètre et de 2 cm de hauteur. Détailler un disque de pâte sucrée de 22 cm de diamètre, le placer dans le cercle et foncer le fond de pâte. Ébarber à ras du cercle. Laisser reposer 24 h.
Enfourner à 150 °C pour 25 minutes.

Le crémeux au chocolat noir grand cru

Faire bouillir le lait et la crème liquide. Verser le tout sur les jaunes d'œufs et cuire à l'anglaise, c'est-à-dire cuire à 83 °C en remuant constamment jusqu'à ce que la préparation épaississe et nappe la spatule. Filtrer immédiatement sur le chocolat finement haché et laisser fondre 1 min. Mélanger à l'aide d'une Maryse afin d'obtenir une texture lisse et brillante.

Le glaçage cacao

Mettre la gélatine dans de l'eau froide. Dans une casserole, faire cuire l'eau minérale, le sucre, le cacao en poudre et la crème liquide à 105 °C en remuant sans cesse. Filtrer. Égoutter la gélatine et l'ajouter au glaçage encore chaud.

Montage et finition

Sur le fond de tarte, déposer sur toute la surface et à la poche à douille unie n° 8, environ 1 mm de crème d'orange de Sovéria et quelques cubes d'aiguillettes d'orange confite.Recouvrir totalement de crémeux au chocolat en bombant légèrement le dessus. Placer au frais pendant 1 h. Réchauffer le glacage entre 35 °C et 38 °C. Sortir la tarte du réfrigérateur. Recouvrir toute la tarte avec le glaçage cacao, lisser les excès de glaçage et déposer la tarte sur un carton or de présentation. Décorer d'1 aiguillette d'orange confite et de feuilles d'or. Conserver au frais jusqu'à dégustation.

ROSEMARY

NATHALIE ROBERT ET DIDIER MATHRAY (PAIN DE SUCRE)

« C'est ringard de dire ça, mais on fait la pâtisserie comme on cuisine »

Didier a passé douze ans chez Pierre Gagnaire, Nathalie six. De leurs années ensemble, ils retiennent le travail de la pâtisserie par les assaisonnements, les décoctions et les infusions. Ils la défendent, cette pâtisserie de cuisiniers-pâtissiers, et Pain de Sucre en est la prolongation divine et nécessaire. Une boutique importante, précurseur du genre en 2004 rive droite, où tout, même les décors, doit être justifié par la composition. Sur le Rosemary par exemple, on trouve comme unique décor des amandes, des framboises et du romarin. Ce gâteau est une jolie synthèse de leur travail, probablement le premier qu'il faudrait manger pour comprendre qui ils sont. Les gens s'interrogent sur le romarin, ce à quoi Nathalie et Didier répondent qu'ils n'ont rien inventé, que les herbes étaient à l'origine plutôt utilisées dans le sucré (confitures, compotes, liqueurs). La fleur d'oranger prend le palais en premier, puis la rhubarbe et les amandes, puis l'acidité des framboises, puis le sablé puis… le romarin. Un gâteau formidable.

POUR 8 PERSONNES

Temps de préparation : 1 h • Temps de cuisson : 15 min • Temps de réfrigération : 12 h

INGRÉDIENTS

Le sablé amande et romarin
- *1 quart de zeste de citron râpé*
- *5 g de brin de romarin haché fin*
- *80 g de beurre*
- *40 g de sucre glace*
- *2 g de fleur de sel*
- *90 g de farine*
- *40 g de poudre d'amandes*

La pulpe de rhubarbe et framboise au romarin
- *4 feuilles de gélatine*
- *500 g de rhubarbe*
- *60 g de framboises*
- *85 g de sucre semoule*
- *1 brin de romarin*
- *20 g de chocolat blanc*
- *150 g de brioche cuite*

Le crémeux orgeat
- *3 g de feuille de gélatine*
- *50 g de lait entier*
- *100 g de lait d'amande sucré*
- *20 g de fleur d'oranger*
- *160 g de crème fouettée nature*

Montage et finition
- *Quantité suffisante de framboises fraîches*
- *Quantité suffisante de romarin*
- *Quantité suffisante de perles croustillantes au chocolat*

PRÉPARATION

Le sablé amande et romarin

Mélanger les zestes de citron et le romarin haché avec le beurre, le sucre et le sel jusqu'à obtenir une pommade homogène. Ajouter la farine et la poudre d'amandes. Laisser refroidir 30 min et abaisser en un carré de 18 cm de côté. Cuire 15 min au four à 150 °C.

La pulpe de rhubarbe et framboise au romarin

Mettre la gélatine dans l'eau froide. Laver et couper en tronçons de 1 cm la rhubarbe. Mettre à cuire dans une casserole la rhubarbe avec les framboises, le sucre et le romarin. Cuire doucement à couvert afin d'obtenir une compote. Retirer le romarin. Ajouter le chocolat blanc, la gélatine ramollie et mixer. Laisser tiédir à température ambiante.

Dans un cadre de 18 cm de côté sur 5 cm de hauteur : disposer au fond le sablé romarin, émietter la brioche dessus et tasser au maximum afin de faire comme un tapis de biscuit. Verser dessus la marmelade de romarin encore liquide et laisser figer au réfrigérateur.

Le crémeux orgeat

Mettre la gélatine dans l'eau froide. Chauffer le lait, ajouter la gélatine ramollie, puis le lait d'amande sucré ainsi que l'eau de fleur d'oranger. Incorporer la crème fouettée et répartir cette mousse dans le cadre. Laisser refroidir plusieurs heures au réfrigérateur.

Montage et finition

Démouler délicatement le Rosemary et le couper à l'aide d'une lame de couteau chaude en 9 carrés. Décorer avec framboises, amandes et brin de romarin.

KOSMIK MILLEFEUILLE

CHRISTOPHE MICHALAK

Une pâtisserie de restaurant déguisée en kosmik rock et ludique

Habité d'un respect abyssal et profond pour ses confrères, Christophe Michalak s'attèle à faire différent pour ne pas reproduire. Il a connu la pâtisserie haute couture et axe aujourd'hui ses produits sur la dégustation, sur le mouvement, sur l'équilibre. Le Kosmik a mis deux ans à naître, ayant pour ambition première de se déguster dans la rue. Loin d'être une simple version verrine d'un entremets monté en hauteur, le Kosmik est un dessert assiette, avec une vraie réflexion sur le dressage des crémeux, la cuisson plus poussée des dacquoises, l'accentuation des croustillants, l'ordre du montage… Comme un restaurant.

POUR 10 KOSMIK

Temps de préparation : 1 h 30 • Temps de repos : 12 h • Temps de cuisson : 1 h

INGRÉDIENTS

Les éclats de caramel salé

120 g de sucre semoule
1,2 g de fleur de sel

La crème diplomate à la vanille (quantité volontairement supérieure)

Crème pâtissière
280 g de lait
6,6 g de vanille en poudre
1 gousse de vanille
0,5 fève tonka
60 g de jaunes d'œufs
43 g de sucre semoule
1,8 g de poudre à crème
0,2 g de sel fin
22,4 g de beurre

Crème chantilly ivoire vanille
174 g de crème liquide
8 g de glucose
8 g de Trimoline
1,5 gousse de vanille
1 g de sel fin
1 g de Pastis
32 g de chocolat blanc de couverture Opalys de Valrhona

La crème chantilly ivoire et vanille

416 g de crème liquide
20 g de glucose
20 g de Trimoline
3 gousses de vanille
2 g de poudre de vanille
1 g de sel fin
1 g de Pastis
78 g de chocolat de couverture Opalys de Valrhona

Le feuilletage caramélisé

1 pâte feuilletée de chez le boulanger (40 x 60 cm)
Quantité suffisante de sucre glace

RÉALISATION

Les éclats de caramel salé

Mettre le sucre dans une casserole sur feu doux. Dès que le sucre a une couleur ambrée, ajouter la fleur de sel puis débarrasser sur une feuille de papier cuisson. Mixer le caramel afin d'obtenir des éclats.

La crème diplomate à la vanille

Crème pâtissière

Faire bouillir le lait avec la vanille en poudre, la gousse de vanille fendue et grattée ainsi que la fève tonka râpée. Dans un saladier, fouetter les jaunes, le sucre et la poudre à crème jusqu'à ce que le mélange blanchisse. Chinoiser le lait bouillant. Mélanger. Remettre dans la casserole et recuire jusqu'à une température de 88° C. Ajouter le sel et le beurre en morceaux, puis refroidir à 35° C. Réserver au réfrigérateur.

Crème chantilly ivoire vanille

Porter à ébullition 1/3 de la crème avec le glucose, la Trimoline, les graines de la gousse de vanille, le sel, et le Pastis. Laisser infuser pendant 10 min à couvert, puis chinoiser sur le chocolat. Mixer, à l'aide d'un mixeur plongeant puis réserver au réfrigérateur pour 2 h. Monter la crème chantilly bien froide à l'aide d'un fouet. Détendre la crème pâtissière au fouet, puis incorporer la chantilly vanille montée. Placer dans une poche à douille. Réserver au frais.

La crème chantilly ivoire et vanille

Procéder de la même manière que précédemment en ajoutant la poudre de vanille. Une fois la crème bien froide la monter au fouet. Placer dans une poche à douille et réserver au frais.

Le feuilletage caramélisé

Mettre la pâte feuilletée sur une plaque entre deux feuilles de papier sulfurisé. Ajouter sur le dessus une autre plaque pour éviter que le feuilletage ne gonfle. Enfourner dans un four à 170° C pendant 35 min. Retourner la plaque, puis cuire à nouveau 8 min. Retirer la plaque du dessus. Ajouter le sucre puis faites cuire 5 min. Détailler en carrés de 5 x 5cm, puis caraméliser à 220° C.

Montage et finition

Au fond de chaque verrine disposer 12 g d'éclats de caramel salé. Au-dessus, à l'aide d'une poche à douille, mettre 60 g de crème diplomate vanille. Ajouter 50 g de crème chantilly ivoire et vanille. Terminer par un carré de feuilletage caramélisé.

CHEESECAKE FRAISE DES BOIS & RHUBARBE

JIMMY MORNET (PARK HYATT PARIS-VENDÔME)

Un jusqu'au-boutisme fructueux, particulièrement notable

Si tout le monde le dit, tout le monde ne le fait pas. Jimmy Mornet dit et « désucre », dit et dégraisse ses gâteaux, et la démarche passe aussi par la forme. Le chessecake par exemple n'aurait pas pu atteindre cet équilibre s'il avait gardé son allure d'origine. Afin d'y loger le maximum de fruits possible, Jimmy monte le cheesecake au cœur, et le recouvre jusqu'au dernier millimètre de fraises des bois, un fruit qu'il adore pour son goût tellement différent des autres fraises, et sa fragilité. À la première cuillère, c'est l'acidité de la compote de rhubarbe qui inonde en premier, suivie par la douceur du cheesecake, puis la fraîcheur des fraises des bois. Le biscuit, lui, accompagne tout du long, discret mais tellement rond, comme un liant idéal et indispensable. Un gâteau sur le fruit, réellement sur le fruit.

POUR 6 PERSONNES

Temps de préparation : 1 h 30 min • Temps de cuisson : 1 h 15 • Temps de repos : 24 h

INGRÉDIENTS

Le streusel noisettes
40 g de farine
40 g de sucre semoule
40 g de poudre de noisettes
40 g de beurre
1 g de sel

Le fond reconstitué
20 g de chocolat blanc
20 g de beurre de cacao
140 g de streusel noisettes
15 g de feuilletine

L'appareil à cheesecake
2 feuilles de gélatine
250 g de fromage frais Philadelphia®
10 g de farine
80 g de sucre semoule
1 œuf
1 jaune d'œuf

La compotée de rhubarbe
125 g de rhubarbe
½ gousse de vanille
20 g de sucre cassonade
1 g de pectine

Montage et finition
200 g de fraises des bois
Quantité suffisante de sucre glace

RÉALISATION

Le streusel noisettes
Pétrir les ingrédients ensemble jusqu'à ce que le mélange soit homogène. Étaler finement entre 2 feuilles de papier sulfurisé à l'aide d'un rouleau à pâtisserie. Enlever la feuille du dessus. Cuire au four à 160 °C pendant 15 min. Mixer après refroidissement.

Le fond reconstitué
Faire fondre le chocolat blanc et le beurre de cacao ensemble. Ajouter le streusel mixé, la feuilletine. Étaler entre 2 feuilles de cuisson sur 5 mm. Mettre au réfrigérateur puis détailler à l'aide d'un emporte-pièce de 6 cm de diamètre.

L'appareil à cheesecake
Mettre la gélatine à tremper dans l'eau froide pendant 20 min. Mélanger l'ensemble des ingrédients. Égoutter puis faire fondre la gélatine au four à micro-ondes. Ajouter la gélatine fondue au mélange.

La compotée de rhubarbe
Dans une casserole, cuire la rhubarbe coupée en morceaux avec la ½ gousse de vanille grattée et le sucre cassonade préalablement mélangée à la pectine. Cuire sur feu doux jusqu'à ce que cela compote. Couler dans des moules demi-sphériques de diamètre de 2 cm. Congeler.

Montage et finition
Couler l'appareil à cheesecake aux ¾ dans les moules demi-sphériques de 4 cm de diamètre. Incruster dedans la demi-sphère de compotée de rhubarbe congelée. Cuire au four à 90 °C pendant 1 h. Congeler le tout pour pouvoir démouler. Coller 2 demi-sphères ensemble. Les disposer sur les fonds reconstitués détaillés à 6 cm de diamètre. Recouvrir de fraises des bois. Saupoudrer de sucre glace.

100 % VANILLE

ANGELO MUSA (PLAZA ATHÉNÉE)

Du goût, de l'élégance, de l'émotion

Angelo Musa au Plaza Athénée fait partie de ces évidences tellement absolues qu'on a l'impression qu'elles sont telles depuis des années. Pâtissier au grand cœur et à la sensibilité débordante, Angelo fait des gâteaux justes et aboutis. Il travaille en mono-parfum, que ce soit du chocolat, de la vanille ou des fruits. Les contrastes se feront sur les textures, mais en ce qui concerne les goûts, s'il décide de parler de vanille, rien ne s'y ajoutera. Son 100 % vanille en est une très jolie version, toute douce et « câlinante » : biscuit vanille, croustillant vanille et fleur de sel, crème vanille et mousse vanille. À la première cuillère de cette composition toute ronde, le goût puissant de vanille inonde, arrive derrière la légèreté foisonnée de la mousse vanille, puis la densité du crémeux vanille, pour finir sur le biscuit et le croustillant amandes pour la mâche et la chaleur, exhaussées et allongées par la fleur de sel. L'envie de revivre cette cuillère est brûlante.

POUR 4 PERSONNES

Temps de préparation : 2 h • Temps de cuisson : 35 min • Temps de réfrigération : 6 h

INGRÉDIENTS

Le croustillant amande vanille
102 g d'amandes blanches
7 g de beurre doux
65 g de chocolat blanc
1 ½ gousse de vanille
1 pincée de fleur de sel
35 g de feuilletine ou de crêpes dentelles du commerce

Le biscuit à la vanille
75 g de poudre d'amandes
45 g de sucre cassonade
30 g blancs d'œufs n° 1
40 g de jaunes d'œufs
1 pièce de gousse de vanille
4 g d'extrait naturel de vanille liquide
1 pincée de sel fin
20 g de crème liquide
63 g de beurre doux
17 g de sucre inverti ou de miel
90 g de blancs d'œufs n° 2
25 g de sucre cassonade
38 g de farine
2 g de levure chimique

La mousse à la vanille
2 feuilles de gélatine
4 gousses de vanille
75 g de crème liquide
10 g de sucre semoule
40 g de jaunes d'œufs n° 1
118 g de chocolat blanc
40 g d'eau
9 g de sirop de glucose
40 g de jaunes d'œufs n° 2
178 g de crème liquide

Montage et finition
Quantité suffisante de poudre de vanille

RÉALISATION

Le croustillant amande vanille

Torréfier les amandes au four à 150° C pendant 20 min. Les laisser refroidir. Faire fondre le beurre et le chocolat blanc. Mélanger intimement avec les graines des gousses de vanille et le sel. Mixer au robot les amandes refroidies jusqu'à obtention d'une pâte épaisse. Ajouter le mélange chocolat, beurre, vanille et fleur de sel dans le bol du robot. Mixer quelques secondes supplémentaires afin d'obtenir un mélange homogène. Verser ce mélange dans un saladier et ajouter la feuilletine en mélangeant délicatement à l'aide d'une Maryse. Étaler ce croustillant entre deux feuilles de papier cuisson sur 2 mm d'épaisseur environ à l'aide d'un rouleau à pâtisserie. Laisser cristalliser ce croustillant au réfrigérateur au moins 1 h.

Le biscuit à la vanille

Mélanger dans un saladier à l'aide d'une spatule la poudre d'amandes avec la cassonade, les blancs d'œufs n° 1, les jaunes, les graines des gousses de vanille grattées, la vanille liquide et le sel. À côté, chauffer légèrement dans une casserole la crème liquide, le beurre et le sucre inverti puis verser sur le mélange précédent en mélangeant toujours. Monter les blancs n° 2 au robot à l'aide du fouet en incorporant le sucre cassonade. Cette meringue doit rester souple.
Procéder au mélange du biscuit. Pour cela incorporer à l'aide d'une Maryse un tiers de la meringue dans le premier mélange réalisé dans le saladier. Ajouter la farine tamisée avec la levure chimique en la versant en pluie. Terminer par le reste de la meringue délicatement. Étaler le biscuit sur une plaque recouverte d'une feuille de papier cuisson à l'aide d'une palette coudée. Enfourner à 170° C environ 15 min. Le biscuit doit être bien doré. À la sortie du four, enlever une des deux feuilles de cuisson du croustillant vanille et l'appliquer sur le biscuit très chaud. Aplanir à la main pour bien faire adhérer le croustillant au biscuit. Ranger ce biscuit au réfrigérateur pour 1 h au minimum. Détailler à l'emporte-pièce des disques de 4 cm de diamètre. Réserver au réfrigérateur.

La mousse à la vanille

Hydrater les feuilles de gélatine dans de l'eau bien froide. Infuser 20 min les gousses de vanille grattées dans la crème

100% VANILLE

ANGELO MUSA (PLAZA ATHÉNÉE)

chaude. Chinoiser l'infusion à l'aide d'une passoire. Y ajouter le sucre et les jaunes n° 1 en mélangeant au fouet. Cuire ce mélange dans une casserole à 82° C.Y ajouter les feuilles de gélatine essorées. Mélanger. Verser cette crème anglaise sur le chocolat fondu. Mixer au mixeur plongeant afin d'obtenir un mélange parfaitement homogène, on obtient alors une ganache à la vanille. Refroidir cette préparation à 30° C. En attendant, porter à ébullition l'eau et le glucose, verser sur les jaunes n° 2, puis recuire le tout à la casserole à 82° C. Verser ensuite ce sabayon dans la cuve du robot et monter à l'aide du fouet jusqu'à complet refroidissement. Monter au batteur la crème liquide jusqu'à ce que la crème tienne sur le fouet. Procéder au mélange en versant un tiers de la crème montée dans la ganache à la vanille refroidie à 30° C. Ajouter un tiers du sabayon puis finir par le reste de crème montée et de sabayon.

Montage et finition

Déposer 4 cercles en Inox de 8 cm de diamètre et de 5 cm de haut sur un plateau recouvert d'une feuille de papier cuisson. Couler dans chaque cercle aux deux tiers la mousse vanille. Y déposer au centre un disque de biscuit et de croustillant. Entreposer au congélateur pour 4 h au minimum. Une fois bien froid, démouler les 100 % vanille en chauffant légèrement les cercles avec vos mains. Les déposer en assiette. Pour le décor, saupoudrer de poudre de vanille achetée dans le commerce ou réalisée maison en mixant au robot des gousses de vanille usagées préalablement séchées au four éteint pendant 1 nuit.

ANGEL CAKE AU CHOCOLAT

NICOLAS PACIELLO (PRINCE DE GALLES, A LUXURY COLLECTION HOTEL)

« Mon objectif, c'est que les gens aient envie de remettre un coup de cuillère illico dans mes gâteaux »

Nicolas Paciello, chef pâtissier, s'en est fait son refrain : le métier de pâtissier, c'est de représenter la gourmandise. Le visuel vient dans un second temps, simplement naturel. Et quand les gens y remettent un coup de cuillère, c'est que c'est bon ! Voilà le point de départ de tous ses gâteaux. Il a créé l'angel cake au chocolat pour Noël, un gâteau presque hypnotisant par sa forme, et complètement régressif une fois ouvert : crémeux chocolat, moelleux du gâteau, cœur coulant qui remouille la cuillère, et croustillant de la pâte sucrée pour la gourmandise. Un Nicolas qui ne prend pas la gourmandise à la légère.

POUR : ENVIRON 12 GÂTEAUX INDIVIDUELS

Temps de préparation : 1 h 30 • Temps de cuisson : 15 min • Temps de réfrigération : 6 h 15

INGRÉDIENTS

La pâte sucrée au cacao
450 g de beurre
420 g de sucre glace
320 g de jaunes d'œufs
800 g de farine type 45
200 g de cacao en poudre

La génoise
65 g de jaunes d'œufs
35 g de sucre semoule n° 1
90 g d'eau
45 g d'huile de pépins de raisin
65 g de farine type 45
20 g de cacao en poudre
2 g de levure chimique
160 g de blancs d'œufs
40 g de sucre semoule n° 2

Le crémeux au chocolat
9 g de gélatine en feuille
960 g de crème liquide UHT à 35 % de MG
960 g de lait
225 g de jaunes d'œufs
90 g de sucre semoule
675 g de chocolat de couverture Manjari de Valrhona

Le glaçage au chocolat
100 g de beurre de cacao
100 g de chocolat de couverture Manjari de Valrhona

Montage et finitions
Quantité suffisante de poudre or

RÉALISATION

La pâte sucrée au cacao

Mettre le beurre et le sucre dans la cuve d'un robot munie de la feuille. Mélanger jusqu'à ce que le mélange soit crémeux et homogène. Verser les jaunes d'œufs. Mélanger. Ajouter la farine tamisée et le cacao. Mélanger. Lorsque la pâte est homogène et se décolle des parois de la cuve, arrêter le batteur. Étaler a pâte sucrée à l'aide d'un rouleau à pâtisserie entre deux feuilles de papier sulfurisé. Détailler des cercles de 5 cm de diamètre. Enfourner à 170 °C pour 20 min environ.

La génoise

Dans un saladier, mélanger les jaunes, le sucre, l'eau et l'huile. Tamiser la farine, le cacao et la levure. Ajouter au premier mélange. Mélanger. Dans la cuve du batteur, monter les blancs en neige avec le fouet. Serrer les blancs en ajoutant le sucre n° 2. Les verser sur la préparation avec les jaunes, puis mélanger à l'aide d'une Maryse. Verser la préparation dans un moule à brioche mousseline. Enfourner à 165 °C pour 25 min. À la sortie du four, laisser refroidir le gâteau dans le moule à l'envers. Démouler à l'aide d'une palette puis détailler des cercles de 5,5 cm de diamètre et 3 cm de haut. Percer le centre avec un tube de 2 cm. Réserver.

Le crémeux au chocolat

Tremper les feuilles de gélatine dans de l'eau froide. Réaliser une crème anglaise. Pour cela, porter à ébullition la crème et le lait dans une casserole. Dans un saladier, fouetter les jaunes et le sucre jusqu'à ce que le mélange blanchisse. Verser une partie du lait bouillant sur le mélange blanchi. Mélanger. Reverser dans la casserole. Cuire sur feu doux, en remuant constamment, jusqu'à ce que le mélange atteigne la température de 83 °C. Réaliser une ganache en versant la crème anglaise chaude sur le chocolat haché. Émulsionner en remuant la préparation. Laisser reposer ce crémeux 6 h au frais avec un film plastique au contact. Mettre la crème au chocolat dans une poche munie d'une douille. Garnir l'espace de 2 cm au centre de la génoise de crémeux chocolat. Avec le reste de crème, pocher des petites pointes tout autour de la génoise. Réserver 15 min au congélateur.

Le glaçage au chocolat

Au bain-marie, faire fondre le beurre de cacao et le chocolat. Utiliser un pistolet à air à une température de 40 °C.

Montage et finition

Mettre le gâteau sur votre plat de service. Déguster.

ENTREMETS MADELEINE

FRANÇOIS PERRET (LE RITZ PARIS)

Une pâtisserie sur la pointe des pieds

Probablement l'un des plus jolis terrains de jeu de Paris, le Ritz s'est offert un pâtissier de la même trempe, inspiré sans fond. François Perret marque son arrivée avec la madeleine, simulacre d'elle-même, un peu comme une folle rencontre entre Proust et Magritte. La première surprise est visuelle, la madeleine ayant toute l'apparence du traditionnel gâteau de thé sans l'être vraiment. La seconde est l'étonnement inéluctable face au contraste entre la taille du gâteau et sa légèreté incroyable à la dégustation.
On le grimperait finalement bien deux fois, cet Everest. La première bouchée se prépare au couteau, dans la longueur, puis avec la fourchette, il faut aller tremper un morceau du gâteau, garni de crème fraîche nature, dans le cœur de caramel de miel de châtaigner pour que tout se passe en bouche.
Six fois de suite en moyenne. Une inouïe nouvelle manière d'aborder la pâtisserie, culottée, emportée, divine.

POUR 3 MADELEINES (ENVIRON 6 PERSONNES)
Temps de préparation : 2 h • Temps de cuisson : 14 min • Temps de réfrigération : 12 h

INGRÉDIENTS

Le sirop à la vanille
150 g d'eau
40 g de sucre semoule
1 gousse de vanille Bourbon

Le biscuit de Savoie
120 g d'œufs
110 g de sucre semoule
60 g de beurre fin fondu
80 g de farine type 45
40 g de fécule de pommes de terre
4 g de levure chimique
40 g d'amandes effilées

La mousse chantilly
1,5 feuille de gélatine
380 g de crème montée (1/3 de crème liquide et 2/3 de crème montée)
1 g de vanille Bourbon
60 g de crème pâtissière
3 feuilles de gélatine

Le crémeux caramel (quantité volontairement supérieure, environ 10 inserts)
4 g de feuille de gélatine
100 g de miel d'acacia
120 g de miel de châtaigner
150 g de sirop de glucose
550 g de crème
2 pincées de vanille Bourbon
140 g de jaunes d'œufs
200 g de chocolat au lait Tannéa

L'appareil à flocage or (quantité volontairement supérieure)
200 g de beurre de cacao
200 g de chocolat blanc Opalys
20 g de chocolat au lait Tannéa
2 g de colorant jaune
Quantité suffisante de colorant en poudre scintillant or

L'appareil à flocage chocolat (quantité volontairement supérieure)
125 g de beurre de cacao
105 g de chocolat noir Carupano
40 g de pâte de cacao

RÉALISATION

Le sirop à la vanille
Mettre l'eau et le sucre dans une casserole. Porter à ébullition. Faire infuser à couvert la gousse de vanille grattée dans le sirop chaud durant 1 h. Réserver au frais.

Le biscuit de Savoie léger
Monter les œufs avec le sucre au batteur. Ajouter le beurre fondu chaud. Tamiser la farine, la fécule, la levure ensemble puis les ajouter à l'aide d'une Maryse au reste du mélange. Graisser légèrement le moule à madeleine (12 cm x 4 cm x 4 cm). Pocher la préparation dans le moule. Parsemer abondamment d'amandes effilées. Enfourner à 160 °C pendant 14 min. Une fois la madeleine refroidie, imbiber à l'aide d'un pinceau avec le sirop à la vanille.

La mousse chantilly
Placer les feuilles de gélatine dans un bol d'eau froide. Tiédir 1/3 de crème liquide puis faire infuser la vanille. Ajouter la gélatine essorée. Lisser la crème pâtissière puis chinoiser le mélange crème, gélatine tiède dessus. Mélanger et chinoiser.

ENTREMETS MADELEINE

FRANÇOIS PERRET (LE RITZ PARIS)

Monter les 2/3 de crème restant. Réserver. Quand le mélange est froid incorporer la crème montée au mélange précédent. Réserver au frais.

Le crémeux caramel

Mettre la gélatine dans un bol d'eau froide. Cuire les miels et le glucose à 150 °C puis décuire avec la crème chaude préalablement infusée à la vanille. Verser une petite partie de cette masse chaude sur les jaunes d'œufs (astuce : le mélange doit être en dessous de 60 °C sous peine de faire une omelette). Remettre le tout à cuire en remuant constamment. Stopper la cuisson lorsque la préparation nappe la cuillère et atteint la température de 83 °C. Essorer la gélatine. L'ajouter à la préparation chaude. Mixer à l'aide d'un mixeur plongeant. Chinoiser. Débarrasser dans un plat à gratin. Filmer au contact et réserver au frais. Dans les moules à madeleine de taille inférieure au montage, étaler à l'aide d'un pinceau une fine couche de chocolat au lait Tannéa. Quand celui-ci est pris, pocher le crémeux caramel refroidi. Bloquer au congélateur.

Astuce : pour les plus gourmands, l'excédent de crémeux caramel sera parfait pour accompagner vos tartines à toute heure de la journée.

L'appareil à flocage or

Faire fondre au bain-marie le beurre de cacao et les chocolats puis ajouter les colorants. Mixer et chinoiser.

L'appareil à flocage chocolat

Faire fondre au bain-marie tous les ingrédients. Chinoiser.

Montage et finition

Dans le moule à entremets madeleine (ici : 12 cm x 8 cm x 8 cm), chemiser le dos de la madeleine de mousse chantilly. Coller le biscuit de Savoie. Lisser avec la mousse chantilly. Dans le moule du dessus, mettre la mousse chantilly. Placer l'insert de crémeux caramel au centre. Lisser de mousse chantilly à ras. Fermer les deux faces du montage. Mettre au congélateur pour environ 12 h. Démouler la madeleine congelée. Planter la madeleine sur une pique en bois puis floquer avec les flocages à 45 °C, d'abord avec le flocage jaune sur le dessus puis avec le flocage noir sur le dessous. Déposer la madeleine sur votre plat de service. Astuce : si vous n'avez pas de moule à madeleine de la taille indiquée pour le montage, le chef vous conseille d'utiliser des cercles à entremets. Un cercle de 14 cm de diamètre et 5 cm de haut graissé pour le biscuit de Savoie. Un cercle de 16 cm de diamètre pour le montage final.

LA TARTE AU PAMPLEMOUSSE

HUGUES POUGET (HUGO & VICTOR)

Un gâteau juteux et léché

Chez Guy Savoy déjà, Hugues Pouget passait son temps à faire des croquis de gâteaux, à imaginer sa boutique, dans laquelle il aurait une vraie carte de desserts, respectant les sous-saisons (figues, mirabelles et cerises ne durant pas trois mois) et les marchés. De ses expériences, il a appris les créations à travers les traditions : les crêpes à la Chandeleur, les bugnes à Mardi gras, les œufs à Pâques… Il voulait ça dans sa boutique. En 2010, c'était chose faite, et, à la sortie de la tarte pamplemousse, la surprise est totale : c'est un véritable carton. Un best-seller dans l'œuf. C'était pourtant risqué, un produit aussi acide et amer à la fois, posé en suprêmes de manière aussi brute. Mais l'objet est particulièrement bien pensé : pâte sablée craquante, crème d'amandes, crémeux au pamplemousse et suprêmes frais. Le croustillant de la pâte arrive le premier, en opposition à l'hyper juteux du pamplemousse, frais et gourmand. La crème d'amandes apporte le moelleux, puis le crémeux pamplemousse, l'inespéré, caresse le tout.

POUR 6 PERSONNES

Temps de préparation : 1 h 30 • Temps de cuisson : 28 min • Temps de repos : 8 h

INGRÉDIENTS

La pâte sablée

88 g de farine de gruau type 45
53 g de beurre
20 g d'œufs
2 g de fleur de sel
33 g de sucre glace
12 g de poudre d'amandes

La crème d'amandes

66 g de sucre semoule
10 g d'eau
20 g de sirop de glucose
33 g d'œufs
100 g de beurre
2 citrons jaunes

Le crémeux pamplemousse

3 g de feuille de gélatine
100 g de jus de pamplemousse rose
75 g de sucre semoule
100 g d'œufs
200 g de beurre
4 g de zestes d'orange
25 g de Campari®

Montage et finition

3 kg de pamplemousses roses

RÉALISATION

La pâte sablée

Tamiser la farine. Couper le beurre froid en cubes. À la main dans un saladier, malaxer la farine et le beurre afin d'obtenir la consistance d'une poudre. Battre un œuf en omelette et peser 20 g. Placer dans le saladier avec le sel. Mélanger. Dès que la préparation est homogène, ajouter le sucre glace et la poudre d'amandes tamisés. Dès que le mélanger est lisse et homogène, former une boule. Filmer au contact. Réserver au frais pour au minimum 5 h. Prendre 170 g de pâte et l'étaler finement au rouleau. Foncer un cercle à tarte de 20 cm de diamètre. Réserver au frais.

La crème d'amandes

Porter le sucre, l'eau et le sirop de glucose à 121° C dans une casserole. Monter les œufs à l'aide d'un batteur muni d'un fouet. Verser progressivement le sirop chaud dessus en conservant le batteur à une vitesse maximale. Lorsque la préparation est tiède, ajouter le beurre en petits morceaux. Dès que le mélange est lisse et homogène, arrêter le batteur. Débarrasser la crème dans un autre récipient et conserver au frais. Sortir le fond de tarte du réfrigérateur. Enfourner à 150 °C pour 20 min afin d'effectuer une pré-cuisson. Mélanger la crème d'amandes avec les zestes des citrons obtenus à l'aide d'une râpe microplane. Mélanger. À l'aide d'une poche à douille, garnir le fond de tarte de crème d'amandes. Enfourner de nouveau à 190° C pour 7 à 8 min.

Le crémeux pamplemousse

Mettre la gélatine dans un bol d'eau froide. Dans une casserole, mettre le jus de pamplemousse, le sucre et les œufs. Cuire sur feu vif tout en fouettant énergiquement afin d'obtenir une crème lisse. Passer la crème au chinois étamine au-dessus du beurre, des zestes d'orange, du Campari® et des feuilles de gélatine essorées. Remuer afin d'obtenir un mélange lisse. Laisser reposer de 2 à 3 h au frais.

Montage et finition

À l'aide d'une poche à douille, garnir le fond de tarte refroidi de crémeux pamplemousse afin d'avoir une épaisseur de 2 à 3 mm. Puis, peler à vif les pamplemousses afin de récupérer les suprêmes. Dresser les suprêmes de pamplemousse afin de former une rosace. Servir très frais.

LA SOURIS PRALINÉ, CITRON & CHOCOLAT

INÈS THÉVENARD ET RÉGIS PERROT (UNE SOURIS ET DES HOMMES)

Une souris et des hommes, des livres et des gâteaux

L'idée de Régis et de sa souris (Inès) était une belle mise en abîme : lire un livre sur les gâteaux en dévorant un gâteau. C'est ce que propose cette pâtisserie artisanale/librairie/salon de thé, avec en prime des conseils personnalisés sur les livres et une gamme de pâtisseries très épurée mais très complète. La souris est devenue le gâteau emblématique. Le couple gianduja/citron fait partie de ces mariages de rêve, tellement idéaux qu'ils n'ont jamais pu se séparer. À la dégustation, les cuillères ne sont pas linéaires, la première étant plus sur le biscuit croustillant et la mousse chocolat au lait noisette, et la seconde commençant à entamer le cœur citron, la surprise qui explose et rend accro.

POUR 4 À 6 SOURIS

Temps de préparation : 2 h • Temps de cuisson : 15 min • Temps de réfrigération : 12 h

INGRÉDIENTS

Le glaçage chocolat au lait

3 feuilles de gélatine
30 g de lait
30 g de crème liquide
100 g de glucose
120 g de chocolat au lait
200 g de nappage neutre

Le streusel noisettes

15 g de sucre roux
15 g de beurre doux
15 g de farine pâtissière
15 g de poudre de noisettes
1 pincée de fleur de sel

Le praliné feuilletine

6 g de beurre doux
14 g de chocolat au lait
48 g de praliné maison
24 g de pailleté feuilletine
8 g de noisettes concassées

Le crémeux citron

22 g d'œufs
9 g de sucre semoule
9 g de jus de citron
2 g de zestes de citron
8 g de beurre doux

La mousse gianduja

½ feuille de gélatine
61 g de lait
14 g de jaunes d'œufs
7 g de sucre semoule
58 g de gianduja
58 g de crème liquide

Montage et finition

Quantité suffisante de chocolat au lait
Quantité suffisante de perles croustillantes

RÉALISATION

Le glaçage chocolat au lait

Hydrater la gélatine dans l'eau froide. Faire bouillir le lait, la crème et le glucose. Verser sur le chocolat fondu. Incorporer la gélatine et le nappage neutre. Mixer, chinoiser, réserver au frais.

Le streusel noisettes

Mélanger tous les ingrédients, étaler sur 2 mm d'épaisseur. Détailler en forme de souris puis cuire au four à 150 °C pendant 15 min. Astuce : congeler la préparation avant cuisson puis s'aider avec un patron en carton pour détailler les formes de la souris.

Le praliné feuilletine

Faire fondre le beurre et le chocolat, ajouter les autres ingrédients. Étaler sur le streusel noisettes sur 1 mm d'épaisseur et faire prendre au froid.

Le crémeux citron

Cuire les œufs, le sucre, le jus et les zestes de citron dans une casserole jusqu'aux premiers frémissements. Refroidir. À 45 °C, ajouter le beurre tempéré, mixer, chinoiser et couler le crémeux dans des formes de demi-sphères. Faire prendre au congélateur.

La mousse gianduja

Mettre la gélatine à tremper dans l'eau froide. Faire une crème anglaise. Pour cela, mettre le lait à bouillir dans une casserole. Fouetter dans un saladier les jaunes d'œufs et le sucre jusqu'à ce que le mélange blanchisse. Verser le lait bouillant. Mélanger. Replacer dans la casserole. Cuire sur feu moyen sans cesser de remuer jusqu'à ce que la préparation épaississe et atteigne 85 °C. Hors du feu, incorporer la gélatine dans la crème anglaise. La verser sur le gianduja fondu. Mixer à l'aide d'un mixeur plongeant. Mettre la crème froide dans la cuve du batteur. Réaliser une crème montée mousseuse. À 30 °C, ajouter la crème montée. Utiliser sans attendre.

Montage et finition

Couler la mousse gianduja à mi-hauteur dans un moule en forme de goutte. Insérer une demi-sphère de crémeux citron. Recouvrir de mousse gianduja. Obturer avec le streusel noisettes recouvert de pailleté feuilletine. Faire prendre au congélateur pendant environ 12 h. Démouler les entremets, les glacer avec le glaçage chocolat au lait à 32 °C. Terminer avec de fins décors de chocolat au lait pour les oreilles et des perles croustillantes pour les yeux et le nez

MONSIEUR SMITH

PHILIPPE RIGOLLOT

Mi-fruit, mi-gâteau, Mister Smith étonne et absorbe

Il a créé ce gâteau en 2007, pour la sélection du Meilleur Ouvrier de France. Le thème était « tarte aux fruits », et Philippe Rigollot a sans hésitation choisi la tarte aux pommes. Mais classique oblige : pas n'importe laquelle, il voulait une rencontre entre fruits cuits et crus, et surtout, un visuel intrigant. Challenge relevé, le jury veut la recette ! Philippe se dit que si ça plaît aux professionnels, ça va plaire aux particuliers. Monsieur Smith se retrouve en boutique, et suit, naturellement, quelques mois plus tard Mrs Smith, sa femme, toute rose. D'extérieur, on pense croquer dans une pomme, et viennent chatouiller le mousseux vanille, la pomme crue et cuite, la pâte bien craquante et beurrée… Apparences trompeuses, au goûter.

POUR 6 TARTELETTES

Temps de préparation : 2 h • Temps de cuisson : 27 min • Temps de réfrigération : 7 h

INGRÉDIENTS

La pâte sucrée
65 g de beurre
75 g de farine type 55
32 g de fécule de pommes de terre
13 g de poudre d'amandes
40 g de sucre glace
½ gousse de vanille
1 g de sel
24 g d'œufs

La crème d'amandes
25 g de beurre
25 g de sucre glace
2,5 g de Maïzena®
25 g de poudre d'amandes
15 g d'œuf
5 g de rhum

La marmelade de pommes
2,5 feuilles de gélatine
120 g de purée de pommes vertes
12 g de sucre semoule
½ gousse de vanille
115 g de pommes granny

La chantilly vanille
118 g de crème fleurette à 35 % de MG
7 g de sucre
¼ de gousse de vanille

Le nappage à la manzana
150 g de nappage neutre
8 g de manzana
Quantité suffisante de colorant vert pistache
Quantité suffisante de colorant jaune citron

Montage et finition
½ gousse de vanille

RÉALISATION

La pâte sucrée
Mettre le beurre en pommade. Ajouter tous les ingrédients et mélanger jusqu'à obtention d'une pâte bien homogène. Mettre la pâte en boule. Filmer au contact. Réserver 1 h au frais. Abaisser à l'aide d'un rouleau à pâtisserie sur 3 mn d'épaisseur et foncer des moules à tartelettes de 8 cm de diamètre. Enfourner à 150 °C pour 15 min.

La crème d'amandes
Mettre le beurre en pommade, puis ajouter toutes les poudres. Mélanger. Ajouter l'œuf battu et le rhum. Dans le fond de pâte sucrée pré-cuit, pocher un peu de crème d'amandes et recuire : enfourner à 175° C pendant 12 min. Laisser refroidir sur une grille.

La marmelade de pommes
Mettre les feuilles de gélatine dans un bol d'eau froide. Dans une casserole, mettre à chauffer la purée de pommes vertes avec le sucre, et les graines de la ½ gousse de vanille. Couper les pommes granny en brunoise. Ajouter la gélatine essorée dans la purée. Mélanger à l'aide d'un mixeur plongeant. Ajouter les dés de pomme. Réserver au frais.

La chantilly vanille
Placer la crème froide avec le sucre et la vanille dans la cuve d'un batteur munie du fouet. La chantilly est prête lorsqu'elle reste accrochée au fouet. Pocher la chantilly dans un moule en forme de dessus de pomme. Congeler la préparation pour environ 6 h.

Le nappage à la manzana
Chauffer le nappage neutre puis ajouter la manzana et les colorants. Mixer à l'aide d'un mixeur plongeant. Utiliser à une température de 30-35° C.

Montage et finition
Garnir jusqu'à hauteur le fond de tarte de marmelade de pommes. Démouler la chantilly vanille et la glacer avec le nappage à la manzana. La déposer sur le dessus de la tartelette. Pour la petite queue de pomme, mettre un morceau de gousse de vanille.

TARTE DULCEY ET ROMARIN

JOHANNA ROQUES (JOJO & CO)

En plein cœur du marché d'Aligre, un rapport gâteaux/prix épatant

Journaliste chez Canal +, Johanna ne pense qu'aux gâteaux, et au bord de l'obsession, elle se lance à la recherche d'un local. Marché d'Aligre ? Inconnu au bataillon pour cette adepte de la rue des Martyrs. Elle visite quand même, c'est le coup de foudre. Jojo and co, à l'époque le nom de ses ventes de gâteaux entre copines, naît en plein cœur du marché, l'accueil y est chaleureux, bienveillant et canaille. Folle du chocolat Dulcey, elle avait très envie d'en faire une tarte, et s'est vite demandé comment atténuer l'excès de sucre. La crème montée sans sucre, infusée (pas qu'un peu) au romarin jouera le rôle d'équilibriste de l'ensemble, et la noix de macadamia caramélisée rappelle que malgré la puissance du romarin, ça reste un dessert gourmand. Le fond de tarte, volontairement surcuit, délivre des notes caramélisées et biscuitées, la boucle Dulcey est bouclée.

POUR 10 PERSONNES

Temps de préparation : 1 h 30* • *Temps de cuisson : 15 min* • *Temps de réfrigération : 12 h

INGRÉDIENTS

La pâte sablée à la noisette
7,5 g de poudre de noisettes
7,5 g de poudre d'amandes
45 g de sucre glace
115 g de farine
1 g de sel
60 g de beurre
25 g d'œufs

La ganache Dulcey
17,5 g de lait
125 g de crème liquide
250 g de couverture Dulcey

La chantilly romarin
125 g de crème liquide
10 g de romarin frais
15 g de mascarpone
1 cuil. à soupe de sucre glace

Les noix de macadamia caramélisées
25 g d'eau
50 g de sucre semoule
50 g de noix de macadamia
1 pincée de fleur de sel

RÉALISATION

La pâte sablée à la noisette

Mélanger dans la cuve du batteur les ingrédients secs avec le beurre froid coupé en petits morceaux. Sabler à la feuille puis incorporer les œufs. Une fois que la pâte forme une boule, la mettre sur le plan de travail. La fraiser, c'est-à-dire écraser la pâte à l'aide de la paume de la main. Cela permet de lier les ingrédients sans pour autant donner du corps à la pâte. Reformer une boule, filmer et placer au frais 1 h. Détailler des disques de pâte pour foncer des cercles de 8 cm. Placer des billes de cuisson dans les fonds de tarte. Enfourner à 180 °C pour 15 min.

La ganache Dulcey

Porter à ébullition le lait et la crème. Verser sur le chocolat Dulcey. Laisser reposer quelques instants puis mélanger et émulsionner au mixeur plongeant. Laisser reposer 12 h au frais.

La chantilly romarin

Porter à ébullition la crème et le romarin. Laisser infuser quelques minutes avant de mettre en boîte en veillant à couvrir le mélange d'un film transparent. Laisser refroidir 12 h avant de monter la chantilly au batteur en chinoisant la crème puis en ajoutant le mascarpone et le sucre glace.

Les noix de macadamia caramélisées

Cuire l'eau et le sucre à 118 °C. Incorporer les noix : elles vont d'abord commencer par sabler puis caraméliser. Lorsque les noix sont bien enrobées de caramel, les déposer sur un Silpat. Ajouter un peu de fleur de sel.

Montage et finition

Réchauffer la ganache Dulcey doucement au four à micro-ondes et la couler directement sur les fonds de tarte. Mettre la chantilly au romarin dans une poche à douille munie d'une douille lisse. Pocher 1 boule de chantilly au-dessus de la ganache Dulcey. Disposer quelques noix de macadamia caramélisées et finir par un bout de romarin.

RELIGIEUSE AU PAMPLEMOUSSE

DOMINIQUE SAIBRON

Un culte religieux pour la religieuse

Dominique Saibron tombe très vite dans la pâtisserie, qu'il préfère instinctivement à la cuisine, appâté par la technicité. La religieuse est son chouchou, ne serait-ce que pour ses deux choux, asymétriques et dodus, appel indécent à la gloutonnerie. À chaque saison son parfum, toujours 100 % pur fruits. L'une de ses plus belles expressions est celle aux agrumes, à la fois douce et acidulée, le duo parfait. Dominique décapite et engloutit la tête, son ultime souvenir d'enfance, qu'il ne laissera jamais au passé. Très bec sucré, il goûte tout, partout, tout le temps.

POUR 6 RELIGIEUSES

Temps de préparation : 1 h 30 • Temps de cuisson : 35 à 45 min • Temps de réfrigération : 3 h

INGRÉDIENTS

Le craquelin
60 g de beurre froid
50 g de sucre cassonade
50 g de farine
Quantité suffisante de colorant liquide jaune citron
Quantité suffisante de graines de pavot

La pâte à choux
100 g d'eau
100 g de lait frais entier
80 g de beurre
4 g de sel
4 g de sucre semoule
120 g de farine tamisée
175 g d'œufs

La crème légère au pamplemousse
5 jaunes d'œufs
40 g d'amidon de maïs
175 g de crème liquide à 35 % de MG
325 g de jus de pamplemousse frais
5 g de jus de citron frais
75 g de sucre semoule

RÉALISATION

Le craquelin
Dans un saladier, mélanger à la main le beurre avec le sucre cassonade, ajouter la farine et le colorant et les graines de pavot. Réaliser une pâte homogène. Étaler finement la pâte entre deux feuilles de papier cuisson. Faire durcir au froid.

La pâte à choux
Dans une casserole, verser l'eau, le lait, le beurre, le sel et le sucre. Porter le mélange à ébullition. Verser le mélange bouillant dans la cuve du batteur puis ajouter aussitôt la farine tamisée. Dessécher l'appareil avec la feuille (vitesse 1 : 5 min et vitesse 2 : 5 min). Incorporer progressivement les œufs en vitesse 2. Sur une plaque de cuisson, dresser à la poche munie d'une douille n° 15 des gros choux d'un diamètre de 7 cm environ. Sur une autre plaque de cuisson dresser à la poche à douille n° 10 des petits choux d'un diamètre de 3 cm environ. Découper à l'emporte-pièce des disques de craquelin (6,5 cm pour les gros choux et 3 cm pour les petits choux). Positionner les disques de craquelin sur vos choux. Cuire les choux à 190° C durant 45 min environ pour les gros et 35 min environ pour les petits.

La crème légère au pamplemousse
Dans un cul-de-poule, mélanger les jaunes d'œufs avec l'amidon et 10 % de la crème liquide. Dans une casserole, porter à ébullition le reste de la crème, le jus de pamplemousse, le jus de citron et le sucre. Verser une partie du mélange bouillant sur le mélange jaunes/amidon et bien mélanger. Reverser le tout dans la casserole et remettre à bouillir tout en remuant de 2 à 3 min. Conserver la crème au froid filmé au contact pendant 3 h.

Montage et finition
Placer la crème légère au pamplemousse dans la cuve d'un batteur. Fouetter la préparation jusqu'à ce qu'elle soit lisse. Mettre la préparation en poche munie d'une douille de 10 cm de diamètre. Garnir chaque chou. Avec une douille sultane, placer 1 point de crème au sommet de chaque gros chou. Placer le petit chou par-dessus et terminer avec une jolie rosace avec une douille cannelée.

ÇHIFFON CAKE À LA VANILLE

YUKIKO SAKKA ET SOPHIE SAUVAGE (NANAN)

La délicatesse

Yukiko et Sophie se sont rencontrées en pâtisserie chez Pierre Gagnaire et ont développé cette envie commune de créer quelque chose ensemble, pour elles-mêmes. Les touches japonaises sont infiniment discrètes chez Nanan, que ce soit sur les gâteaux, la viennoiserie, le pain, les quiches… Tout a sa place, tout est à l'envie. Le chiffon vanille est de loin le gâteau le plus japonais de la boutique, gâteau qui n'avait d'ailleurs jamais eu pour ambition de briller sous les projecteurs. Pour Yukiko, c'était surtout le gâteau familial qu'elle faisait à la maison, trop simple et trop personnel pour être en boutique. Et puis finalement, il en dit beaucoup, ce gâteau, plus moelleux qu'une éponge et blindé de vanille fraîche, enrobé d'une première couche de crème vanille ultra-fine et d'une autre couche de chantilly. C'est peut-être ceux-là, finalement, qui mettent tout le monde d'accord.

POUR 4 PERSONNES

Temps de préparation : 1 h • Temps de cuisson : 30 min

INGRÉDIENTS

La pâte à gâteau

60 g de jaunes d'œufs
60 g de sucre semoule
1 gousse de vanille
30 g d'huile végétale
40 g d'eau
75 g de farine
120 g de blancs d'œufs
1 noix de beurre

La crème chantilly

20 g de sucre glace
200 g de crème fleurette liquide à 35 % de MG

RÉALISATION

La pâte à gâteau

Blanchir les jaunes d'œufs et 2/3 de sucre. Ajouter les graines de la gousse de vanille. Ajouter l'huile et l'eau en fouettant. Tamiser la farine sur le mélange et mélanger sans trop insister. Monter les blancs en neige avec le sucre restant. Incorporer les blancs montés délicatement dans le mélange précédent. Beurrer un cercle de 16 cm de diamètre. Sur une plaque recouverte d'une feuille de papier sulfurisé, déposer un moule à chiffon cake. Garnir le moule de la préparation. Enfourner dans un four préchauffé à 170 °C. Cuire pendant environ 30 min. Dès la sortie du four, retourner le gâteau. Réserver.

La crème chantilly

Placer le sucre glace et la crème froide dans la cuve d'un batteur munie du fouet. Monter la chantilly. Astuce : la chantilly est prête lorsqu'elle reste accrochée au fouet. Masquer le gâteau avec la chantilly et décorer en formant des boules à l'aide d'une douille unie.

SABLÉ BRETON CHOCOLAT ET NOISETTE

YANNICK TRANCHANT (NEVA CUISINE)

« J'aime rassembler toutes les textures dans mes gâteaux, on s'ennuie sur le mou ! »

Neva, au-delà de ses assiettes extraordinairement bien cuisinées, est un temple secret de la pâtisserie, des desserts à l'assiette aux gâteaux montés. Épurée, gourmande et éclatée, la pâtisserie de Yannick Tranchant ne ressemble qu'à elle-même, et n'a rien à envier aux boutiques parisiennes. Généreuse, honnête et franche dans ses goûts, ses gâteaux vont au bout du bout : « Quand on met de la vanille dans un gâteau, on ne rigole pas et on met de la vanille, c'est pareil pour tout ! » La tarte aux fraises incarne pour Yannick le gâteau qui fait rêver par excellence, avec des fraises et des fraises des bois. Sur le chocolat, c'est pareil, il joue sur les textures et livre une tarte considérablement aboutie. Tous les éléments sont au maximum rapprochés au moment du dressage, pour que tout se joue en même temps dans la cuillère, la mousse, la ganache, les noisettes caramélisées, le sablé breton, la fleur de sel, tout.

POUR 6 SABLÉS

Temps de préparation : 1 h • Temps de cuisson : 20 min • Temps de réfrigération : 4 h

INGRÉDIENTS

Le sablé breton

250 g de beurre pommade
100 g de sucre glace
2 g de fleur de sel
40 g de poudre d'amandes
40 g de cacao
30 g de jaunes d'œufs
190 g de farine

La chantilly au chocolat

100 g de chocolat de couverture Madong
200 g de crème liquide

Le crémeux au chocolat

500 g de crème anglaise
380 g de chocolat Madong

Montage et finition

Quantité suffisante de noisettes torréfiées
Éclats de meringue

RÉALISATION

Le sablé breton

Dans un batteur, mélanger le beurre pommade, le sucre, la poudre d'amandes, le sel et le cacao. Puis ajouter les jaunes d'œufs et la farine. Obtenir une pâte homogène. Abaisser la pâte sur une épaisseur de 0,5 cm. Cuire au four dans un cercle beurré de 20 cm de diamètre à 170° C pendant 20 min.

La chantilly au chocolat

Mettre le chocolat au bain-marie, monter la crème en chantilly mousseuse puis mélanger les deux masses et mettre en poche munie d'une douille cannelée.

Le crémeux au chocolat

Tiédir la crème anglaise et ajouter au chocolat préalablement fondu au bain-marie. Émulsionner l'ensemble et réserver au frais au minimum 4 h.

Montage et finition

Pocher sur le sablé breton des rosaces de chantilly chocolat et alterner avec le crémeux chocolat pour obtenir un ensemble harmonieux. Ajouter des noisettes torréfiées et des éclats de meringue.

KOUGLOF
STÉPHANE VANDERMEERSCH

N'a d'alsacien que son kouglof en boutique, irréprochable

De ses années en tant que tourier chez Pierre Hermé, Stéphane Vandermeersch aura retenu le savoir-faire, entre autre, de la pâte feuilletée parfaite. Formidablement bien accueilli par un quartier friand de tradition, Stéphane épate avec ses galettes, millefeuilles et tartes, et un beau jour, c'est le kouglof qui brille. Le boulanger s'amuse quotidiennement des origines alsaciennes que les gens lui prêtent, par son nom, en fait flamand, et son kouglof, qu'il a simplement appris chez Fauchon. Il avoue modestement que pour les Alsaciens, son kouglof n'en est pas un, car plus beurré, plus humide, plus fourni que le traditionnel. Plus gourmand, aussi, il en devient un gâteau à lui tout seul, moelleux, sucré, beurré, craquant sur les fruits secs, fondant à cœur... Jusqu'à 600 kouglofs par semaine, tous les moules sont beurrés et moulés à la main, le résultat est palpitant.
Un gâteau qui reste.

POUR 4 PERSONNES

Temps de préparation : 1 h • Temps de repos : 14 h • Temps de cuisson : 30 à 45 min

INGRÉDIENTS

Le sirop à bostock
500 g d'eau
75 g de sucre semoule
65 g de poudre d'amandes
45 g d'eau de fleur d'oranger

La pâte pour le kouglof
250 g de farine
25 g de sucre semoule
5 g de sel
10 g de levure fraîche
150 g d'œufs
8 g d'eau de fleur d'oranger
135 g de beurre pommade
100 g de raisins secs
1 petite poignée d'amandes
1 petite poignée de noisettes

Montage et finition
Quantité suffisante de beurre clarifié
Quantité suffisante de sucre glace

RÉALISATION

Le sirop à bostock
Dans une casserole, porter à ébullition l'eau et le sucre. Incorporer la poudre d'amandes et l'eau de fleur d'oranger. Laisser refroidir. Conserver au réfrigérateur.

La pâte pour le kouglof
Mettre la farine, le sucre, le sel, la levure et les œufs dans la cuve du batteur. Pétrir la pâte 4 min en première vitesse. Ajouter l'eau de fleur d'oranger et 125 g de beurre pommade. Pétrir 6 min en deuxième vitesse. Arrêter et ajouter les raisins. Reprendre le pétrissage en première vitesse afin d'obtenir un mélange homogène. Débarrasser et réserver au froid pendant 12 h à 5 °C.

Le lendemain, prendre la pâte et la détailler. Beurrer le moule avec le beurre pommade restant. Disposer quelques amandes entières et quelques noisettes au fond du moule. Bouler la pâte à kouglof. La mettre dans un moule avec la soudure vers vous. Faire pousser 2 h à 30 °C.
Enfourner à 180 °C de 30 à 45 min selon la taille. Démouler et laisser refroidir.

Montage et finition
Tremper légèrement votre kouglof dans du beurre clarifié, puis dans le sirop à bostock. Égoutter. Saupoudrer légèrement de sucre glace.

M

MORI YOSHIDA

L'excellence à la japonaise, au service de la pâtisserie française

Il fait partie de ceux qui, en un battement de cils, ont conquis Paris. Discret, appliqué, infiniment passionné, Mori Yoshida n'a en boutique que des gâteaux aboutis, exactement tels qu'ils méritent d'être. Il ne connaît pas l'à-peu-près, et applique à chacune de ses créations, du bonbon de chocolat au Mont-Blanc en passant par le cake et le millefeuille, la même dextérité. Ayatollah du goût, il s'est très vite dessiné un nom, qu'il honore au quotidien. Corps, âpreté, couleurs naturelles, acidité, saisonnalité : son langage quotidien. Le M, signature du chef, est une superposition de textures merveilleusement complémentaires et parfaitement équilibrées. Une crème d'érable, toute douce et justement dosée en sucre, une mousse chocolat-érable, légère, nuageuse, en deux temps sur le palais, une confiture de mandarines, pimpante et révélatrice, un biscuit noisettes, fondant et long en mâche, et la nougatine noisette, résistante, craquante et hyper gourmande. Un esthète du genre.

POUR 4 PERSONNES

Temps de préparation : 2 h 30 • Temps de cuisson : 20 à 25 min • Temps de réfrigération : 12 h

INGRÉDIENTS

Le biscuit Joconde et noisettes
93 g de poudre de noisettes
56 g de poudre d'amandes
93,5 g de sucre glace
112 g d'œufs
50 g de blancs d'œufs n° 1
30 g de farine
75 g de beurre
62,5 g de blancs d'œufs n° 2
35 g de sucre semoule

La nougatine noisette
45 g de sucre semoule
37,5 g de beurre
15 g de sirop de glucose
11 g de crème liquide
100 g de noisettes entières

Le perlée de clémentine
5 clémentines
50 g de sucre semoule

La crème caramel au sucre d'érable
34 g de sucre d'érable
112 g de crème liquide
37 g de jaunes d'œufs
12 g de cassonade
2 g de gélatine
42 g de crème fouettée

La mousse au chocolat au sucre d'érable
102 g de crème fouettée
22 g de sucre d'érable
45 g de crème liquide
18 g de jaunes d'œufs
11 g de cassonade
57 g de chocolat de couverture Guanaja de Valrhona

Le glaçage chocolat
46 g de chocolat de couverture Guanaja de Valrhona
14 g de praliné noisette
125 g de crème liquide
17 g de trimoline
14 g de sucre semoule
17 g de sirop d'érable
4 g de gélatine

Montage et finition
Quantité suffisante de chocolat de couverture Jivara de Valrhona

RÉALISATION

Le biscuit Joconde et noisettes

Peser et tamiser ensemble la poudre de noisettes, la poudre d'amandes et le sucre glace. Verser ces poudres dans la cuve du batteur. Ajouter les œufs et les blancs d'œufs n° 1. Monter cette préparation à l'aide d'un fouet. Pendant ce temps, tamiser la farine. Faire fondre le beurre au bain-marie dans un grand bol. Préparer une meringue bien ferme, pour cela mettre les blancs d'œufs n° 2 dans la cuve de votre batteur munie du fouet. Fouetter l'ensemble pour qu'il devienne mousseux. Ajouter le sucre semoule petit à petit pour ne pas faire retomber la meringue. Dès que la première préparation est bien montée, prélever un tiers. Mélanger ce tiers au beurre fondu dans le grand bol à l'aide d'un fouet. Ajouter la farine tamisée délicatement à l'aide d'une Maryse au deux tiers restants de la préparation toujours en travaillant dans la cuve mais avec vos mains. Reverser le tiers avec le beurre dans les deux tiers avec la farine et délicatement mélanger. Couler la pâte à biscuit dans un cadre sur une plaque de 30 cm x 40 cm recouverte de papier cuisson. Enfourner à 170° C pour 20 min. Lorsque le biscuit est bien refroidi, retirer le cadre et la feuille de papier cuisson délicatement. Détaillez une bande de biscuit de la largeur et de la longueur de la base de votre moule à bûche. Réserver sur une grille.

La nougatine noisette

Mettre dans une grande casserole le sucre semoule, le beurre et le sirop de glucose. Cuire sur feu moyen jusqu'à obtention d'une jolie couleur brun clair. Ajouter la crème liquide chaude et mélanger. Astuce : la crème doit être chaude afin de limiter les projections dûes au choc thermique. Ajouter les noisettes. Mélanger et débarrasser la nougatine sur une plaque recouverte d'une feuille en silicone. Enfourner à 160° C de 20 à 25 min. Lorsque la nougatine est bien refroidie, sur une planche à découper coupez grossièrement des morceaux de 1 cm. Réserver.

MORI YOSHIDA

Le perlée de clémentine

Éplucher et laver les clémentines. Les couper en petits dés. Les mettre dans une casserole, ajouter le sucre. Faire bouillir le tout, tout en mélangeant pour éviter que le fond n'accroche. Laisser refroidir. Couler la préparation dans une poche à douille. Réserver au frais.

Crème caramel d'érable

Mettre dans une casserole le sucre d'érable. Cuire jusqu'à obtention d'un caramel brun. Décuire en ajoutant la crème liquide chaude. Mélanger dans un bol les jaunes d'œufs et la cassonade à l'aide d'un fouet afin de blanchir le mélange. Verser un tiers du caramel d'érable sur le mélange jaunes d'œufs-cassonade. Mélanger et reverser le tout dans la casserole. Mélanger jusqu'à obtenir la texture d'une crème anglaise, c'est-à-dire que la préparation doit napper la cuillère. Hors du feu, ajouter la gélatine préalablement ramollie. Mélanger. Réserver la crème d'érable jusqu'à ce qu'elle atteigne une température de 10° C. Monter la crème fouettée à l'aide d'un batteur. Attention de ne pas trop la monter, elle doit rester mousseuse. Lorsque la crème d'érable à une température de 10° C, incorporer délicatement la crème fouettée à l'autre mélange. Utiliser aussitôt. Chemiser votre moule à bûche de 15 cm de long et de forme triangulaire d'un film plastique. Couler au fond une petite couche régulière de perlée de clémentine. Puis coulez par-dessus votre crème d'érable. Le moule doit être rempli seulement à moitié. Laissez prendre au moins 6 h au congélateur. Démouler l'insert une fois qu'il est congelé. Réserver au congélateur.

La mousse au chocolat d'érable

Monter au batteur la crème fouettée pas trop ferme. Dans une casserole, caraméliser le sucre d'érable et décuire avec la crème liquide. Mélanger dans un bol les jaunes d'œufs et la cassonade. Procéder alors comme une crème anglaise : verser un tiers du caramel d'érable sur le mélange jaunes d'œufs-cassonade, bien mélanger et reverser dans la casserole pour obtenir la texture d'une crème anglaise. Lorsque la texture est bonne, verser la crème sur le chocolat noir, émulsionner. Enfin délicatement incorporer la crème fouettée à la crème au chocolat. Utiliser aussitôt. Nettoyer et chemiser de nouveau avec du film plastique le moule à bûche de 15 cm de long et de forme triangulaire. Couler dans le moule la mousse au chocolat d'érable. Récupérer l'insert congelé. Le placer délicatement au centre de votre mousse au chocolat. Parsemer régulièrement de morceaux de nougatine à la noisette. Refermer avec la bande de biscuit en prenant soin de bien appuyer pour que le biscuit adhère bien à la mousse. Laisser prendre au congélateur pour au moins 6 h.

Le glaçage chocolat

Dans un grand bol, peser ensemble le chocolat et le praliné. Dans une casserole, faire bouillir la crème liquide, la trimoline, le sucre et le sirop d'érable. Hors du feu, ajouter la gélatine préalablement ramollie et bien mélanger. Procéder alors comme pour une ganache en versant petit à petit la crème sur le chocolat et le praliné en émulsionnant à l'aide d'une spatule. Réserver.

Montage et finition

Préparez votre glaçage en le chauffant à une température de 26° C. Mélanger bien pour qu'il ait une texture parfaitement homogène. Démouler l'entremets congelé. Retirer le film et le déposer sur une grille au-dessus d'un plat à gratin. Verser en une fois et de manière régulière le glaçage sur l'entremets. Tapoter la grille pour enlever l'excédant de glaçage. Déposer l'entremets sur un plat de présentation. Réaliser des décors en chocolat à l'aide du chocolat de couverture Jivara tempéré. Déposer délicatement vos décors en chocolat sur la pointe de l'entremets avant que le glaçage ne sèche complétement.

CAKE CHOCOLAT NOISETTE
À LA MÈRE DE FAMILLE

La belle intemporelle, nécessaire et irremplaçable

Et si c'était elle, la boîte à secrets ? À la Mère de Famille, toute première chocolaterie/confiserie de Paris (1761), a plus d'un tiroir à son armoire. Chocolats, bonbons, nougats, calissons, biscuits, gâteaux, glaces, pralinés, fruits confits... Une sorte de grimoire du sucré, totalement authentique et pourtant complètement actuel. La gamme est classique mais parfaitement réalisée, avec à chaque fois ce bon goût d'à l'ancienne, nostalgique et irrésistible. Le cake de l'écureuil, réalisé en toute détente, avec les amandes et noisettes caramélisées et enrobées de chocolat de la boutique, en est l'exemple idéal. Une bonne pâte à cake à base d'excellents produits et d'une recette traditionnelle, dans laquelle on vient jeter, avant le passage au four, des noisettes et amandes caramélisées, enrobées de chocolat. Une irrésistible confiserie dans un irrésistible gâteau donne un goûter régressif et parfaitement gourmand. La Mère a tout bon. Comme toujours..

POUR UN CAKE DE 6 PERSONNES

Temps de préparation : 20 min • Temps de cuisson : 45 min

INGRÉDIENTS

L'appareil pour le cake
100 g de noisettes émondées
3 œufs
100 g de sucre semoule
11 cl de crème liquide
60 g de miel
45 g de chocolat noir à 70 % de cacao
100 g de farine
6 g de levure chimique
60 g de poudre d'amandes
16 g de poudre de cacao
60 g de beurre fondu

RÉALISATION

Concasser les noisettes. Fouetter les œufs et le sucre jusqu'à ce que le mélange blanchisse légèrement. Faire chauffer la crème et le miel jusqu'à frémissement, y faire fondre le chocolat. Mélanger. Une fois que le mélange est homogène, verser dans le mélange sucre et œufs. Ajouter la farine, la levure chimique, la poudre d'amandes et le cacao. Incorporer le beurre fondu et 80 g de noisettes. Chemiser un grand moule à cake de papier sulfurisé. Verser la pâte et parsemer les noisettes restantes. Enfourner 5 min à 200 °C. Inciser le dessus du cake. Enfourner à nouveau 40 min à 155 °C. Démouler à la sortie du four.

ADRESSES

L'Éclair de génie* • *Christophe Adam
13, rue de l'Ancienne-Comédie, 75006
Autres adresses sur : leclairdegenie.com

Café Pouchkine* • *Julien Alvarez
64, boulevard Haussmann, 75008 Paris
Autres adresses sur : cafe-pouchkine.fr

Un Dimanche à Paris* • *Nicolas Bacheyre
4-6-8, cours du Commerce Saint-André, 75006 Paris

Shangri-La* • *Michael Bartocetti
10, avenue d'Iéna, 75116 Paris

Les Étangs de Corot* • *Yannick Begel
55, rue de Versailles, 92410 Ville-d'Avray

Mad'leine* • *Akrame Banallal
Points de vente sur : www.madleine.fr

Nicolas Bernardé
2, place de la Liberté, 92250 La Garenne-Colombes

Utopie* • *Erwan Blanche et Sébastien Bruno
20, rue Jean-Pierre Timbaud, 75011 Paris

Acide Macaron* • *Jonathan Blot
24, rue des Moines, 75017 Paris

Sébastien Bouillet
15, place de la Croix-Rousse, 69004 Lyon
Autres adresses sur : www.chocolatier-bouillet.com

Blé Sucré* • *Fabrice Le Bourdat
7, rue Antoine Vollon, 75012 Paris

Yann Brys
www.yannbrys.fr

Casse-Noisette* • *Jeffrey Cagnes
35, avenue de l'Opéra, 75002 Paris

Liberté* • *Benoit Castel
39, rue des Vinaigriers, 75010 Paris

Gontran Cherrier
22, rue Caulaincourt, 75018 Paris
Autres adresses sur : www.gontrancherrierboulanger.com

La Maison du Chocolat* • *Nicolas Cloiseau
225, rue du Faubourg Saint-Honoré, 75008 Paris
Autres adresses sur : www.lamaisonduchocolat.fr

Mon Éclair* • *Grégory Cohen
52, rue des Acacias, 75017 Paris

Philippe Conticini
Laboratoire : 59, boulevard Camélinat, 92230 Genevilliers
Plus d'informations sur www.conticini.fr

La Pâtisserie par Cyril Lignac
24, rue Paul-Bert, 75011 Paris
Autres adresses sur : www.cyrillignac.com

Yann Couvreur
137, avenue Parmentier, 75010 Paris

T Xuan* • *Yuelin Cui et Pierre-Henri Boissavy
56, rue la Fayette, 75009 Paris

Des Gâteaux et du Pain – Claire Damon
63, boulevard Pasteur, 75015 Paris

Sébastien Dégardin
200, rue Saint-Jacques, 75005 Paris

Laurent Favre-Mot
12, rue Manuel, 75009 Paris

Pâtisserie Foucher* • *Jean-François Foucher
12, rue au Fourdray, 50100 Cherbourg-Octeville

Foucade* • *Marjorie Fourcade
17, rue Duphot, 75001 Paris

Jacques Génin
133, rue de Turenne, 75003 Paris
Autre adresse sur : www.jacquesgenin.fr

Colorova* • *Guillaume Gil
47, rue de l'Abbé-Grégoire, 75006 Paris

Stéphane Glacier
66, rue du Progrès, 92700 Colombes

Le Meurice* • *Cédric Grolet
228, rue de Rivoli, 75001 Paris

Boulangerie BO • Olivier Haustraete
85 bis, rue de Charenton, 75012 Paris

Pierre Hermé
4, rue Cambon, 75001 Paris
Autres adresses sur : www.pierreherme.com

Jean-Paul Hévin
231, rue Saint-Honoré, 75001 Paris
Autres adresses sur : www.jeanpaulhevin.com

Mokonuts • Moko Hirayama
5, rue Saint-Bernard, 75011 Paris

Terroirs d'Avenir • Shinya Inagaki
8, rue du Nil, 75002 Paris

Le Bristol • Laurent Jeannin
112, rue du Faubourg Saint-Honoré, 75008 Paris

Amami • Antoaneta Julea et Sayako Tsuji
12, rue Jean-Macé, 75011 Paris

Ernest et Valentin •
Logan et Bradley Lafond
225, rue de Charenton, 75012 Paris

Gâteaux Thoumieux •
Alexis Lecoffre et Sylvestre Wahid
58, rue Saint-Dominique, 75007 Paris

Les Souris dansent • Yann le Gall
16, rue Marie Stuart, 75002 Paris

Pièr-Marie Le Moigno
8, rue Victor-Masse, 56100 Lorient

Moulin de Bassilour • Gérard Lhuillier
Quartier Bassilour, 64210 Bidart

Bontemps • Vincent et Fiona Leluc
57, rue de Bretagne, 75003 Paris

Raoul Maeder
158, boulevard Berthier, 75017 Paris
Autre adresse sur : www.raoulmaeder.fr

Maison Chaudun • Gilles Marchal
149, rue de l'Université, 75007 Paris
Et Gilles Marchal : 9 Rue Ravignan, 75018 Paris

Pain de Sucre •
Nathalie Robert et Didier Mathray
14, rue Rambuteau, 75003 Paris

Christophe Michalak
60, rue du Faubourg-Poissonnière, 75010 Paris
Autres adresses sur : www.christophemichalak.com

Park Hyatt Paris-Vendôme • Jimmy Mornet
5, rue de la Paix, 75002 Paris

Plaza Athénée • Angelo Musa
25, avenue Montaigne, 75008 Paris

Prince de Galles – Nicolas Paciello
33, avenue George-V, 75008 Paris

Ritz Paris • François Perret
15, place Vendôme, 75001 Paris

Hugo & Victor • Hugues Pouget
40, boulevard Raspail, 75007 Paris
Autres adresses sur : www.hugovictor.com

Une Souris et des Hommes •
Inès Thévenard et Régis Perrot
17, rue de Maubeuge, 75009 Paris

Philippe Rigollot
1, place Georges-Volland, 74000 Annecy

Jojo & Co • Johanna Roques
Marché d'Aligre Beauvau, place d'Aligre, 75012 Paris

Dominique Saibron
77, avenue du Général-Leclerc, 75014 Paris

Nanan • Yukiko Sakka et Sophie Sauvage
38, rue Keller, 75011 Paris

Neva Cuisine • Yannick Tranchant
2, rue de Berne, 75008 Paris

Stéphane Vandermeersch
278, avenue Daumesnil, 75012 Paris

Mori Yoshida
65, avenue de Breteuil, 75007 Paris

À la Mère de Famille • Sophie et Jane Dolfi
35, rue du Faubourg-Montmartre, 75009 Paris
Autres adresses sur : www.lameredefamille.com

© Alix de Beer

Après un master en entrepreneuriat et quelques années entre les cuisines et l'événementiel, **Raphaële** crée son blog enrangdoignons.fr en 2014 et se lance, à 24 ans, dans sa toute première société. Journaliste gastronomique pour des magazines et professeur de communication en gastronomie, elle crée également une agence de placement de chefs, de conseils et de partenariats. *À la Folie* est son premier livre, suite à une immersion dans les gâteaux grâce à sa collaboration au magazine *Fou de Pâtisserie*.

REMERCIEMENTS

Merci à Julie Mathieu, toute première à m'avoir fait confiance, sans qui je n'aurais jamais écrit ces pages.
Merci à Muriel et Claire pour leur soutien sans faille.
Merci à mes parents pour leur amour débordant.
Merci à Laure Martin pour son travail et son optimisme à toute épreuve.
Merci à Romain pour sa patience quotidienne.
Merci à mes amis pour leur éternelle fidélité.
Merci à Nicolas.
Merci à tous les pâtissiers pour leur bienveillance, leur gentillesse et leur générosité.
Merci à Rachael, merci à Thomas.
Merci à Stéphane pour son grand cœur.
Merci à ma famille pour toute son affection et à ma Dany pour ses inondations de tendresse.
Merci à David, Antoine et Camille pour leur ouverture et leurs nerfs si doux !
Merci à toutes les personnes avec qui j'ai eu la chance de travailler pour leur place si douillette.
Merci aux chefs pour leur immense richesse.
Et tout d'abord merci à Marie Baumann de m'avoir permis d'écrire ce livre.

Création graphique et mise en page : Claire Morel Fatio
Collaboration éditoriale : Laure Martin
Secrétariat d'édition : Sophie Greloux